Software Testing Management

Life on the Critical Path

Thomas C. Royer

The MITRE Corporation

P T R Prentice Hall
Englewood Cliffs, New Jersey 07632

Royer, Thomas C.
    Software testing management : life on the critical path / Thomas C.
Royer
        p. cm.
    Includes bibliographical references and index.
    ISBN 0-13-532987-6
    1. Computer software—Testing—Management. I. Title.
QA76.76.T48R68   1993
005.1′4—dc20   92-12095
                                                                    CIP

Editorial/production supervision
    and interior design: *Ann Sullivan*
Cover Design: *Wanda Lubelska*
Buyer: *Mary Elizabeth McCartney*
Acquisitions Editor: *Paul W. Becker*
Editorial Assistant: *Noreen Regina*

The publisher offers discounts on this book when ordered
in bulk quantities. For more information, write:

        Special Sales/Professional Marketing
        Prentice-Hall, Inc.
        Professional Technical Reference Division
        Englewood Cliffs, New Jersey 07632

Printed in the United States of America
10 9 8 7 6 5 4 3 2 1

ISBN 0-13-532987-6

Prentice-Hall International (UK) Limited, *London*
Prentice-Hall of Australia Pty. Limited, *Sydney*
Prentice-Hall Canada Inc., *Toronto*
Prentice-Hall Hispanoamericana, S.A., *Mexico*
Prentice-Hall of India Private Limited, *New Delhi*
Prentice-Hall of Japan, Inc., *Tokyo*
Simon & Schuster Asia Pte. Ltd., *Singapore*
Editora Prentice-Hall do Brasil, Ltda., *Rio de Janeiro*

For Donna, whose faith in me kept me from giving up on this book, and whose love made writing it for her something special.

Contents

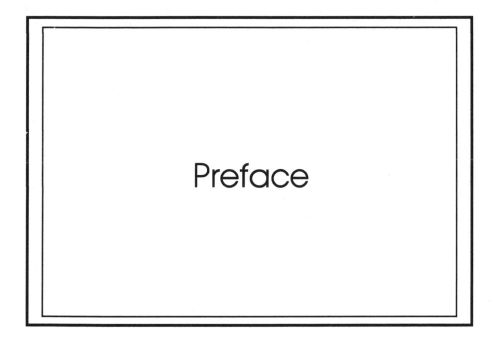

Preface

Testing software is a task of contradictions. Academics tell us that testing is the "search for errors." Management, on the other hand, directs us to "prove that it works."

What do we do? If we find errors, and they're easy to find, we're seen as somehow impeding progress. But proving that it "works" isn't so easy either. Mostly because no one knows what "works" means.

And beyond that, we're given budgets and schedules prepared by others, by people who are filled with the optimism of the developer ("Everything will work fine") or the urgency of management ("Get this program out the door. Now.").

This book has been written to guide the software tester (or the tester's boss) into and through a test program that satisfies both goals, finding errors and proving that it works, while doing it within responsible time and cost constraints.

How do we do that? First, by understanding the entire development process. Next, by planning. Third, by designing efficient test cases. Fourth, by executing the tests in an efficient way using automation and tools wherever possible. And fifth, by monitoring schedule and cost and by being responsible for the money we spend and the time we take. *Software Testing*

Management: Life on the Critical Path is organized around these five elements of testing.

We begin at the beginning, discussing the things that software testers work with: requirements, errors, faults, and failures. When we understand what requirements are (and what our specific requirements are), we can design a test program that evaluates the software against its real objectives: the user's needs. And when we understand errors, faults, and failures and how erroneous software gets developed, we can design a test program that looks for mistakes before the bad code exists.

In Chapter 2, we look at the software development process, not because we're discussing software development, but because that process is the musical score that defines the end product—the project manager and the software manager (the conductor and the concert master) can interpret the score, but they can't fundamentally change it; and all the performers, the developers, the testers, and the others, had better be ready when their parts are cued. Besides, by understanding the process, the test manager can see where testing and other quality functions can be accomplished before the on-machine testing begins. It's at this point that we realize that testing is much more than executing code against some test cases—it is continually evaluating the software product, regardless of its stage of development, against its requirements as they're understood at that time.

After reviewing the development process, we look, in Chapter 3, at the test organization and its place in the total development organization.

When these testing fundamentals, requirements, errors, faults, failures, the development process, and the test organization, are understood, we can move, in Chapter 4, to the most important single task of the test manager: planning. Planning is not writing a document entitled "Software Test Plan." It's deciding what testing is to be done, when it will be done, who will do it, and how the inevitable errors and retesting will be handled. When the planning is done, the Test Plan document can be written, and, in Chapter 5, we discuss two: the Software Verification Plan defined by the IEEE in IEEE 829–1983, and the Software Test Plan defined by the U.S. Department of Defense in DOD–STD–2167A.

When planning is complete, detailed test design begins, and, because requirements drive test case design, Chapter 6 starts that discussion with the subject of "fuzzy" requirements—those requirements that provide no hard pass/fail criteria for the final software product.

Chapter 7 addresses a very unique testing topic: prioritization of requirements. Specifically, in any development effort, not all requirements are equally important. By analyzing system and software failure modes for those that could seriously interfere with human safety or user operations, we can identify critical requirements in a software specification so that we can follow those requirements, continually verifying them, throughout the development process.

In Chapters 8 and 9, the subject is test case design, first as applied to software components, then as applied to complete subsystems. The topics reviewed are test case design and scenario generation.

Chapter 8, "Test Case Design," concentrates on "black box" and "glass box" (or "white box") testing approaches. Since extreme black box testing (functional testing) and extreme glass box testing (structural testing) are both impossible for nontrivial programs, most testers opt for a hybrid approach to testing. But without a good understanding of the theories behind black box and glass box testing, they often settle on a less than satisfactory hybrid. This chapter points out the essential attributes of each technique and closes with a series of suggestions for combining the best aspects of the black box and glass box approaches.

Chapter 9, "Scenario Generation," concentrates on test cases for complete systems (or large subsystems). The emphasis here is on being sure that the end user's operational needs are satisfied and, an important adjunct, that the user can be convinced that those needs are satisfied. An extensive example of scenario generation is taken from the world of air traffic control. This example shows how to build a scripted scenario around the user's tasks and missions while still ensuring that the requirements of the software specifications are met. Such a scenario can be used by commercial software developers as a product demonstration or by government contractors for qualification testing.

With test cases in hand, the tester needs software. Waiting until the developers say it's done isn't a good idea. Mostly because it's never done. So the test manager needs to know how to work with an incomplete and evolving software system. That's the subject of Chapter 10, "Integrating the Software."

In some organizations, integration is done by developers; in others, it's done by integration specialists; and in still others, it's done by the test team. Regardless of who does it, the test manager and the manager's team must have input into the integration process because the result of that process should be a software system that will pass the test team's test cases. Independent testing is all well and good, but an integration effort without significant input from the testers only leads to a second integration effort after the errors are removed. Chapter 10 suggests strongly that the test team's qualification (or acceptance) test cases and procedures be used by the integrators, whoever they are, as the basis for integration testing while the software is assembled.[1]

Testers and test managers working in the custom software environment (that is, as contractors for an agency like the U.S. government) eventually

---

[1] "Assembled" is perhaps a poorly chosen word because it has a very specific software meaning in addition to its more broadly understood development meaning. In this case, we mean assembled in the sense of "plugged together."

must demonstrate the compliance of the software with the contract specifications. These demonstrations are called *formal demonstrations* or *formal tests*. In most cases, these formal demonstrations are conducted in accordance with a rigid protocol. Chapter 11, "Formal Demonstrations," is an extensive discussion of the choreography and protocol necessary to conduct a successful demonstration even if the buyer is less than completely enthusiastic about the product (a situation that occurs more frequently than it should).[2] Test managers working in the commercial arena will find some useful ideas in this chapter, too, since they often get the assignment of developing the sales demonstration for the new product. Commercial sales demonstrations and custom development formal tests have a lot in common—they must be oriented to the user's or buyer's problem and they must show all the features of the software product in the best light.

The last people to automate their work are the ones who automate everybody else's work: the software developers. And among software people, testers are the last of the last. But a number of useful tools do exist that can assist the tester and the test manager. Chapter 12, "Test Tools," was the last one written because the state-of-the-art in tools, test or otherwise, is rapidly changing. But even if the state-of-the-art does overtake the descriptions of Chapter 12, it closes with an extensive discussion, including a checklist, of tool evaluation. So we're always prepared.

Some kinds of software are particularly difficult to test. Mostly because the development methodologies are so new. Expert systems and other software products which are described as artificial intelligence software are difficult to test because they are often created to solve problems that are not fully understood or not fully described (don't have complete requirements specifications). Chapter 13 takes up the peculiarities of the most common of these, expert systems, and suggests ways to attack the testing of them.

One of the hottest topics in current software literature is that of software reliability. While advances are being made, the industry is still undecided on the exact definition of reliability for software. And they're even more undecided on how to apply whatever definition they have to a specific project. Now, strictly speaking, reliability isn't a tester's responsibility (other than, perhaps, to measure it in accordance with someone else's instructions), but the reality of the situation is such that the tester is looked to for advice on how to implement a reliability program for a software development effort. So the tester has to know about software reliability: what it is, how to predict it, and how to measure it. We take up those subjects in Chapter 14.

---

[2] If the software doesn't work, we would expect the buyer to be unenthusiastic, and rightly so. But too often the contractual environment is such that an adversarial relationship between customer and contractor arises. In such cases, the software test manager can do a lot to minimize tension and to reduce the natural tendency of the buyer to resist accepting the software.

The last three chapters in the book address subjects about which testers are notoriously weak: management. Specifically, they take up the topics of estimating testing costs, measuring and reporting cost, and schedule status. If testers can't do that, they're doomed to a life of no respect from project and corporate management. Good cost and schedule management is easy for the tester who knows how.

While there has been a significant effort to maintain consistent form and style throughout the book, there has been an even stronger effort to make each chapter as self-contained as possible. This self-containment has brought about a certain amount of repetition, but it permits an individual with limited time to read the chapter addressing a specific problem without concerning himself or herself with context or prerequisite subject matter.

I would like to give special thanks to Don Mick, who made it possible for me to devote full time to testing; to Tom Gagne, who taught me how to focus; and my wife, Donna, who kept me going.

Chapter 1

Requirements, Errors, Faults, and Failures

Before we can discuss testing, we need to understand what we're trying to accomplish. This chapter looks at the principal concerns of the software tester: requirements, errors, faults, and failures. Without an understanding of each, the test engineer will have difficulty developing a coherent and directed test program.

1.1 REQUIREMENTS

Requirements are obligatory functions to be provided and properties to be possessed by the software or the hardware/software system. Generally, requirements come to the software development team in the form of a written list, but there are other ways in which sets of requirements can be stated.

For example, every time a computer manufacturer elects to provide the UNIX[1] operating system or a UNIX look-alike for a new computer processor (a process called *porting*), the list of obligatory functions is embedded in the copy of UNIX that existed previously. The new UNIX must have all the

[1] UNIX is a trademark of AT&T.

properties of the old UNIX minus one (it doesn't necessarily have to work on the old processor) plus one (it must function on the new processor).[2]

However requirements come to a software developer, the set of them is called a *specification*. The specification that defines the properties of the entire software or hardware/software system is called a *System Specification* or, sometimes in military situations, an *A-Specification*. Before the system can be delivered to a customer, the developer must ensure that all requirements in the System Specification are satisfied. But the System Specification is not the only specification.

As the development engineers examine the requirements of the System Specification, the available hardware and software products, the current state-of-the-art in software and system development, they begin to envision a complete system, composed of many pieces, hardware and software. As the designers settle on the system's *architecture,* they begin to assign responsibility for satisfaction of the System Specification's requirements to individual components. This process is called *requirements allocation*. Of course, the overall requirements as stated in the System Specification are quite high level, and it is likely that several components are assigned shared responsibility for many of them. Additionally, these high-level requirements cannot always be implemented directly so some "lower-level" requirements may be needed to flesh-out the problem solution. As an example, let's consider an air traffic control (ATC) system.

Air traffic control systems are responsible for, among other things, detecting and tracking aircraft as they approach designated locations. While detection and tracking are not the same thing, they are very interrelated. Radars attached to the ATC system are continually detecting objects. The location of each detected object is then compared with the position of previously detected objects. For each detected object that was previously known, the old and new positions provide data that can be used to predict future positions and, hence, make future comparisons with detected objects. The process of predicting positions and recognizing known objects is called "tracking." Detected objects that were previously unknown are considered newly detected, and their positions will be compared with those of objects detected during the next scan of the radar.

System level requirements for a new air traffic control system will include the successful detection of objects of certain minimum sizes and the tracking of objects of interest with a specified accuracy.

The designer of this ATC system will probably come to the conclusion that a predominantly hardware component, a radar, is best suited to detecting objects. Radars emit pules of microwave energy at regular short intervals and sense the return of that energy when it is reflected from some object.

---

[2] Of course, by now, so many UNIX ports have been done that most vendors have indeed written them down.

Depending on the accuracies required, the air traffic control designer will probably also decide that a computer/software combination is the best component for doing the actual tracking of the detected objects. Additionally, the designer will come to the conclusion that some sort of communication device is required between the radar and the computer and software.

From an air traffic control system doing detecting and tracking, the designers have progressed to three lower level components: a radar, a computer/software component, and an interface device.

The computer/software component is, in fact, two components: the computer and the software. The computer must execute instructions with sufficient speed and precision to permit the software to perform its tasks, which in this case are the association of detected objects with known ones and the prediction of future object positions from past positions. The specific algorithms employed by the software engineers creating the software component will depend on the capability of available computers and on the nature of the data presented by the radar through the interface device.

The chosen algorithm for, say, object recognition, and the speed and accuracy with which it must execute, will become requirements of the software component or module that performs the task.

As we've moved from the system level requirement down to the object recognition algorithm within a piece of code, we've *derived* requirements from higher level ones and at each step along the way, the derived requirements are binding upon the component (hardware, software, or both) that is assigned to implement them. Figure 1.1 illustrates this derivation process.

If requirements are correctly analyzed and subordinate requirements accurately derived and properly *allocated* to the constituent components of the system, then by ensuring that each component satisfies its own requirements, whether derived or not, the developers will construct a system that satisfies the highest level requirements, the system requirements.

Of course, that's in a world where things are "perfect," and "proper," and "correct." The real world is not perfect; and that leads us to the subject of errors.

1.2 ERRORS

Errors result from human mistakes. Designers create errors when they misinterpret the user's or customer's requirements; programmers create errors when they write incorrect code; users create errors when they operate a system in ways not intended by the designer or builder.

Often, improperly stated requirements are the cause of misinterpretation.[3] For example, a requirement which states that "the system shall period-

---

[3] See Chapter 6, Fuzzy Requirements.

COMPONENT	REQUIREMENT
Air Defense System	Detect objects Track objects
Radar Component	Detect objects Transfer objects to interface component **(derived)**
Interface Component	Receive object coordinates from radar **(derived)** Convert coordinate data to form appropriate for computer/software **(derived)** Transfer object coordinates to computer/software **(derived)**
Computer/Software Component	Receive object coordinates from interface component **(derived)** Compare object coordinates with predictions for known objects **(derived)** Predict new positions for all known objects **(derived)**
Computer Component	Execute instructions with sufficient speed **(derived)** Provide adequate precision for selected algorithm **(derived)**
Software Component	Compare object coordinates with predictions for known objects **(derived)** Predict new positions for all known objects **(derived)**

Figure 1.1　Requirements derivation.

ically report aircraft position to the operator'' is subject to misinterpretation because, among other things, the word ''periodically'' is often used incorrectly.[4]

Again, most software systems with a nontrivial human interface are required to display the current date (or transaction date, etc.). Interesting things happen depending on where the system will be used and where the designer/implementer comes from. For example, Americans display the date as

$$mm/dd/yy$$

That is, month followed by the day of the month followed by the year. Europeans, on the other hand, use the form

---

[4] Periodically means ''at regular intervals,'' but many people use the word to mean ''when necessary'' or ''when available.''

dd/mm/yy

If we think about how naturally and unthinkingly we write the date, it's pretty easy to see how an American programmer writing code for a system to be implemented in Europe might generate one or more sets of "erroneous" dates.[5]

Errors originating with the users of a system are generally beyond the control of the development agency,[6] so the developer's primary responsibility is in the location and removal of design and implementation errors.

1.3 FAULTS

Faults occur when, in response to a real-world stimulus (input), a previously undetected error in design, implementation, documentation, or training causes the system or software to behave in other than the correct or expected manner. The incorrect date format in the above example manifests itself as a fault only when the operator or the environment causes the system to display the date; until that time, the error is only an undetected (*latent*) one.

Much of the time, manifestation of a software system fault is the result of executing untested code or the result of executing that code in the presence of input data or an operating situation that were not previously tried. However, faults also occur (or, more precisely, reoccur) when previously unobserved errors are initiated. In the case of our date display, for example, we may not even notice that the displayed date is in American rather than European format; it remains for our customer to point out the fault.

1.4 FAILURES

Failures happen when faults keep a system from accomplishing its mission. Errors cause faults which may or may not cause failures. That's where the difficulties arise.

A coding error in the tracking routines of an air defense system may keep that system from successfully tracking an incoming missile. If that missile initiates (or could have initiated) an attack, then the system has failed its mission. But a coding error in the display routines may cause the date to be displayed incorrectly (European rather than American or vice versa);

---

[5] While the precise format of the displayed dates should be stated in the software's specifications, it often is not. However, the fact that the system is to operate in Europe is sufficient to impose implicitly a requirement for the dd/mm/yy format on the display software.

[6] The developer does have some responsibility in implementing a clear human interface which is designed with the abilities of real users in mind, and for providing sufficient documentation.

unless the system is doing interest calculations or some kind of aging analysis, this won't result in a failure of mission, only in an inconvenience to the operator.

Complex systems comprised of many more-or-less autonomous subsystems require careful definitions for faults and failures. The failure of a particular component (a true failure because the component cannot fulfill its specific part of the mission) may not result in a system failure because the mission of the component is not critical to the mission of the total system or because the total system has redundant components or because fault-tolerant software components prevent the consequences of the failure from propagating themselves throughout the rest of the system. For example, the operations centers for most air traffic control systems contain a large number of controller consoles. If the software in any one of the consoles fails, the total system can be reconfigured in such a way that those consoles that remain operational take over the functions of the failed one. Then, provided the stimulus which caused the original console failure does not occur in the reconfigured system, the air traffic control facility remains operational and, hence has not itself failed.

This becomes the tester's dilemma: find errors but (at least in management's view) only those that result in failures, unless, of course, they result in the inability to satisfy requirements. The precise definition of faults and failures becomes critical when estimated and observed reliability figures are used for evaluating designs and in deciding when a software system is ready for delivery. Chapter 14, Software Reliability, goes into considerable additional detail on the subject of errors, faults, and failures.

Chapter 2

The Software Development Process

A Canadian once said that living close to the United States is like sharing a bed with an elephant: no matter how benign its intentions, when it rolls over, you feel it and you may get hurt. It's sort of like that in the software development and testing world.

The U.S. government is the largest single purchaser of software in the world. It therefore has enormous influence on methods used to develop software and on the terms used to describe it—even in the commercial software arena. The U.S. government and its agencies have established a number of policies and standards which are intended to bring some consistency to the software development process, and these standards, rightly or wrongly, affect the way in which software development is viewed by all. If nothing else, standards like DOD–STD–2167A [U. S. Department of Defense 1988] have served to establish the taxonomy of software development.

Before the software testing process can be studied, we need to understand how software is developed. Even more important, it is necessary to establish a common terminology by which the processes of development and testing can be discussed.

2.1 THE SOFTWARE DEVELOPMENT PROCESS

Software or system development begins when someone identifies a problem. It could be that current methods and tools are no longer capable of handling the existing world, or the world has evolved in such a way that a new situation exists. In commercial software development, the person who identifies the problem is often a marketing specialist or someone who specializes in examining a user's needs. In contracted software development, the one identifying the problem is quite frequently the eventual user of the system.

In any event, once a problem has been identified, a proposed solution is devised. In the commercial arena, this requires an examination of existing software, the perceived needs of the user, and an analysis of the products likely to be developed by competitors; and always an eye is kept on the potential cost of the product and the size of the market.

It's not too different in the contracted world: one or more potential developers are asked to submit proposals documenting a solution to the identified problem. The contractor proposing to develop a workable solution to the problem for the lowest, or at least a reasonable, cost is selected and a contract is awarded. In the commercial arena, this selection is made by the potential buyers and users by comparing the costs and benefits of the existing or announced products of the various competitors; the product offering the "best bang for the buck" is selected.

The principal difference between the commercial and contracted (some might say "custom") software world is that the contracting software buyer makes a decision based on a proposal while the commercial buyer decides, usually, by comparing existing or nearly existing products.

The actual processes of code and implementation do not differ between the contracted and custom development worlds except that a custom developer is expected to keep his or her customer well apprised of design and progress through a series of reviews and data submittals, while the commercial developer generally keeps such information confidential.

Commercial and custom software developers approach testing in similar fashions, too. Each progresses from low-level testing, where coders "unit test" individual units or modules, to higher levels of testing, where more and more pieces of the evolving product are brought together. Eventually, a "complete" software system is tested for compliance with the initial specification or design goals (the ability to solve the user's problem). Finally, the product is made available to real users for real-world shake-down and for an evaluation of usability.

Confusion arises because commercial and custom developers have devised different terms for these various stages of testing. Both groups generally call the lowest levels of testing "unit testing" and "integration" testing.

TABLE 2.1 Commercial and Custom Testing Terminology

Contracted	Commercial
Development Test and Evaluation (DT&E)	Alpha Testing
Unit Testing	Unit Testing
Integration Testing	Integration Testing
Formal Qualification Testing (FQT)	
Initial Operational Test and Evaluation (IOT&E)	Beta Testing
Operational Test and Evaluation (OT&E)	

Beyond that, though, things get complicated. Table 2.1 compares the terminology of the custom and commercial software developer. Table 2.1 implies that there is no equivalent of the custom developer's Formal Qualification Test (FQT). This may or may not be true. Almost always, there is an internal evaluation before a product is released to beta testing. The degree of formality of this evaluation, however, is by no means standard and there is certainly no agreement on the name of this process.

Although we begin by addressing commercial software development, the discussion that follows concentrates on contracted software development for the U.S. government, particularly the U.S. Department of Defense. It does so because of the degree of rigor imposed by the U.S. military and because the terminology imposed is the most universally understood. Commercial readers are encouraged to follow along and to mentally translate the terms used to their own experience based on the previous discourse.

2.2 COMMERCIAL SOFTWARE DEVELOPMENT

As defined here, commercial software development involves either design and implementation of software for internal use by a company or organization, or creation of a software product for commercial sale to external users. In either case, as with contracted software, the process begins with the identification of a problem or a lack of capability and the first thing the software organizations should do is document the features and capabilities the new software system must have. This documentation is prepared in conjunction with the end users, the marketing group, or a combination, and is called a *specification*. The degree of rigor and formality imposed on developers of software for the U.S. government has often led software people not in that environment to shy away from written specifications. But that's a bad idea. The specification defines the target, and without one, no one can be sure when the software is done. To be sure, the specification may spell out a system that is inadequate to solve the problem at hand, but without that specification, developers and testers have no target at all.

When an organization undertakes the development of software, it and its management should negotiate the activities and processes to be used in that development. This list of tasks is called a *Statement of Work* in the custom world. By itemizing individual activities, it becomes possible for the parties involved, the developers who will do the work, and management who will pay for it, to see the total scope of effort through the same eyes. Too many programs get in trouble because the parties involved have different understandings of the job to be done. This list of tasks should do the following as specifically as possible:

- Define the authority of the specification;
- Clearly identify what is to be delivered;
- Define the internal reviews to be performed during the development process and the parties that must approve requirements and design;
- State testing documentation and activities that must be performed, including the kind of final demonstration that must be accomplished prior to the new software becoming fully operational;
- Define the documentation to be prepared by the development organization; and
- State the conditions that constitute project completion (including, for example, permissible numbers of known errors at product release) and identify who makes that decision.

Finally, the software developers and their management and users (if the software is for internal use) negotiate and agree on a *schedule*. The schedule is more than a statement of intended release dates. It is developed using the planning techniques described in Chapter 4 and identifies when *each phase* of the development process should begin and end, when testing is to begin, when the software is to be released for alpha testing and beta testing, and when shipments of an operational system are to begin.

Commercial software teams and their managers frequently resist the preparation of specifications, statements of work, and schedules (at least detailed ones) because "things keep changing," "we're at the mercy of the competition," "the user doesn't know what he wants." Well, all of these documents can be changed when the environment changes, but without them, there is no real way of evaluating the effect of a change. After all, it's only worthwhile to complete development of a product if the profit from its sale or the savings from its use exceed the cost of design, implementation, and maintenance.

2.3 SOFTWARE DEVELOPMENT FOR THE GOVERNMENT

The government's system acquisition cycle begins when a government agency (the Air Force, for example) determines that a need exists—that some situation or threat is not being adequately met by existing systems. If the need is deemed real and important, and if funds are available for a new system, then a contract will be awarded to a contractor.

The remainder of this chapter identifies the events that occur during the performance of a contract by a typical software development contractor. Included are definitions of terms and concepts often heard by project personnel but frequently not understood.

2.3.1 The Contract and Its Components

The relationship between a contractor and its customer (the U.S. government in this case) during the life of a project is defined by a contract. The term "contract" is all-inclusive since all aspects of the project are defined by it. In actual practice, however, the word has been used to identify just one part of the project definition: the contract instrument itself. Other parts of the contract (in the largest sense) are the *Statement of Work* (SOW), the *Contract Data Requirements List* (CDRL), the *Specification*, and the *schedule*. Each of these is discussed in detail below.

Figure 2.1 shows the relationship of these four documents to each other. The fifth component, the schedule, is discussed with the contract instrument.

The contract instrument. The contract instrument, which will be referred to from here on simply as the contract, defines the general nature of the project and is the document that controls and governs all others. Most contracts contain standard or uniform clauses that define the general ground rules under which the project is to be operated. Among other things, the standard clauses

- Define the contracting parties (the specific government agency and the contractor) and their relationship to each other;
- Define the manner in which the contract may be modified and the types of approval needed for such modifications;
- Define guarantees and warrantees to be provided by the contractor;

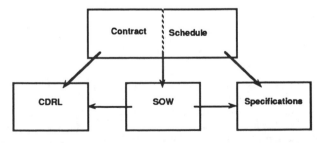

Figure 2.1   Relationship of the contract documents.

- Define requirements for using domestic items within the delivered product.

In addition to the standard clauses, and perhaps more important, the contract defines specific items to be delivered, the dollar value associated with each item, and the rules for payment.

The contract identifies the cost responsibility and spells out contractor and government options should either party not perform in accordance with the terms and conditions of the contract. Some common types of cost responsibility are

- Fixed Price (FP), in which the contractor is obligated to provide the product or service for the negotiated price. Any additional cost incurred in providing the product or service is the responsibility of the contractor and any savings incurred during the project may be retained by the contractor.[1]
- Cost Plus (CP), in which the entire cost for providing the product or service is borne by the customer, with the contractor receiving a fixed or set fee for the effort it has expended.
- Incentive Contracts, in which the contractor and the government share some of the risk for cost overruns but in which the contractor's fee may be increased if it can realize cost savings.
- Time and Materials and Level of Effort, in which the contractor expends a fixed amount of effort at some fixed rate.

The final component of the contract is the schedule. Although not normally stated in the detail necessary to actually manage a program, the schedule defined in the contract shows key dates for reviews of designs, and the like, and most important, for the delivery of a product. By making the schedule part of the contract, the government has ensured that the contractor is legally obligated to deliver software as stated. One of the first tasks of the software development manager (and, indeed, all managers in the contractor's organization) is the preparation of a detailed schedule which will ensure that the stated milestones are met.

Members of test organizations may never see the contract itself, but they frequently need to know information in it.

---

[1] The contractor is not quite so free to set a price as it might at first appear. The U.S. government is aware that, in the case of sole-source procurements, contractors can insulate themselves from any risk by merely inflating their prices, and that for competitive contracts, contractors can insure a win simply by "low-balling" the competition. Consequently, the government has instituted procedures for reviewing prices for realism and fairness. "Defective pricing" is illegal.

The Statement of Work (SOW).   The contract Statement of Work (SOW) defines the specific tasks that the contractor must perform in order to fulfill its contractual obligations. The SOW is subordinate to the contract, but takes precedence over the other contract documents. The SOW identifies specific tasks such as

- Construction of the product in accordance with the specification(s);
- Preparation and maintenance of schedules;
- Provision of a full-time program manager;
- Preparation of training and logistics programs;
- Preparation and conduct of reliability, quality assurance, and configuration management programs;
- Development and conduct of packaging and installation plans and programs;
- Conduct of design reviews;
- Use of military standards (MIL–STDs);
- Conduct of a test program.

The testing task usually defines both the hardware and software test efforts. Of particular interest to members of the test organization are requirements for tests or demonstrations which are not normally performed by the contractor (e.g., operational checkout) and any indications of the degree of formality necessary for the lower levels of tests.

The Contract Data Requirements List (CDRL).   The Contract Data Requirements List (CDRL) is a list of all data and documentation that the contractor must prepare and deliver to the customer. The CDRL

- Identifies the document title;
- Indicates the date of delivery for the document and whether or not draft copies must be submitted for customer comment prior to submission of the final version;
- Specifies the *Data Item Descriptions (DIDs)* to be used in preparation of the document, and any exceptions to the DID that will be in effect;
- Indicates whether the customer must approve the document as submitted;
- Indicates the number of copies of the document to be delivered and the customer organizations that are to receive them.

Entries in the CDRL may list specific paragraphs from the SOW which are applicable to the preparation of the document. Comments or instructions

may also be included which alter or modify the usual interpretation of the
SOW or other relevant documents such as military standards.

DIDs are government prepared guidelines to be used in the preparation
of documents. DIDs usually provide a specific outline for the document and
describe the exact nature of the information that is to be included in each
section.

If the CDRL provides the contractor with no relief from the DID requirements, then the document is prepared exactly to the DID specifications.
If a particular CDRL says something like "contractor format is acceptable,
content in accordance with DID," the document should still follow the general format guidance of the DID since approval of the document may be
needed from someone who just happens to like the DID format regardless of
what the CDRL says (the contractor may be within its rights, but most of
the time the hassle isn't worth the savings of using its own format).

Many contractors have prepared "generic" versions of most commonly
required software documents. These generic documents should be prepared
using the DIDs associated with the latest existent government military standards (e.g., DOD–STD–2167A).

The specification.   The specification defines the physical and functional characteristics and performance requirements of the system or product
that the developer is to build. Generally, a high-level specification is available
at the time of contract award or project start. This high-level specification is
the *System Specification* or *A-Specification*. It is a statement of the customer's perception of the problem to be solved and the customer's idea of
one solution to that problem.

During the early stages of a project, the requirements of the highest
level specification are analyzed and a system architecture is developed which
consists of one or more *hardware configuration items (HWCIs)* and one
or more *computer software configuration items (CSCIs)*. Each identifiable
configuration item is assigned the task of fulfilling a subset of the stated
requirements. Specifications are written for each of these CIs. The specification for a software CI is a *Software Requirements Specification (SRS)*, or a
Computer *Program Performance Specification (PPS)*, or a *Part I Development Specification,* or a *B5 Specification*. Each of the CIs is, in turn, analyzed in a similar manner until requirements have been defined for all identifiable pieces of the final system. This decomposition process is called
requirements allocation.

The terms used to describe a CI specification are specific to the company doing the development, the particular branch of the DOD for whom the
developer is working, and the specific military standards imposed on the job.
DOD–STD–2167A is the currently mandated standard for software development for all *mission critical computer resources,* but software developers

DOD–STD–2167A	DOD–STD–2167	DOD–STD–1679A	MIL–STD–483
System/Segment Specification	System/Segment Specification	System/Segment Specification	System/Segment Specification
Software Requirements Specification	Software Requirements Specification	Program Performance Specification	Part I Development Specification
Interface Requirements Specification	Interface Requirements Specification		
System Design Document	Top-Level Design Document	Program Design Specification	Part II Product Specification
	Low-Level Design Document		
Interface Design Document	Interface Design Document	Interface Design Document	Interface Design Document
	Data Base Design Document	Data Base Design Document	
Software Product Description	Software Product Specification	Program Description Document	
Version Description Document	Version Description Document	Program Package Document	
Software Test Plan	Software Test Plan	Computer Program Test Plan	CPCI Test Plan
Software Test Description	Software Test Description	Computer Program Test Specification	
	Software Test Procedures	Computer Program Test Procedures	CPCI Test Procedures

Figure 2.2 Document terminology comparison.

may still encounter others. Figure 2.2 allocates specification terminology to specific government standards.

The System Specification defines the requirements for the entire system including hardware and software. Each lower level specification defines requirements for a single CI or, at the next level, component. In custom software development, the requirements specified are legally binding on the element being developed, and testing of each element can, and should, be performed against the individual specification without referring to a higher level one.[2] Figure 2.3 depicts the requirements allocation process and shows the testing that is done at each level. In the commercial world, the specifications can be treated a bit more informally, but with an understanding that the looser one is with the specification, the more debate there will be about whether or not the project is done.

The schedule.   The schedule establishes the dates for key events during the system development process. In addition to the product delivery

---

[2] Although most of the test case development described in this book will keep the higher level specifications well in view.

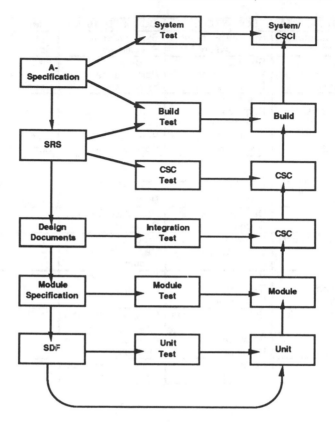

Figure 2.3   Testing at any level.

date (or dates, if multiple deliveries are involved), the schedule defines the dates for key reviews and document deliveries. Contractors expand the contract schedule when preparing their project management plans. These detailed schedules are delivered to the customer as part of periodic program status reviews. Like the other contract documents, the contract schedule can't be changed without a contract modification. However, the lower level or detailed schedules change often as program management makes adjustment in the development process.

2.4 THE PROJECT LIFE CYCLE

Every software development program goes through a process of definition, design, implementation, testing, and, possibly, maintenance which is called the *project life cycle*. The steps in this life cycle are similar from project to project and form a subset of a larger process called the *system life cycle*.

While not every program will include all of these steps and some may call them by different names, the steps are as follows:

1. *Requirements definition* in which the requirements of the highest level specification are analyzed, system CIs are identified, and requirements are allocated to them.
2. *Top-level design* in which the high-level components of each CI are identified and the communication between components and CIs (the interfaces) is defined.
3. *Detailed design* in which the structure of each component identified in the preliminary design is analyzed and all constituent units and their requirements are defined.
4. *Coding and unit testing* in which each of the units of the system is coded, compiled, and tested for compliance with its functional requirements.
5. *Component integration and testing* in which components are constructed from their constituent units and tested for compliance with their specified functional and performance requirements.
6. *CI level testing* in which entire portions of the system (sometimes the entire system) are constructed and tested for compliance with the requirements of the CI and system specifications.

As the software proceeds from one phase to the next, it is continually examined to ensure that the right product is being developed. The process of examining the results of each phase for consistency with the previous phase is called *verification*. The process of examining the final product for compliance with the initial problem statement (the specification) is called *validation*.

Each of the phases within the project life cycle is discussed in more detail below.

2.4.1 Requirements Definition

The primary goal of the requirements definition phase of a project is the identification of precisely what is to be constructed.

The first step in requirements definition involves understanding the problem: Why is this software system being developed? Why has this customer come to the developer? Why has the developer committed a large amount of money to the design and implementation effort? With a clear understanding of the problem, the developers can better and more quickly implement the specified solution, if it is truly a solution, or they can identify better solutions.

It is important, too, to understand the customer's priorities. There may be technical problems that arise later in the project requiring actions that make a complete problem solution impossible. If that happens, a developer may still be able to come up with a useable product by concentrating on the most important aspects of the problem, as seen by the customer, and deferring or eliminating others, always with the customer's approval.[3]

2.4.2 Top Level Design

During top-level design, the basic architecture of the system is determined. The process usually involves analysis of the functions of the system or CI and assignment of those functions to specific components. The communication between components (the *interfaces*) is determined and the details of communication with the outside world (the *human interface* and the link to any external hardware or software) are completed.

The software engineers doing the top-level design often prepare *data flow diagrams,* showing the way data moves about the system, and *structure charts,* showing system architecture and component interfaces. This information is included in a preliminary version of the *Software Design Document (SDD) or a Top-Level Design Document (TLDD).*

When complete, or nearly so, the top-level design is presented to the customer at a *preliminary design review (PDR).* In the commercial world, the preliminary design review is, or should be, conducted by the developer's technical and marketing staff. Successful completion of the PDR permits the project to proceed to the detailed design phase.

2.4.3 Detailed Design

During low-level design, the internal logic for each component identified in the top-level design is developed. Detailed data structures are developed and the units that compose each component are identified and designed. The primary output of the low-level design phase is the final *Software Design Document (SDD),* or a *Low-Level Design Document (LLDD).* The design document expresses the system design using *program design language (PDL)* or, more rarely, *flow charts.* The design information for each unit within the system is extracted from the SDD and included in a *Software Development File (SDF)* or *Unit Development Folder (UDF)* or a *Programmer's Notebook,* together with any information which might be of interest or importance to the person who codes the unit. There is an SDF for each unit in the system.

---

[3] For contracted software, the approval of capability deferral must be explicit. For commercial developments, the approval comes only after the decision is made and a reduced capability product is shipped; if the reduced capabilities are desirable, the customer still buys; otherwise, the customer doesn't.

When complete, or nearly so, the detailed design is presented to the customer at a *Critical Design Review (CDR)*. Once again, the commercial effort will or should enforce internal review of detailed design by presenting the complete system configuration to a technical review team which includes market experts. Successful completion of CDR is necessary before the coding and unit test phase can begin.

2.4.4 Coding and Unit Testing

During the coding and unit test phase of a project, the software developers actually construct the components of the system. A software engineer is assigned responsibility for one or more units. This engineer converts the design contained in the SDFs into code.

When the code is complete and has compiled without error, the development engineers conduct a *code walkthrough* or *peer review* with one or more other engineers. The purpose of the walkthrough is the detection of errors before the unit enters any part of the test phase. When the code walkthrough has been successfully conducted and all action items resulting from it have been cleared, *unit testing* begins. The degree of formality imposed on the walkthrough process varies from organization to organization. Some companies are adherents of the very formal *structured walkthrough* described by Yourdon [1978]; others rely on team leaders and other senior software engineers to implement the inspection.

During unit testing, the development engineer executes the developed code in order to verify that the unit's performance matches that specified in the unit design specifications. The test data and test software used during this verification process is documented in the unit's SDF. On some projects, a *test walkthrough* is conducted. This test walkthrough reviews the test data and test cases to ensure that the unit has been thoroughly verified or that the test data and test cases are adequate to verify proper operation of the unit (depending on whether the walkthrough is conducted after or before the test).

Successful unit testing is required before the unit is eligible for component integration. At this time, the unit will normally be placed under *configuration control* so that changes to it can be monitored and communicated to all members of the development and integration teams who are using it.

2.4.5 Component Integration and Testing

During the component integration and testing phase, the software system is actually constructed from its constituent units. Depending on the strategy selected by the team doing the integration, major pieces of the software begin to appear as stand-alone elements to be combined at a later stage *(bottom-up integration)* or as a partially working, but incomplete, system *(top-down integration).*[4]

Since each unit has successfully undergone unit testing and, therefore, functions in accordance with its own design specifications, component integration and testing concentrates on the proper functioning of the interfaces between units and on the ability of the integrated components to satisfy the requirements of their functional specifications.

Errors detected during this phase of system development usually require changes in the previously tested units and, therefore, a return to unit level testing for some of them. This implies that the unit testing and component integration phases of system development overlap in time and are not discreet or unrelated activities.

Component integration and testing is usually performed by a team consisting of members of the development staff and members of the formal test team if there is one. Many of the test cases to which the components are subjected are similar to those that will be performed during CI level testing. Indeed, this phase of development also serves as a time to debug the formal procedures to be used during CI testing.

Each configuration item must successfully undergo component integration and testing before it can proceed to CI level testing.

2.4.6 CI Level Testing

CI level testing for software culminates in a formal demonstration of the correct functioning of the CI undergoing test. A formal demonstration is conducted using approved test procedures. This demonstration is performed with the customer in attendance. A formal CI level demonstration is usually called a *Formal Qualification Test* or *FQT*. An FQT, or its equivalent, must be performed on each CI before it is qualified for integration into a complete system. Completion of FQT brings about formal configuration control involving the customer; that is, each change to a CI that has completed FQT must be approved by the customer.

Until the term FQT was presented, the previous paragraph was very careful to use the word "demonstration" instead of test. The reason for this is simple: a test is a search for errors; a demonstration is a show. During a test, the discovery of an error, whether suspected or unexpected, means success. During a demonstration, no errors are desired, certainly no unexpected ones, and one that is detected is actually a threat to system acceptance.

During CI level testing, the configuration item under test is subjected to the approved, or about to be approved, test procedures with the intent

---

[4] Bottom-up and top-down are very broad terms. More detailed discussion of integration can be found in Chapter 10.

of eventually being able to execute the procedures without exception. The procedures are derived from the development specifications and provide a mechanism for demonstrating that each specified function of the CI is present and operates correctly. The procedures are, in effect, the test team's interpretation of the functions of the system (and, since they are approved by the customer, they can be considered a correct interpretation); this is compared with the development team's interpretation (the code) and any deviations indicate a need to change the code or, possibly, the original requirements.[5]

2.5 CHANGING THE CONTRACT

System development is a human endeavor and, as such, is subject to error. It will frequently happen that the contract (this time in its very broadest sense) fails to completely or consistently define the scope of a project or activity. This situation can come about for any of several reasons, but the two most common are (1) the magnitude of the problem to be solved was not fully understood and, hence, there are more or different requirements to be satisfied, or (2) the solution of the original problem has revealed possibilities for solving related problems and the customer or developer management desires that those solutions be implemented in conjunction with the current effort.

When such changes become necessary, an adjustment to the contract must be made. The contractor can deviate from the terms stated in its existing contract only at its own risk. That is, without assurance from the customer, either in the form of explicit direction or a negotiated contract modification, there is no legal assurance that the company will be reimbursed for its efforts or that the delivered system will satisfy the requirements of the customer or its users.[6]

Some contract changes are more administrative than substantive, but all are important. Assume, for example, that system development has been delayed, perhaps because the customer did not approve design documentation when submitted, and that delivery cannot be accomplished until two months after the date called for in the contract. In this case, even though the customer may be at fault, a contract modification is required because, without it, the late delivery would put the contractor in default of its contact and make it, at least in theory, liable to the penalty clauses of that contract.

---

[5] That's a pretty strong statement. In actual fact, about as many errors show up in the test procedures as show up in the code. However, most of the procedure errors (at least those that result from requirements misunderstandings) are corrected by the time the customer approves the test procedures.

[6] Even if the contract is followed exactly, the system may still fail to satisfy the customer or the users, but, in that case, the contractor is in a position to defend the system it built as being the one requested by the customer.

Administrative changes of this latter type can be made fairly simply, assuming that they are mutually agreed to by the contractor and the customer and assuming that they have no, or at least minimal, impact on the government's cost. Such changes are usually handled by project administrative and contract personnel; the software test engineers are seldom directly involved (although they may have to estimate new schedules, etc.).

Changes involving an increase in effort (usually referred to as a *change of scope*) are handled very much like the original proposal. That is, all involved project personnel, including the test personnel, are asked to evaluate the change and to estimate the cost of its implementation, including the impact that it will have on already completed work. This estimate of cost is used to prepare an *Engineering Change Proposal (ECP)* which is submitted to the customer for review. If the ECP is approved, the contract, including SOW, CDRL, Specification, and schedule, is updated and the technical implementation of the change can begin.

Commercial developers and testers are well advised to treat changes of scope in a similar manner since the ECP process makes the reestimation and rescheduling of activity a specific and defined task.

The time between submission of an ECP and its approval by the customer can be an awkward one for software developers and, particularly, software test engineers because the development team's concept of the system (as defined in the ECP) is different from the legal definition of the system (as stated in the existing contract). Individuals writing documents that will be submitted to the customer during this "limbo" stage must always be careful to reflect the existing contract even though that may not agree with the latest knowledge about the system (they must also be careful to include the cost of changing these documents in the ECP estimates).[7]

2.6 THE PROJECT REVIEW CYCLE

No software system should be developed in a vacuum and large ones in particular require constant discussions between the developers, the customer, and the users.[8] In order to ensure frequent interchange between these

---

[7] Documents may be submitted which reflect upcoming changes, but only with customer approval. If such documents are prepared, their relationship to future changes should be explicitly mentioned in the transmittal letter that accompanies them.

[8] Note that the customer is frequently not the user. It often happens that an organization such as the Air Force's Electronic Systems Division (ESD) or the Navy's Space and Naval Warfare Systems Command (SPAWAR) is selected by the using community to procure the actual system. This is done for a number of reasons, but usually because the procuring agency is better qualified to handle the contractual aspects of the acquisition process. It often happens that the procuring agency does not really understand the technicalities of the user's problem and, hence, ends up with a less than perfect system. The contractor can find itself in a difficult position at such a time, but must always remember that its customer is the procuring agency.

groups, a series of formal reviews is conducted with the purpose of guaranteeing that all parties understand the problem to be solved and the solution that is being developed. The specific dates for conducting the reviews are given in the contract.

For custom software developed for the U.S. government, MIL–STD–1521B [U.S. Department of Defense 1985] defines the minimum subject matter that must be discussed at each review. The paragraphs below don't repeat the material of that standard, but address the content of each review in terms of the understanding that should result at the end of it.

For commercial or internal software development, the project reviews will be similar to the formal ones mandated for U.S. government contracts. Even though some topics may be omitted or glossed over, the commercial developer without an established review procedure can do worse than to orient his or her project reviews after those defined in MIL–STD–1521B.

During the course of a review, questions or points of discussion will come up that cannot be resolved immediately. When this happens, an *action item* will be generated and assigned to either the contractor or the government. The review is not considered complete until all action items are resolved.[9]

The most common reviews are discussed below.

2.6.1 Requirements Reviews

Requirements reviews are intended as a forum to ensure that all parties understand the problem to be solved and the proposed approach to solving it. From the software developer's point of view, there are several requirements reviews:

1. System Requirements Review (SRR), which has as a goal the mutual understanding of the requirements placed on the entire system, hardware and software, by the user's needs and the System/Segment Specification;

2. System Design Review (SDR), which seeks agreement on the partitioning of requirements among the various hardware and software subsystems or configuration items; and

3. Software Specification Review (SSR), during which the requirements as stated in each Software Requirements Specification are discussed and agreed to.

---

[9] In reality, some action items will remain open for several reviews. The principal purpose of the action item system is to ensure that all questions, whether from the customer or the contractor, are recorded and that someone is assigned responsibility for resolving them.

At the SRR, the contractor will present the details of the problem, including key requirements from the customer specifications, will review the approach to the problem as described in the proposal submitted to the government, and will ask for clarification of points that could not be addressed previously because of the presumably competitive nature of the system procurement.

At the requirements reviews, the contractor may point out areas where the problem solution, as indicated by the specifications, appears to be less than optimum or where the specifications are either self-contradictory or not in agreement with the current technical state of the art. At this time, also, the contractor may suggest changes to the system specification which will clarify the points raised.[10] If general agreement about the changes can be reached, then the contractor and customer will begin preparation of an ECP.

Successful completion of the requirements reviews is the prerequisite for beginning the preliminary design phase.

2.6.2 Preliminary Design Review

The Preliminary Design Review (PDR), gives the customer a chance to review the results of top-level design activity. The highlights of the PDR are the presentation of the top-level system architecture, including a detailed discussion of the user interface and component communication requirements of the system. The basic testing approach for the system is presented at this time.

Many new systems include significant amounts of new hardware as well as software, and the PDR discussions focus about equally on both aspects. Depending on the area perceived by the customer as the riskiest,[11] more or less attention will be given to the software development effort.

The preliminary Software Design Document and the Software Test Plan will have been submitted to the customer before the commencement of PDR, and these documents, along with their hardware counterparts, will form the basis for the discussions. Action items from the requirements reviews will be discussed and any items that are still open will be given added emphasis.

The results of the PDR will be a series of action items to both the contractor and the customer which are directed toward clarifying requirements or design points. Resolution of these action items is necessary to

---

[10] It is important that the specification be modified as soon as these kinds of problems are noted. If such modifications are not made, then the resulting system (which will reflect reality and the state of the art, rather than the specification) will violate the requirements and the contractor will be in technical default of the contract.

[11] Software has been treated as the riskiest system element recently, but experience is showing that this is more perception than reality: new hardware shows up on the critical development path about as often as does software.

formally complete the PDR (although an informal completion will usually result at the end of the meetings). A successful PDR is necessary for initiation of the detailed design phase.

2.6.3 Critical Design Review

Just as the PDR is intended to provide the customer with insight into the preliminary or high-level design, the Critical Design Review (CDR) gives information about the detailed design of the software system.

At the completion of the PDR, major system components had been identified and the interfaces between these components and between the system and the user had been established. The low-level design phase then proceeded to identify the specific units which comprise these components and to establish the algorithms and detailed logic for them. This information is documented in the software design specifications, which are delivered prior to the CDR and which form the basis for much of the discussion.

At this stage of the software development process, the customer is concerned with ensuring that the software design is consistent with the system requirements established at the Requirements Review and with the overall architecture established at PDR. Additionally, the customer will begin to press for resource allocation information such as memory budgets and timing details.

Test personnel present the latest details of the test program at CDR, but the driving document and, hence, depth of discussion vary from program to program. For some projects, the test engineers will have submitted test procedures for the software and discussion will center around these documents; on other programs, the key test documentation will be a test specification or test description document or, possibly, an updated test plan. While functional details exist at CDR and, therefore, test procedures are possible, it is usually too early to provide all of the information necessary for an executable set of procedures. Test engineers faced with producing procedures for CDR should be resigned to extensive revision of them as software development and verification proceed.

A successful CDR is necessary before the development team may proceed with the coding and unit testing effort.

2.6.4 Test Readiness Review

Historically, testing activity has been reviewed as part of the software development reviews at PDR and CDR and formal testing began when the contractor declared that the system was ready for it. DOD–STD–2167A has identified the necessity for a separate review of the software test effort. The new review does not directly address test planning or procedure development, but, rather, the question of whether the system is ready to be subjected to formal testing. Test plans are, of course, reviewed for completeness, and any failure of the customer to approve these documents is examined closely. Additionally, however, the status of the ongoing unit and integration testing is discussed, particularly the amount of software integrated, the number of identified *trouble reports*, and the number of open trouble reports.[12] The government's purpose in initiating the TRR is to avoid the tendency to begin formal testing just because the schedule says it's time and, at the same time, to minimize the probability that a troubled system will be accepted just because a test has been conducted.

2.6.5 Configuration Audits

Software testers are often called upon to support two additional reviews: the Functional and Physical Configuration Audits. Each has as a goal the insurance that the software product is complete as delivered.

Functional Configuration Audit (FCA).   The Functional Configuration Audit (FCA) is intended to demonstrate that, at some point during the testing (Qualification), each requirement has been addressed. If the traceability of requirements to design and test has been carefully documented (and automation makes this relatively easy), then the FCA is a straightforward activity.

Physical Configuration Audit (PCA).   During the Physical Configuration Audit (PCA), delivered code is compared against the delivered documentation. The purpose of the PCA is to ensure that the delivered product matches the delivered documentation.

The level of detail at the PCA can be excruciating. If, for example, a coding specification indicates that an iteration is to be implemented using the DO-WHILE, and the code shows a REPEAT-UNTIL, then a discrepancy has been identified and a change (with the necessary retesting, if the code is changed) must be made.

2.6.6 Internal Reviews

The customer is not the only one interested in the progress of the software development process. Contractor management also wants to know what is going on, and a number of reviews will take place for the purpose of keeping them informed.

---

[12] These two are different numbers. The number of identified trouble reports gives some clue to the general quality of the software as written: lots of problems imply lots more problems. The number of open trouble reports, especially when compared to the number opened initially, gives an indication of the severity of the errors.

The number and type of review varies from contractor to contractor and from division to division within contractors and, to some extent, depends on the size of the contract and whether or not it appears to be in trouble. In other words, big programs in trouble get reviewed a lot more frequently and in more detail than small ones that aren't.

Internal reviews tend to be centered on financial questions, but thinking of them as simply dollars-and-cents concerns is misleading. Asking how much money has been spent and at what rate is another way of asking if the development team is applying the right amount and kind of resources to a program. Management is as concerned with spending enough as it is with spending too much since, after all, failure to apply sufficient effort to a program during development will almost certainly mean financial problems later on (fixing problems, lost business because of a poor or incorrect product, etc.).

There are frequently internal technical reviews, too. These are intended to ensure that a system is well thought out and up to the appropriate state of the art before any presentation is made to the customer. Again, the number and size of these reviews is very much company, division, and project dependent.

All software test engineers will be involved in internal technical reviews, but in many organizations only the test manager is involved in the financial ones. All testers should be prepared to give input to the test manager regarding resources, both manpower and time.

REFERENCES

U.S. DEPARTMENT OF DEFENSE, 1985. MIL–STD–1521B (USAF) "Technical Reviews and Audits for Systems, Equipments, and Computer Software," June.

U.S. DEPARTMENT OF DEFENSE, 1988. DOD–STD–2167A "Defense System Software Development" (with DIDs), February.

YOURDON, E., 1978. *Structured Walkthroughs*. Yourdon, New York.

Chapter 3

The Test Organization

In this chapter, we consider the role of the test organization during the life of the software development activity.

3.1 TEST ACTIVITY DURING THE DEVELOPMENT CYCLE

During each of the software development phases described in Chapter 2, there are one or more related software testing phases. These are discussed in the following sections.

3.1.1 Requirements Definition

During this phase of a project, the mission-level requirements of the software system are finalized and then allocated to its various components. This phase corresponds exactly to the requirements definition phase for development. As the software development engineers are allocating high-level requirements to lower-level ones, each requirement is reviewed for testability. The goal of the review process is to ensure that the resulting specification(s) contain only requirements that (1) are stated using contractually agreed to language;[1] (2) provide clear, precise performance parameters; (3) can be realistically verified; and (4) are agreed to by the customer or the release organization. Each of these testability criteria is further discussed below. The primary output of the requirements definition phase is one or more specifications for the software: a specification for each subsystem or configuration item.

Standardization of language.   The language used in stating a requirement is important because it provides a mechanism for separating hard requirements, those properties of the software that must be satisfied, from those properties that are desirable but not mandatory. Groups developing software for nongovernmental applications can use whatever language conventions they desire as long as they provide a means of accurately differentiating mandatory requirements from design goals. For companies that have no such standard, the language of the U.S. Department of Defense has much to recommend it. Paragraph 3.2.3.6 of MIL–STD–490A [U.S. Department of Defense 1985] states:

> Use "shall" whenever a specification expresses a provision that is binding. Use "should" and "may" wherever it is necessary to express non-mandatory provisions. "Will" may be used to express a declaration of purpose on the part of the contracting agency.

This paragraph defines the way the government looks at the statements of requirements contained in specifications: each statement containing the word "shall" represents a contractually binding requirement on the system and, hence, one that must be formally demonstrated as a condition of system acceptance.

In reviewing a requirement for testability, the test organization must consider whether a statement is truly a functional or performance requirement of the system or whether it is a statement of design that has been included in the specification because of customer pressure or a desire to impress the customer with the progress that is being made in system construction. If the statement is a legitimate requirement, then it should be accepted. If, on the other hand, the statement expresses design information, then the test organization should recommend that it be removed from the specification or its wording be changed to something less obligatory.

One last comment on standard language is appropriate. The easiest way to keep track of requirements is with some sort of data base—in other words, automation. For large systems, the original entry of requirements in the data

---

[1] The tester doesn't, of course, really care what words are used, but it is important to be consistent in the wording of requirements so that they can easily and unambiguously be extracted from the specification.

base is so labor intensive that many organizations don't do it. But again, automation is the key. Either by processing an electronic specification document or by optically scanning a paper specification and then processing the result of the scan, the requirements entry process can be made doable. But for a software tool to successfully identify requirements and transfer them to a data base, there must be some reliable means of actually identifying the requirements. The easiest way to do this is with simple sentences and standardized language—using "shall."

Clear, precise parameters.   Frequently a specification will contain a statement something like "The system shall respond in a timely manner." In this situation, the definition of the word "timely" can become a serious point of discussion between the customer and the contractor, particularly if the specification contains no other timing or response information.[2] In reviewing a requirement for testability, the test organization should consider the ease with which a set of pass/fail criteria can be written for the demonstration in which that requirement is verified. If the pass/fail criterion is not evident from the requirement as worded, then the requirement is not testable; any criterion developed for the purpose of demonstration will not have the force of the specification behind it.[3]

Realistic verification.   One will occasionally encounter clear and precise requirements that cannot be verified because the verification method defined in the specification is not consistent with the requirement itself.

Consider, for example, a requirement such as "The magnetic tape system shall be capable of storing and retrieving data for up to 180 days." Although it is poorly worded, this requirement is a reasonable one for a system that contains magnetic storage. If, however, the specification's verification matrix requires that this requirement be verified by demonstration (i.e., actually storing and retrieving data), then the requirement becomes untestable because the verification process will require six months to complete.

In reviewing a requirement for testability, the test organization should consider the verification method, whether specified or expected, for consistency with the requirement statement.

Customer agreement.   Any capability of the software system for which the customer and contractor can agree on a verification method is a testable requirement.

---

[2] Fuzzy requirements such as this are discussed in Chapter 6.

[3] Or the test procedure document will take the place of the specification for the purpose of definitizing that particular requirement. Splitting system definition between two documents, one of which isn't even identified as a specification, will almost assuredly lead to configuration management and contractual problems.

3.1.2 Test Planning

Once the software requirements are defined, the development and test organizations can, at least in theory, go their separate ways: development begins the (high-level) software design process and the test organization begins test planning.

The test plan is a road map through the software test process; it does not necessarily define how any particular test is to be done, but it identifies when and with what resources all tests are to be done. The development of the test plan is not trivial and a complete process is given in Chapter 4. It is important to point out, however, that considerable thought must be put into the test process before the plan document is committed to paper. The test process is developed in a series of steps:

1. Identify requirements to be tested.
2. Associate each requirement to be tested with a software unit or group of units.
3. Establish a verification sequence. That is, determine the most convenient and convincing order in which to demonstrate requirement compliance.
4. Identify the aggregates of software necessary to perform each test step.
5. Establish a sequence diagram showing the order of testing.
6. Identify supporting material and resources necessary to perform each test.
7. Attach dates and durations to each resource and verification step.
8. Review the plan and perform one or more iterations of the planning process.
9. Partition the software into blocks or builds for testing.
10. Write the plan.

The test plan document is written after the planning process is complete and presents the results of that process as well as additional information about the protocol of test conduct and the specific responsibilities of customer, contractor, and other organizations.[4]

3.1.3 Test Description

The test description is to testing what the design specification is to the development groups: it addresses each test identified in the test plan and defines precisely how that test will be accomplished. Information included

---

[4] See Chapter 5, "The Test Plan Document."

in the test description includes software and hardware configurations, ranges of input values to be used and expected software responses, data collection methods and analysis techniques, accept/reject criteria, and regression test guidance.[5]

For programs being developed according to the general guidelines of MIL–STD–483 [U.S. Department of Defense 1985],[6] the data defined here for the test description must be included in the test plan. Since submittal of the test plan is generally required before some of this information is available, the test engineer is left with a problem for which there is no really satisfactory solution.

Programs being developed using the Navy standards, MIL–STD–1679 or DOD–STD–1679A, or DOD–STD–2167 or DOD–STD–2167A will generally have a separately deliverable test description (called a test specification by DOD–STD–1679 and –1679A) which is deliverable at a time more consistent with the nature of the information it must contain.

The information in the test description must be approved by the customer. Since this data is the primary input to the test procedure development process, it is important that agreement is reached early in the development process. The most common time for delivery of the description is either just prior to the Critical Design Review (CDR) or just after it with a presentation and discussion of the document at that review.

3.1.4 Test Procedure Development

Development of detailed test procedures for use in demonstrating that the software system complies with its requirements is not a trivial task. But, if the planning and specification of the tests and demonstrations has been done properly and if there is general agreement between customer and contractor, procedure development is at least straightforward.

Test procedures should be stand-alone documents which require minimum knowledge of the workings of the software. Each action to be taken by the test conductors and each response by the system should be defined. If the precise response of the system cannot be predicted ahead of time, then the acceptable range of responses should be indicated and a place should be included in the procedure document to record the actual response.

Reality occasionally interferes with the generation of such test proce-

---

[5] See Chapter 8 "Test Case Design."

[6] MIL-STD-483 (without a revision letter—this comment does not apply to MIL-STD-483A) is a configuration management standard and, as such, does not directly address the software development or testing process. It and its associated data item descriptions (DIDs) do, however, define the content, format, and level of detail expected in development and design specifications and test plans and procedures.

dures: not enough time remains to develop a stand-alone document. When this is the case, and with customer concurrence, it may be acceptable to develop "expert-level" procedures. Expert-level procedures are test procedures that require some degree of familiarity with the system or its internal workings on the part of the test team and the test witnesses. If there is a good working relationship between the developer and the customer, expert-level procedures can significantly reduce the amount of time required to get a software system accepted; but such procedures have several drawbacks:

1. Because system knowledge is required to execute and, therefore, to understand the test process, the contractor must rely on the customer to provide witnesses with an appropriate level of system knowledge.

2. Because each input to and each response from the system is not clearly defined, disagreements can arise regarding the appropriateness of an input or the correctness of a response. This is a particular danger where human interfaces are involved.

3. Also because each input to and response from the system is not defined, analysis of trouble reports becomes difficult. The development engineer assigned to respond to a problem is dependent for data upon the description provided by the test engineer and may be unable, because of lack of detail, to reproduce the situation using the test procedures. This particular difficulty can be somewhat ameliorated by using some kind of recording function to keep track of actual test input and system response.

4. Test procedures for different programs or configuration items may contain different levels of detail. Such an inconsistency may cause difficulty in obtaining procedure approval from even a sympathetic customer.

If it appears that because of insufficient time expert-level procedures will be required, some sort of top down or phased procedure development should be initiated. Using this technique, the test descriptions are first converted to "super expert" test procedures. More detail is then added to each procedure so that all procedures remain consistent with each other. At any time, the set of procedures may be declared "finished" and delivered.

3.1.5 Verification

Verification is the process of locating errors in both software and test procedures. While true verification should not begin prior to the establishment of configuration control over the developed software, some level of it can start as soon as the test organization has faith that the software configuration is reasonably stable.[7]

At this time, the test organization begins running the software in accordance with the test procedures. Early in the verification process, many failures will result because of errors in the procedures, but as time progresses, the majority of the identified errors will be in the program or programs under test.

During the verification process, the test organization must be aware that formal test procedures, because their ultimate purpose is as a vehicle for software acceptance, are generally useful only for locating the type of error where the software fails to satisfy an explicitly stated requirement. The search for a second kind of error, where the software does something it's not supposed to do, is more informal in nature, although the test engineers should take care to maintain sufficient discipline that tests are repeatable.

Retesting.   Very few tests are executed only once. Indeed, most tests are executed many times in the process of evaluating software and finding and removing errors. The first time a test is executed, a common result is that the software "fails the test"; that is, it doesn't generate the expected response. When this happens, the tester prepares a problem report, the developer analyzes the problem and prepares a fix. The fix is applied to the software and the test is reexecuted to see if the fix is correct. This reexecution is referred to as *retesting*.

Technically, *any reexecution* of a test falls into the category of retesting. Most commonly, though, the term "retesting" is used to mean the reexecution of a previously failed test.

Regression testing.   When a change is made to a software configuration (whether the application of a problem fix, the addition of an enhancement, or the upgrade of a component to reflect a change in the hardware environment), the prudent software practitioner will want to run some "health checks" to ensure that the change has not had any inadvertent side effects. These health checks are referred to as *regression tests*. Strictly speaking, the only rigorous regression test is a complete reexecution of all previously passed tests (suitably modified to account for the change just made to the software). This is because some changes result in very subtle faults whose effect on previous tests is difficult to predict in advance; the retest is necessary.

---

[7] Stability, in this case, might involve faith that a specific development team or team leader will not permit random or risky changes in a component without notification to all who might be using it. This is, of course, a form of configuration control, but most people don't use the term.

Frequently, though, testers and developers identify a set of test cases that are particularly adept at locating problems or showing proper operation. In interactive drawing programs, for example, a regression test case might be a particularly complicated drawing; in a word processing application, the regression test case might require the editing of a long document with very complex paragraph and typographic characteristics.

Testers working in a contract software situation (where formal testing before the customer is needed) should, at the time a software change is planned and designed, identify to the buyer the regression testing to be done to ensure that the modification has no unanticipated side effects.

3.1.6 Demonstration (The Show)

Sometimes called validation or acceptance testing, the formal execution of approved test procedures, technically a *Formal Qualification Test* (*FQT*), for the purpose of obtaining customer acceptance of the software is not truly a test. Indeed, the goal of the demonstration is precisely the opposite of that in testing: no error (certainly no unexpected error) should be found. The final demonstration is a very carefully rehearsed show in which each of the required capabilities of the software is demonstrated and in which no surprises should arise.

3.1.7 Reporting the Results

At the conclusion of testing (including the final demonstration), a test report is written. This report documents the results of the test process. It discusses any deviations from the test plan, description, or procedures that occurred, and any problems that were encountered (and their disposition). The report includes all output from the formal test process including the master copy of the test procedures with all recorded results and *red-lines*.[8]

The test report contains a narrative summary of the test process and may include recommendations for product improvement or enhancement.

Finally, the test report contains a statement of completion which is signed by contractor and customer representatives. This statement is not a declaration of acceptance by the customer, but simply an acknowledgement that the test was conducted as indicated in the red-lined procedures and that the test data and problem reports, with their dispositions, accurately describe

---

[8] Red-lines are manual corrections to a document that indicate changes mutually agreed to by contractor and customer but that could not be incorporated into the official release of the document either because of time or because the changes were developed while the document was in use (as with test procedures). See Chapter 11, "Formal Demonstrations."

the test process. The final acceptance of the system comes after the customer organization has reviewed the test report.

3.2 THE INDEPENDENCE OF TEST

Generally speaking, a programmer should avoid testing his or her own program and an organization should not test a software system that it has designed and developed. The reasons for this are more psychological than technical.

Because testing is the search for errors, it is a destructive process in that it threatens the design and implementation of the program. It can be extremely difficult for a programmer to intentionally destroy the product of many hours (or days or weeks) of work. It may even be difficult for a programmer to truly believe that errors exist.

Second, the program may contain errors due to the programmer's misunderstanding of the problem statement or the program specification. If this is the case, it is likely that he or she will carry that misunderstanding through into the test process. As Glenford Myers points out in *The Art of Software Testing* [1979], this does not mean that a programmer cannot successfully test his or her own code, only that it is more difficult than for another party.

A common problem for the software developer who is assigned to test his or her own software is *point of view:* the programmer has difficulty thinking like the user or the user environment. For example, when a user perceives that a program is taking too long to respond (to a display request, for example), he or she may, before the first action completes (a) repeat the original request, (b) cancel the request, (c) do something else. The program must be able to handle each situation without crashing. The typical developer, however, may not think of interrupting the program operation with another request because he or she knows what's going on inside the computer: if it's a complicated data retrieval, it's natural that it take a long time, so wait.

The argument against an organization testing its own software system is similar to that for an individual programmer, but it has an added consideration: the programming organization is largely measured by management on its ability to produce a program on time and for a given cost. Testing, when approached using the destructive definition, is seen as a threat to cost and schedule goals because a successful test then becomes one that locates an error rather than one that fails to do so.

The question then arises as to who should do the actual testing of the software or system under test. The degree of independence given to the test team can range from none when, despite the arguments against the situation, the development organization does its own testing, all the way to complete independence where an independent contractor is given responsibility for testing. The latter extreme is sometimes referred to as *Independent Verifica-*

tion and Validation (IV&V), although true IV&V involves more than just testing. True IV&V is almost never done without customer insistence (and customer funding) and even when it is imposed, some amount of development testing is done anyway just to avoid embarrassment. AFSC/AFLC Pamphlet 800–5 [U.S. Department of Defense 1988] contains guidance for establishing the need for true IV&V and also identifies the tasks to be performed by the IV&V agency. Under most situations, the highest degree of independence is achieved when testing is done by a group within the contractor's organization which is administratively isolated from the development team.

Of course, one needs to keep in mind that testing is an expensive activity and the people tasked with keeping costs under control, namely the program managers, will want control of the people spending the money. This means, of course, that program management will resist too much independence. A compromise will then become necessary.

One such compromise is to assign a test manager from an independent group of specialists. This individual is given responsibility for establishing the test program and for designing and overseeing the implementation of specific tests. As a specialist, the test manager brings to the program the independent point of view that is needed for effective testing. The test manager can be allocated a testing budget and given accountability for keeping the testing program within its bounds (in other words, there is a single point of accountability for testing costs and for testing effectiveness). The remainder of the test team, the people who actually write test procedures and do the hands-on shake-down of the software can be assigned from the development team as they complete their design and implementation tasks.

Such a compromise has a number of advantages: (1) it keeps valuable software developers associated with a program (as a hedge against emergency) after their nominal development tasks are done; (2) it puts the people with the best "nuts and bolts" knowledge of the software to work digging out the problems (subject to the independent look of the test manager); (3) it teaches the development staff about testing; and (4) the administrative independence of the test manager protects the test team from the pressure, intentional or inadvertent, to shortcut testing while the budget accountability of the test manager provides incentive to do efficient testing.

Such a staffing compromise only works, though, when the staffing requirements for design and implementation decline at roughly the same time that the requirements for testing increase. This is often the case when a developer has contracted to build a customized, "one of a kind," system such as an air traffic control or air defense system. In situations where long-term development is done, or where the programming staff is charged with designing and implementing a series of products, test specialists are about the only answer.

REFERENCES

MYERS, G. J., 1979. *The Art of Software Testing*. Wiley–Interscience, New York.

U.S. DEPARTMENT OF DEFENSE, 1985. MIL–STD–483A (USAF) "Configuration Management Practices for Systems, Equipment, Munitions, and Computer Programs," Department of the Air Force, 4 June.

U.S. DEPARTMENT OF DEFENSE, 1988. AFSC/AFLC Pamphlet 800–5 "Software Independent Verification and Validation (IV&V)," AFSC/AFLC, 10 May.

U.S. DEPARTMENT OF DEFENSE, 1985. MIL–STD–490A "Specification Practices," 4 June 1985.

Chapter 4

Planning
the Test Process

This chapter addresses the problem of planning a software test program. The term "planning" is used here to mean the process of thinking about the "what" and the "how" of actually verifying that the software performs in accordance with imposed requirements. Most of the process defined in this chapter precedes the actual writing of the document which carries the name "plan."

4.1 PLANNING STEPS

Each of the steps in the development of the test plan is explored in detail in the following sections. The specific steps addressed are as follows:

1. Identify the requirements.
2. Associate requirements to software units.
3. Establish a verification sequence.
4. Identify the software aggregates required for requirement verification.
5. Establish a sequence diagram.

6. Identify supporting material.
7. Attach dates and durations.
8. Iterate.
9. Partition the system into blocks and builds.
10. Write the plan.

4.1.1 Analyze the Requirements

The first step in the test planning process is the identification of the specific requirements to be verified. If a specification exists, the usual case in custom or contracted software development, the requirements come from it. If no specification or list of requirements exists, too frequently the case in commercial software development, the first task is to create one.

Obligatory requirements are identified within the Requirements section (usually Section 3) of most specifications by the presence of the word "shall." Most military specifications include a *verification cross reference index (VCRI)* in the Quality Assurance or Verification section (usually Section 4) which identifies all subsections of Section 3 that the specification author considers to contain binding requirements. If such a VCRI exists, it is the starting point for the requirements identification process. If a VCRI doesn't exist, one should be created.

Build a detailed verification index.   A VCRI is a table containing one entry for each requirement addressed by the body of the specification. As generally presented in system and component level specifications, each entry of the VCRI corresponds to a subsection within the requirements description section of the document. Each requirement entry in the VCRI defines a general method for verification (usually inspection, analysis, demonstration, or test as defined below) and a level of testing (for example, configuration item level, system level, or installation level).

Computer-based spreadsheets and data base management systems make keeping track of the VCRI easy, after the initial entry of the requirements. This initial entry can be quite labor intensive, and has, in the past, often discouraged testers from using automation or even from the preparation of the VCRI itself.

If the specification is particularly well written with only one requirement per subsection and a single subsection per requirement, the initial identification of requirements is complete and the test planning process may proceed to the next step. The more likely case, however, is that each subsection states several obligations of the software or system and the test planner must perform further analysis of the specification before the initial identification is finished.

Consider, for example, the excerpt from a military specification shown in Figure 4.1. This example is extracted from U.S. Air Force specification 404L-50464-S-104. The paragraph quoted includes eight sentences containing the word "shall," and which, therefore, potentially define requirements. Three of these are easy to identify since they are included in the enumerated subparagraphs a, b, and c. Of the five remaining, four define obligations of the software/system and one, the last in the initial subparagraph, merely provides a lead-in to the list that follows. A more thorough discussion of the tester's analysis of requirements is given in Chapter 6.

In a complete list, all seven of the binding requirements of the above

```
3.3.8.5  Message Generation
     The generation of error/diagnostic messages shall
make  a  distinction between (1) the requirements for on-
line messages to facilitate real-time fault isolation re-
quired to maintain the system in operational status and
(2) the logging of fault messages onto system files for
the category of faults which require isolation and cor-
rection but can be addressed off-line and do not degrade
the system performance.  The required processing time to
identify and generate an error/diagnostic message either
for on-line or off-line isolation and correction shall
not degrade the operational requirements for the system.
All messages shall be date/time stamped, and there shall
be no message output to any device while another message
is being output to the same device, unless the error
causes program termination.  The following additional re-
quirements shall apply to message generation:
     a.  Processor message and advisory formats shall
not require additional interpretation by the operator,
such as table lookups and references to documentation,
with the exception of lengthy diagnostic procedures to be
followed by the operator following abnormal termination.
     b.  No computer program shall generate a message or
advisory identical to one generated by the OS or by an-
other program.
     c.  Off-line error messages shall contain as a min-
imum the following information:
                          .
                          .
                          .
          [There follows an enumerated list]
                          .
                          .
                          .
```

Figure 4.1 Excerpt from a typical specification.

Req No.	Paragraph	Requirement Summary	Method I A D T	Level M S P F
0340101	3.4.1.1	Software shall provide control to pedestal servo-motors iaw Interface Spec 4704-37-84-A	T	F
340102a	3.4.1.2	Pedestal control software shall convert joystick pressure to turn rate iaw $r = k\ arctan\ p$	I	M
340102b	3.4.1.2	Turn rate shall never exceed 70 mils/sec	D	M P F

Figure 4.2   Verification matrix.

example would be contained in the VCRI together with the verification method and the level at which the requirement will be verified.[1] Figure 4.2 contains an example of such an expanded VCRI.

An additional note is in order here. The continual pressure by customers for detail in a specification, coupled with the contractor's desire to demonstrate progress, frequently leads to the inclusion of design detail in delivered requirements documents. This information is invariably expressed using the contractual word "shall." The tester may or may not decide to include verification of this design information in the final test procedures (the usual recommendation is not to include it), but it is very important that such information be identified and noted in the plan. Design detail that will not be tested should be identified as such in the master or expanded VCRI.

If a spreadsheet or data base is used to maintain the VCRI, it is often useful to attach one ore more *keywords* to each requirement in order to classify it. When preparing test cases and test scenarios, the test manager will want to group related requirements together. The tester is limited only by his or her imagination when it comes to these classification keywords. Some possible categories are:

- Functional *versus* performance
- Functional area (graphic, tracking, communication)
- Requirement granularity (low-level, high-level)
- Criticality (safety-related, mission-critical)

Establish verification methods.   Finally, a verification method must be associated with each requirement to be verified or validated. The usual choices are inspection, analysis, demonstration, and test,[2] but there is no consensus as to the meanings of these (a fifth method, certification, and

---

[1] The eighth, the lead-in paragraph, should also be included, but with the notation "NR" for "No Requirement." In fact, it's not a bad idea to include every sentence including the word "shall" in the VCRI.

[2] DOD-STD-2167A recognizes the techniques *Inspection, Analysis, and Demonstration.*

a sixth, implication, are occasionally useful). Each is discussed below, but the tester is advised to be flexible about the names of the method attached to specific requirements since, after all, it is the sequence of procedure steps actually executed that is important, not the name or tag given to the method.

Inspection.   Inspection is verification by visual examination. For software, inspection is most commonly used to verify compliance with coding standards and conventions and to verify that the error-handling logic exists for errors that cannot easily be brought about or simulated (they will eventually have to be created, but perhaps after the software is integrated with its attendant hardware). The implementation of a specified algorithm may be verified by inspection (although the proper functioning of that algorithm will generally have to be verified by other means). While the test planner should not avoid inspection as a verification method, he or she should be aware that customers tend to see extensive use of inspection as lacking in rigor.

Analysis.   Analysis is verification by calculation. For example, one might verify a memory usage specification by obtaining sizes of individual components from program listings or a link map, then calculating the system memory usage by adding these figures. The preceding example notwithstanding, analysis is almost never used by itself. Generally, it is used in conjunction with one of the other verification methods, specifically Test. DOD–STD–2167A, in fact, identifies the verification method Analysis as a combination of the former methods Test and Analysis and holds that when the success or failure of a test cannot be determined without posttest data review, then the method used is called ''Analysis.''

Demonstration and Test.   Demonstration is verification of a requirement by execution of the software: the software is actually executed and its reaction to systematically presented input stimuli is observed. The key in the definition is that the action of the software must be *unarguable*. Either the software did what it was required to do or it didn't. The only data recording mechanism is a simple ''Yes/No'' box in the test procedure or the test data sheet.

Test (prior to the definition changes of DOD–STD–2167A) is verification by repeated execution or verification by execution and analysis. Not that these are the same thing, but, rather, both of these verification methods have been tagged with the title test at one time or another. The usual differentiation between demonstration and test was determined by the number of points from the input space which were examined (the number of test cases): if one or a very few points were used, the method was called ''demonstration''; if a large number of points from the input space were used, it was ''test.''

It was a common misconception that a numerical requirement can only be verified by test. Such is definitely not the case. For example, a requirement that an air traffic control system track at least 100 aircraft simultaneously can be verified by demonstration: present it with 100 aircraft and either it will track them all simultaneously or it will not. However, another requirement on the same air traffic control system, namely that it track those aircraft with a specific accuracy, will require verification by test since such a verification will undoubtedly be statistical in nature, requiring the tracking of several hundred aircraft, not all necessarily simultaneously, and the posttest comparison of known and tracked positions for each.

As stated earlier, it is advisable that the tester not be too wedded to the names of verification methods, particularly where analysis, demonstration, and test are concerned. Some customers seem to believe that test is more thorough than demonstration and, therefore, preferable as a method. Since the tester generally has a specific set of test procedure steps in mind (a set that will be used regardless of name), it is just as well to be flexible about the names of the methods.

Certification.   Certification is a verification method that is related to inspection and demonstration. It requires executing a set of test steps, or otherwise verifying a requirement, prior to the formal verification process and then presenting the customer with a certification of the compliance of the system with the addressed requirement. Verification by certification is frequently done as part of hardware testing when the equipment or expertise necessary for the verification is not readily available to the test team (environmental and TEMPEST[3] testing, for example), but is seldom done for software. Since certification implies that the customer won't see the product actually execute, there may be some reluctance on his part to accept the method.

A logical place to use certification in software testing is in the verification of the ability of interactive systems to properly process erroneous input. In the case of an air traffic control system, for example, the number of erroneous combinations of operator input which can arise is extremely large, and the formal verification and validation can take a long time, especially when exhaustive combinations of errors are involved. It is often more efficient to perform this validation on the final software prior to the initiation of the formal qualification tests with the developer's Quality Assurance personnel and, possibly a buyer representative, as the test witnesses. At FQT time, then, a certificate of compliance with error-handling requirements together with the configuration management attestation that the software has not changed can be presented to the buyer.

---

[3] TEMPEST (and the name isn't an acronym for anything) testing is done on hardware to ensure that the equipment does not leak radiation which might compromise the nature of the activities being performed by it. It is possible, for example, to analyze the radiation from a terminal that generates its display by stroke-writing and reconstruct the contents of the on-screen display.

Implication.   Verification by implication assumes that satisfactory demonstration of the compliance of a system with a specific requirement implies that all lower (derived) requirements are also satisfied. If accepted by the customer, implicit verification is an ideal method for use in some "chicken and egg" situations referred to elsewhere in this chapter. However, implicit verification can be carried to ridiculous extremes (track an aircraft, for example, and implicitly verify all requirements in an air traffic control system) and customers are often reluctant to accept it.

As a general rule, during the initial execution of any formal test, the tester should plan to limit the use of verification by implication to those few situations where it is absolutely necessary. When planning regression tests, however, implication can save a lot of retest time by quickly providing assurance that software in areas not related to recent problems has not been affected by the fixes for those problems.

The tester using implication should be prepared to present rigorous proof of the validity of the implicit verification in support of a test plan that includes it.

Implicit verification may not be accepted by a buyer for the initial qualification testing of a software system, but it may be useful later as a means of keeping retesting and regression testing from getting out of hand after changes have been made.

4.1.2 Associate Requirements to Elements

Once a complete list of requirements has been developed (as described in the preceding section), it is necessary to identify a specific piece of software with each of the requirements to be verified. The design documents or the help of the software designers will be necessary in order to perform this task. At this stage in the planning process, it is desirable to identify the smallest controllable element uniquely identified with the requirement under consideration. That is, if a specific unit has been associated with that function, then the name of that unit should be added to the expanded VCRI as part of the matrix entry for the function or requirement. If, however, the smallest identified piece providing the function is a major component, configuration item, or even a complete system, then that name should be included in the VCRI entry. The completed version of the expanded VCRI is frequently called a *traceability matrix* since it can be used to ensure that all binding requirements are traceable to one or more software units and vice versa. The concept of a traceability matrix is shown in Figure 4.3A. The traceability matrix is normally very sparse since most elements do only a few functions and most requirements are addressed by only a few elements. If the matrix were maintained as shown in Figure 4.3A, it would be extremely unmanageable. In practice, traceability information is usually attached to the

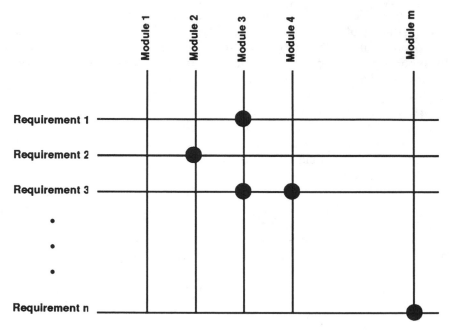

Figure 4.3a   A conceptual traceability matrix.

verification matrix to form a traceability matrix like that shown in Figure 4.3B.

The initial version of the traceability matrix will probably provide the first benefits of the test program: it will identify some requirements that have not been allocated to software elements. While such a revelation may not help the tester win a popularity contest, knowledge that something has been omitted from the system allocation or design is significant and will save time and money later in the project.

A few points about the matrix generated up to this point are in order.

Req No.	Paragraph	Requirement Summary	Method I A D T	Level M S P F	Modules Needed
0340101	3.4.1.1	Software shall provide control to pedestal servo-motors iaw Interface Spec 4704-37-84-A	T	F	CDTRK (full CSCI
340102a	3.4.1.2	Pedestal control software shall convert joystick pressure to turn rate iaw $r = k$ arctan p	I	M	CMRATE
340102b	3.4.1.2	Turn rate shall never exceed 70 mils/sec	D	M P F	CMRATE, CMJOY

Figure 4.3b   An implemented traceability matrix.

First, it is important to note that many specification requirements will actually be dependent on several software elements,[4] *each of which should be explicitly listed in the chart.* The tester should be extremely careful about identifying too large an element (e.g., a major subsystem) since it may be the case that everyone assumes that the element is performing the task, but no units have been specified specifically for the function under consideration. Additionally, if too large an element is identified as being responsible for a function, it will be difficult to perform any formal or semi-formal verification of that function without the entire element.

Also, be wary of software elements that the developers claim are necessary for system function, but that are not traceable to any specific specification requirement. Truly orphan code has no place in a system since the development, checkout, and maintenance of that code will cost time and money which is better allocated elsewhere. Keep in mind, too, that it is very often the case that rather than no requirements justifying the element's existence, there are *a great many requirements.* Operating systems and utility packages very often fall in this category.[5]

Finally, the traceability matrix is susceptible to the old computer maxim "Garbage in, garbage out." If it's not correct or maintained, it quickly moves past the misleading stage to that of being dangerous.

4.1.3 Establish a Verification Sequence

The requirements traceability matrix generated in the preceding two steps of the planning process lists requirements in specification order which is essentially the order in which the author(s) of the specification thought of them. It's generally very difficult and nearly always wasteful to actually demonstrate these requirements if the tests/demonstrations are executed in that order.

The third step in the development of a workable test plan is the selection of the desired sequence for the verification of requirements. At this stage, the selection is made with an eye toward logical sequence and flow: What would give the greatest assurance that the system is actually working?

A sequence of verification steps always flows more smoothly and is more convincing when each verified requirement establishes a foundation for the ones that follow. For example, a customer develops a much warmer feeling about an interactive data base system when the data entry and display

---

[4] Performance requirements are addressed by all elements that reside in the process or processor subject to them.

[5] The system must satisfy *all* requirements and the operating system is the glue that holds all the other elements together. Hence, all requirements, at least all addressed by a particular processor, justify the operating system. Think, also, if the developers change the operating system, how many requirements are potentially affected?

routines are verified before their use in verifying the data base retrieval mechanism. Too, such a sequence is helpful because the previously tested software is used as a *tool* for testing the rest of the software. Similarly, customers like to see simulation software verified as providing an adequate model of the real world before the output of the simulation is used to test and verify application software which ultimately must interact with that real world. The keywords attached to the requirements in the verification matrix are useful for identifying these sequences.

In the process of arranging the verification, one will almost always come across one or more "chicken and egg" situations in which the complete demonstration of one capability is dependent on a second which in turn is dependent on the first. If possible, these dependent requirements should be lumped together and demonstrated as a single test case. If such a grouping isn't possible or convenient, then the test engineer should select a sequence that is. Customers recognize that such situations exist and, while they may not agree with a specific sequence, they'll at least be sympathetic to the situation and will generally be open to suggestions.

A final caution, when planning a verification sequence: the tester should keep a close eye on the development sequence. You can't test what you don't have.

4.1.4 Identify Software Aggregates

Once a candidate sequence of verification has been established, the test engineer must identify the largest unit that will ever be needed to verify each requirement. Here, the word largest is interpreted to mean "At most we will need . . ."

This identification of software aggregates is done in order to determine the level of testing/demonstration that is appropriate for each requirement. The VCRI in the governing specification may give guidance as to the level of verification for each requirement. In that case, the specification guidance should be used as the initial selection. If the specification gives no guidance, or if the specification contains multiple requirements per VCRI entry, some of which are clearly not suited for the indicated level, then the test engineer should select that level of verification which seems most efficient and reasonable. It's generally desirable to perform verification at the lowest level that is consistent with project requirements.

When the largest unit necessary for verification of each requirement has been identified, the traceability matrix (expanded VCRI) should be updated to include this information and each requirement should be allocated to a level of testing that is consistent with the largest unit required.

At this time, the sequence of tests should be reviewed for consistency. This is done because the sequence of test levels must be from that requiring the smallest units to that requiring the largest ones.

4.1.5 Establish a Sequence Diagram

At this point in the test program planning process, a candidate sequence of test events has been developed (probably not the final sequence, but a start), and test methods and levels have been assigned to each requirement. The traceability matrix or expanded VCRI appears as shown in Figure 4.3.

The next step in the planning process is the preparation of a test sequence diagram. Such a diagram or "bubble chart" is shown in Figure 4.4; it identifies graphically the order of requirement verification. Each bubble on the chart represents an event or the existence of a thing (a software or hardware component or a document, for example).

Verification activities are shown as circles or bubbles which are marked with some identifier indicating the activity being performed.

Lines on the chart represent time flow and dependency: Two bubbles connected by a line show that the activity represented by the first must be completed (or exist) before the second can be completed (or exist).

Verification of unrelated requirements is shown by parallel sequences on the diagram, with all of the unrelated prerequisite requirements leading to a bubble representing the verification of the next dependent one.

The version of the sequence diagram that is drawn during this step in the planning sequence only shows the dependency of each test sequence on the previous ones. Identification of external needs is deferred to the next step.

Several computer-based tools exist which can assist in the preparation of the sequence diagram or network. If such tools are available, the test engineer should seriously consider using them. Since the diagram is a work-

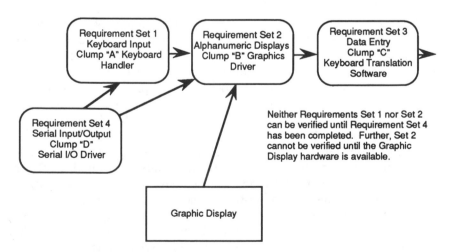

Figure 4.4 Sequence diagram.

ing document and not generally deliverable, its exact form is unimportant; the engineer is free to choose any aid that provides the most assistance.

4.1.6 Identify Supporting Material

Software cannot be successfully tested unless the test organization has in its possession the necessary elements. Also, a successful verification of adherence to requirements is not possible unless the development organization has performed unit level testing to ensure that what was built agrees with what was designed. The final step in this development process is the placing of the software units under project configuration control.

The test sequence diagram developed in the previous planning step is, in actuality, a dependency chart which identifies prerequisite events that must be accomplished prior to the execution of other events. It follows, then, that since testing is dependent on the completion of the development process for software units or sets of units, this completion should be marked on the chart and tied to the dependent events.

But software units aren't the only items or events that might be required before testing can take place. Some other items that frequently are needed are discussed in the following subsections.

Support software.   Special support software such as test drivers, test stubs, special analysis programs, debuggers, or simulators are often required to run software verification, particularly when the level of test is such that complete systems or stand-alone subsystems are not available. It takes time to develop or pre-verify such software, and the dependency of final verification/test on this activity should be shown.

When software is tested *top-down,* missing components are replaced with pieces of test software called *stubs.* When software is tested *bottom-up,* the test software items are called *drivers.* All software developers are familiar with the problem of expending more effort getting a test driver to work than on the deliverable code. Stubs have been promoted as simple test items that can be written with much less effort than for drivers. Indeed, the alleged simplicity of stubs is one of the biggest reasons for the popularity of the top-down process. But all may not be what it seems.

When a stub is used as the replacement for existing subordinate code, it will have to respond realistically to *any* request made of it from the software under test. Consider our air traffic control system. If we are testing the aircraft tracking module in a top-down manner, we will eventually face the problem of designing a stub that will provide the software under test with the observed position of an aircraft (so that the tested component can predict where the airplane will be on the next observation). We have several possibilities:

1. The stub could return the same position every time it's called;
2. The stub could return a random value each time;
3. The stub could return a position simulating straight line motion;
4. The stub could simulate a more complex motion.

Case 1 is the simplest, but it isn't the best for testing the tracking modules. Air traffic control systems are designed to treat objects with zero velocity as unmoving.[6] If the stub returns the same position every time, the component under test (if it works properly, and we will want to test that, too) will draw the conclusion that the object being reported is stationary. In Case 2, the tested software will see "noise" and will (or should) ignore the reported positions. The straight-line stub of Case 3 will turn out to be useful for a great deal (perhaps most) of the software testing, but it won't stress the tracking module very much since it is acceleration that stresses the performance of mathematical filters. If the tester elects the complex stub of Case 4, he or she is close to crossing the line between simple test software and simulation.

It has been argued that the total amount of test software developed for a project will be the same regardless of the test direction (bottom-up or top-down). The tester may develop a few very complicated drivers or many relatively less complex stubs.

Computers.   Software can't be verified without a working computer. In fact, the computer must be in more than working condition: it must be verified or qualified in its own right. Unless the target computer is a specially developed one, this verification usually consists of execution of the vendor's diagnostics and is, therefore, a simple process, but it must be done; it must be done formally; and the configuration of the computer at the time of software verification must be the same as when the computer itself was verified (in some applications, it can't ever have changed since verification). Completion of computer verification should be shown on the dependency diagram.

New hardware.   Just as the computer used for software verification must itself be verified, any special hardware, whether purchased or newly built, must be verified before it can be used for software formal verification. This dependency must be shown on the sequence chart.

It is here with new or special hardware that the test engineer is most likely to encounter the "chicken and egg" situation described above: the software is the best vehicle for verifying the hardware and the hardware makes it easy to verify the software. Which? There's no correct answer; the test engineer must select the most appropriate sequence.

---

[6] And helicopters aren't really stationary.

Personnel.   When additional human resources or human resources with special talents are required to verify software, that requirement must be included on the sequence diagram at the appropriate location. Several categories of personnel may be needed:

- Test engineers to actually execute the tests;
- Software engineers to write the support software needed to do the testing and to help in the analysis of problems and, often, the development of work-around processes for use in testing until the software can be corrected; and
- Hardware engineers to support, maintain, and analyze the computers and other hardware needed during software testing.

With respect to the development of test software, keep in mind that since test stubs and drivers are frequently more than simple "I passed this way" pieces of code, the development rate for even moderately complex software often is lower by an order of magnitude from that anticipated by the test manager. That's one reason why it is worthwhile considering using someone other than the actual testers—who will be busy doing other things—to write test tools.

Test procedures.   Because he or she is responsible for writing them, the test engineer usually assumes that the required test procedures will be available at the time of testing. What is frequently forgotten is that customer agreement to test procedures is necessary prior to the commencement of any formal test. Formal approval is not normally required since test procedures are subject to red-lining up to and including the time of test, but no test should begin without a written agreement from the customer or a representative that the procedures as submitted are acceptable for the purposes of test conduct. Even though it's usually stated in the contract, this dependency very definitely should be included in the sequence diagram.

4.1.7 Attach Dates and Durations

The sequence diagram that has evolved from the planning to date should ultimately define precisely when each requirement defined in the project's governing specifications will be verified. In the state it is as described to this point, it can't do that since only event dependency is shown, not event duration. Some indication of event duration must now be added to the chart.

Availability dates for items and events not under the direct control of the test organization must be obtained. In a project's early planning stage, it is usually difficult to get a hardware or software development engineer to commit to a specific date for anything other than large aggregates of hardware or software (it's human nature to want to retain as much flexibility to oneself as possible) and those large aggregates are seldom smaller than configuration items (occasionally major components or subsystems).

At the same time that the availability of prerequisite items is being estimated, the test engineer must estimate the time required to prepare for and conduct each test. Early in a project, it is almost as difficult to estimate test duration as it is for a developer to estimate code availability. It must be kept in mind that no test is run only once. Each test will be executed a number of times while errors are being located in both the software and the test procedures; each test should be dry run once for the in-house Quality Assurance organization (on some programs this is mandatory); and each test will be executed once with the customer present.

When planning, we don't want a schedule that we can make *with 100 percent certainty,* and likewise, we don't want one *we can never make.* The goal is a schedule with a *50/50 chance of success.*

4.1.8 Iterate

Of course, the plan at this point isn't completely correct. In fact, after the first version of the annotated and dated sequence diagram is prepared, serious inconsistencies with internal and external expectations and dates will be apparent. Some of these will exist because the original ideas and plans were wrong, and some will exist because of changes in the contract that occurred during the first part of the planning phase.

The means of correcting such problems and inconsistencies is repetition or iteration: go back to the beginning and repeat the process.

The second, third, and subsequent passes through the planning sequence will be easier than the first since they will generally be maintenance passes over the plan, but they are equally important since they provide the final details and the polish to the plan.

The process of iterating through the plan sequence will be a never ending one since schedule changes, product enhancements, and so on are always being made. The time to stop iterating (at least until a major change in contract scope comes about) is when all major errors have been removed from the plan sequence and when the degree of change between the latest iteration and the previous one has been minimal.

4.1.9 Partition into Blocks and Builds

Only now is it possible to partition the various components of the software system into blocks or builds. As used here, the terms "block" and "build" are essentially synonymous and mean an accumulation of capability.

Proposals and early customer presentations frequently contain a build sequence which many development groups attempt to keep "cast in concrete." However, one can't make what is really only an intermediate packaging decision until such time as the development sequence and, most important, the availability of modules and, hence, capabilities, is determined. It may, for example, appear to make logical sense to incorporate six units into a build until one observes that the last unit of the six will not be available until two months after the others. The build packaging for a software system should be selected in order to provide both early verification of requirements and an even pacing for the verification process.

While such a decision cannot be made in a vacuum, the partition of a system into blocks and builds is essentially an integration and testing decision that needs to be coordinated with the order and timing of the arrival of software units from the developers. Unfortunately, it is common for the development teams to more or less unilaterally define builds and for the integration and test teams to scramble around trying to accommodate those definitions. It is important to remember, however, that a build is a grouping of functions that is defined in order to provide early evidence that software requirements are being met: a build is a verification mechanism.[7]

4.1.10 Write the Plan

Only now, when the planning process for the test program has reached the very advanced stage of having a completely defined event sequence and a logical build packaging, is it possible to write the document that deserves the title "plan."

Most test plans written by defense contractors are prepared in accordance with a Data Item Description (DID) and the software test plans are usually prepared to DIDs DI–T–3703A (an Air Force DID used in conjunction with MIL–STD–483), DI–T–2142 (a Navy DID used in conjunction with MIL–STD–1679 or DOD–STD–1679A), or DI–MCCR–80014A (used with DOD–STD–2167A). Test plans for commercial products do well to follow the outlines provided by the Institute of Electrical and Electronic Engineers (IEEE), specifically, IEEE standard 829–1983, "Software Verification Plan."

The actual writing of the plan to the outline defined in a DID requires some thought even though the actual test planning process is complete. The reason for this is that the document addresses the actual mechanics and protocols of test conduct in addition to the sequence and order of tests. These mechanics and protocols define the amount of customer participation expected by the contractor and, consequently, give the customer insight into

---

[7] On projects with considerable schedule risk and with critical requirements for timely delivery, the build sequence can be set up to permit early *phased* deliveries of the software. But testers and developers do well to remember that the project goal is the completion of the *total* product, not a series of partial deliveries.

the amount of visibility into any given test he or she can expect. If the test plan has been well thought out and if the sequence developed during the execution of the planning steps defined in this chapter is a truly attainable one, it is generally advisable to give the customer as much visibility into the test process as can be done commensurate with his or her level of interest in and understanding of the test being conducted.

The Air Force DID DI–T–3703A, especially in some of its tailored versions, requires definition of such testing details as ranges of inputs and outputs to be used, specific analysis techniques to be used, and other items which generally are not available until some amount of design work has been accomplished. While this information must eventually be developed by the test team, it is more logically and correctly deferred to a Test Specification (as defined under MIL–STD–1679 or DOD–STD–1679A) or a Test Description (as defined under DOD–STD–2167 and –2167A). Deferring the definition of specific parameters, and the like, to a later document permits submission of a complete test plan which can be reviewed and approved by the customer in the general time frame of the Preliminary Design Review. If this additional information must be included in the test plan document itself, then the contractor is faced with several not totally desirable alternatives:

1. Delay the detailed decisions until their correct time sequence by inclusion of TBDs (to be determined) in the test plan and maintain the plan in draft status until such decisions are made;
2. Write "fiction" to fill the required but unknown parts of the plan document and then issue change pages as the additional information becomes available;
3. Be noncompliant with the DID; or
4. "Pass the buck" to some future document (usually the test procedures) by including in the test plan DID-compliant but empty forward referencing phrases such as "specific ranges of input data will be included in the test procedures."

None of the possibilities enumerated above is really a solution to the problem of having to define test details before the necessary data is available, but numbers (1) and (4) are probably the least undesirable. The "buck-passing" referred to in (4) is only possible if the customer has been forewarned that such an approach is to be taken and is in general agreement with it. If the customer disagrees with this deferment of specifics, then the contractor is really only left with possibilities (1) or (2), with the former being preferable.

4.2 SUMMARY

A Test Plan is more than just a document that is written to fulfill a contractual requirement. It is a road map to be used by the software test team in negotiating the complex process of software testing.

This chapter has presented a detailed process for generation of a workable test program which can be presented to a customer in a test plan document. Each step in the generation of the plan and, ultimately, the plan document, is important, but none is so important that it can singly be identified as controlling the planning process. If, however, there were to be one step identified as more important or requiring more thought than the others, the first, requirements definition, would be that one.

Chapter 5

Writing
the Test Plan

Once the planning process described in Chapter 4 is complete, the tester can go ahead and write the document titled "Test Plan." This chapter discusses the contents of a good Test Plan document. Each paragraph of the two most commonly requested Test Plans is described. The two plan formats are

- The Test Plan defined the by Institute of Electrical and Electronic Engineers (IEEE) in 829-1983, *IEEE Standard for Software Test Documentation* [IEEE Computer Society 1983]; and
- The Software Test Plan defined by the U.S. Department of Defense in DOD–STD–2167 and DOD–STD–2167A [U.S. Department of Defense 1988].[1]

If a good job of planning has been done, a great deal of the information called for by these outlines will be directly available. Indeed, in a certain

---

[1] This is one of several cases where the rather marked difference between DOD-STD-2167 and what should have been a minor revision, DOD-STD-2167A, will become important. Strictly speaking DOD-STD-2167 is obsolete, but its Test Plan format is of interest because (a) some contracts still exist with that version of the standard applied, and (b) that document format has some interesting features.

sense, the annotated sequence diagram, together with the expanded requirements matrix developed during the planning process of Chapter 4, are a test plan. But some administrative and contingency details are missing.

Both the IEEE standard plan and the Test Plan derived from DOD–STD–2167A are intended to be part of a complete set of documents describing the design, development, and testing of a software product. However, the IEEE plan is somewhat more self-contained and, therefore, able to stand alone. So we shall start with it.

5.1 IEEE 829-1983

IEEE 829-1983 "describes a set of basic test documents which are associated with the dynamic aspects of software testing (that is, the execution of procedures and code)." That definition, from the standard itself, is compatible with testing as we've been discussing it.

In what follows, we have occasionally simply quoted the appropriate subparagraph of the section of IEEE 829–1983 discussing the Test Plan. In most cases, though, we have deliberately used different words and have added some amplifying material. Where we have quoted the standard directly, the text is enclosed in quotation marks.

5.1.1 Section 1—Test Plan Identifier

"Specify the unique identifier assigned to this test plan."[2] This, of course, says almost nothing. What is the identifier assigned to a test plan? On some projects, this will be a simple title: "Test Plan Kingdom of Argonia Air Traffic Control System." On other projects, the identifier will specify which of several tests the plan addresses: "Stress Test Plan for the Kingdom of Argonia Air Traffic Control System." And on still other projects, the identifier will indicate a specific subsystem of the complete product and may also limit the scope of a test to a particular subset of tests: "Maximum Throughput Stress Test Plan for the Operator Interface Computer Software Configuration Item for the Kingdom of Argonia Air Traffic Control System." And if incremental development and testing is being used, this test identifier makes that clear, too: "Build 5 Test Plan for the Operator Interface Computer Software Configuration Item for the Kingdom of Argonia Air Traffic Control System." If formal configuration management nomenclature (that is, numbers) have been assigned to products and documents, these should be indicated in this paragraph.

---

[2] Quotations from IEEE Standard 829-1983 are used with the permission of the IEEE Computer Society Press.

In an IEEE-format plan, the identifier serves to limit the scope of the document to a specific test or series of tests.

5.1.2 Section 2—Introduction

The introductory section of the Test Plan is a convenient place to put in context both the software product and the tests described in the plan. The author of this section should consider briefly describing the product's purpose, its place in the grander scheme of things, the method of software development (a life cycle diagram is appropriate here), the high-level product architecture (using a block diagram), and the need that caused the product to be developed.

A list of project references can, and probably should, be included in the introduction to the test plan. The IEEE standard suggests the following documents, if they exist, be referenced in the highest level test plan:

1. Project authorization
2. Project plan
3. Quality assurance plan
4. Configuration management plan
5. Relevant company and customer policies
6. Relevant company, customer, and industry standards
7. Next higher level test plan

Be careful about differentiating between items actually referred to in the plan and those listed for informational purposes.

5.1.3 Section 3—Test Items

"Identify the test items including their version/revision level. Also specify characteristics of their transmittal media which impact hardware requirements or indicate the need for logical or physical transformations before testing can begin (for example, programs must be transferred from tape to disk)."

Here there may be some repetition of information from Section 1. We specifically identify the item and configuration to be tested: "The Single Console Configuration of the Operator Interface Computer Software Configuration Item for the Kingdom of Argonia Air Traffic Control System."

Note that the standard requires that the version/revision level of the software be specified. This can be a problem. Commercial software is usually released as version 1.0, and subsequent releases will be 1.1, 1.2, . . . (or whatever the configuration control process mandates. The Test Plan author can specify the release version or the maintenance version) in which case the version/revision level referred to by the standard will be known at the time of the initial release of the plan. If, on the other hand, the Test Manager and the approving organization wish that the internal version numbers for all the components comprising the test items be stated, the initial release of the Test Plan will necessarily contain a void (usually filled by the letters "TBD" for "To Be Determined). The actual versions will be listed either in an addendum to the Test Plan or in a revision issued just prior to the actual test.

In addition to identifying the item(s) by name (and, possibly, by model number, etc.), we further specify it by referencing the requirements and design documentation. Documents suggested by the standard for reference are

1. Requirements specification
2. Design specification(s)
3. Users' guide
4. Operations guide
5. Installation guide
6. Incident or problem reports relating to the test items

It's probably not a good idea to include *internally generated* incident reports (reports developed by the contractor in the process of design or planning) since with good planning these will be resolved by the time of actual testing. However, externally generated problem statements which have a bearing on the actual use and operation of the software system (an aircraft accident report, for example) are appropriately included.

Finally, it's important to be very clear about what is *not* to be tested. If, for example, the entire air traffic control software component is being tested (an extreme case, admittedly) except for the communication subsystem which links the system to other countries, then, to avoid misleading readers of the plan, that exception should be clearly stated.

5.1.4 Section 4—Features To Be Tested

"Identify all software features and combinations of features to be tested. Identify the test-design specification associated with each feature and each combination of features."

The term "feature" may need some clarification. Usually, we interpret it as a major function or capability or performance characteristic specified in the requirements specification for the software component being tested.[3] The level of feature will, to a certain extent, be a function of the position of the item under test in the overall software and system hierarchy. One thing to keep in mind, though, is that the features defined must have definitions that

---

[3] IEEE 829-1983 defines software features as "A distinguishing characteristic of a software item (for example, performance, portability, or functionality)."

are meaningful to all those interested in the test, particularly the customer or buyer of the system. That means that the test plan author should keep his or her features list oriented toward the end item. For our Argonian air traffic control system, this might include

1. Aircraft tracking
2. Hand-off of aircraft control from one operator to another
3. Operator control of the format and layout of his or her display
4. Degraded operation
5. Handling of emergencies

Such internally generated functions as "task scheduling" or "window drawing" are important, but their operation will be evaluated with customer or user recognized ones.

Writing this section is not easy; however, the Verification Cross Reference Index (VCRI) developed during the planning process should significantly shorten the process, particularly if keywords have been used to classify the requirements listed in it.

5.1.5 Section 5—Features Not to be Tested

When they don't plan to do something that a customer might expect, many software testers, and other software engineers, are tempted just to say nothing. The idea is that if the customer signs off on the test plan with those things missing, then they've agreed to defer those test cases to some later date. Well, that might be the case, but it's not a good way to do business. If you don't intend to do something, then say so. That way there's no misunderstanding.

The list of features not tested will have a similar appearance to Section 4's list of features to be tested. In this list, though, it's a good idea to state why the features are omitted and when they will be tested. Performance features, for example, are often omitted from lower level tests (such as for subsystems) because the performance of one function can be adversely affected by other pieces of the system.

5.1.6 Section 6—Approach

"Describe the overall approach to testing. For each major group of features or feature combinations, specify the approach which will ensure that these feature groups are adequately tested. Specify the major activities, techniques, and tools which are used to test the designated groups of features."

There will probably be several subsections in this section. The tester will take the list of features to be tested, or the list of requirements (the

Verification Cross Reference Index, or VCRI, of Chapter 4), and assign them to test scenarios or test runs.[4] Each of these test runs (that's what the standard means by "groups of features") will be described ". . . in sufficient detail to permit identification of the major testing tasks and estimation of the time required to do each one."

It is important that the readers of the Test Plan understand exactly what is being tested and how thoroughly. Since the planning and plan writing are done early in the project, the natural tendency is to "hedge" the commitment by skimping on detail. But customers and reviewers have to make their own plans, and the only data they have about the test is that supplied in the Test Plan. Hence, the requirement to "Specify the minimum degree of comprehensiveness desired [What absolutely *must* be accomplished by the test]. Identify the techniques which will be used to judge the comprehensiveness of the testing effort (for example, determining which statements have been executed at least once). Specify any additional completion criteria (for example, error frequency). The techniques to be used to trace requirements should be specified." Requirements tracing, by the way, can usually be adequately described by sorting the requirements in the VCRI according to the scenario or feature group and including it with the Test Plan. In addition, the plan should indicate that each detailed procedure step will identify requirements as they are verified.

5.1.7 Section 7—Item Pass/Fail Criteria

"Specify the criteria to be used to determine whether each test item has passed or failed testing." This sounds easy, and it may be. In some situations, it will be possible to merely make a general statement that the results specified in the test procedures will be accomplished *exactly*. In other words, there is no margin for error.

In cases where there is no Test Description Document or Test Specification, the tester may have to list each test item (in a sort of expanded verification matrix) and identify exactly what input situations will be set up and exactly what results are expected. The latter situation is a lot of work, especially early in the program (when a Test Plan is normally written).

More likely, though, the tester will want to specify the number of requirements or functions that may go unverified while still declaring the overall test a success. A statement such as "The item shall be deemed to pass the test if the number of unvalidated requirements at the end of all scenarios is less than three (3) and if no safety-related requirement remains unvalidated." The exact numbers should be negotiated with the customer or system buyer.

The tester might consider defining several categories of "failures,"

---

[4] See Chapter 9, "Scenario Generation."

including such things as *catastrophic failure, serious failure, failure,* and *inconvenience*.[5] The pass/fail criteria stated in the Test Plan would then state the maximum number of each type of failure which are permitted while still considering the test a success. In this situation, catastrophic failures (those that will keep the software system from fulfilling its mission or that might represent safety risks) and serious failures (those that seriously limit the usefulness of the software) are usually not permitted.

Additionally, the tester should address the manner in which the failed requirements that are permitted to remain will eventually be corrected and then revalidated. With certain categories of failure, the entire test (with possible abbreviations) might have to be repeated. For other types of failures, either a specially designed test or an altered version of a future test might suffice.

Keep in mind, though, that even though the presence of errors might not disqualify a software system from proceeding to the next phase of existence (including, possibly, shipment), there should be some plan for eventually dealing with those errors.

5.1.8 Section 8—Suspension/Resumption Criteria

"Specify the criteria used to suspend all or a portion of the testing activity on the test items associated with this plan. Specify the testing activities which must be repeated when testing is resumed." The tester must consider two situations: normal suspension of the test, as at the end of a day; and abnormal suspension, as would be necessary because of a hardware malfunction.

Normal suspension.   While a formal test is a highly choreographed affair that could, at least in theory, be timed to the last nanosecond, the normal case is that its duration is much more variable. If there is any possibility that a test could be suspended, the tester should plan to mark a number of possible termination points in the Test Procedure documents. In this case, the Test Plan will indicate the point or points after which suspension is possible. In scenario-oriented testing where a very long functional scenario results in the verification of many test items or requirements, these suspension points will normally come at the conclusion of each scenario and the procedure should so note. It's important to remember, too, that when a test is resumed, a great deal of the system's data base and operating context may require restoration. This needs to be considered when selecting the suspension points and when planning for the restoration itself.

---

[5] If the tester decides to categorize the types of errors or failures, then he or she is well advised to be careful with both the definitions and with the use of the term "failure." See, for example, Chapter 1 "Requirements, Errors, Faults, and Failures."

Abnormal suspensions. At any time, something could happen that prevents test continuation. What happens, for example, if the power fails during a software endurance run, even though no specific deficiencies in the software have been detected? Obviously the tester can't predict in advance when these events might occur, but he or she should still make some provisions for suspension and resumption. If normal suspension points are to be included in a test, a reasonable approach would be to specify that, upon an abnormal test suspension, the test will be resumed at the most recently passed resumption point, assuming that such a resumption is still possible, that is, assuming that the restart situation hasn't been destroyed by test steps that occur after the resumption point.

5.1.9 Section 9—Test Deliverables

What does the customer get when testing is complete? IEEE 829–1983 lists all of the test documentation, some of which we don't discuss in this book:

1. Test plan
2. Test design specifications
3. Test case specifications
4. Test procedure specifications
5. Test item transmittal reports
6. Test logs
7. Test incident reports
8. Test summary reports
9. Test input data and test output data should be identified as deliverables
10. Test tools (for example, module drivers and stubs) should also be included

The one thing that IEEE 829-1983 omits is that these items should be listed only if (a) their preparation is within the scope of the project, and (b) the tester actually intends to prepare them. Test design specifications and test case specifications may actually be part of the same document (with a very different title).

One should, of course, also include the tested software as part of the test deliverables.

5.1.10 Section 10—Testing Tasks

"Identify the set of tasks necessary to prepare for and perform testing. Identify all intertask dependencies and any special skills required."

Each bubble on the sequence diagram developed during the planning process (Chapter 4) is a task. In Chapter 16 on Status Accounting, we suggest (insist on) writing a detailed description of each of these tasks. These descriptions can be included in the Test Plan.

5.1.11 Section 11—Environmental Needs

Environment is *everything* required to test the software except for the software itself. All the support hardware and software identified during planning (in the previous chapter) should be listed here. Of all the paragraphs in 829-1983 about the Test Plan, this is the clearest; little extra is needed. However, it is useful to list the kinds of items the standard is requesting and make an occasional amplifying comment.

"The physical characteristics of the facilities including the hardware, the communications and system software, the mode of usage (for example, stand-alone), and any other software or supplies needed to support the test." In a nutshell, what is the setup? The easiest way to satisfy this requirement is with a simple sentence or two: "The test will be conducted at the Air Defense Laboratory of the Government Systems Division of Super Software, Inc. The HyperCyber 404 processor with OS9/90 executing in stand-alone mode will be the host computer during test execution. In addition, an Ethernet™ communication line to a satellite Moon300 workstation running UNIX™ will be required. A test configuration block diagram is shown in Figure . . ." Among other things, this section lets management know if anything exotic is needed for the test.

"Also specify the level of security which must be provided for the test facilities, system software, and proprietary components such as software, data, and hardware." Many testers neglect to consider security (and the lucky ones don't have to worry about it), but of all the hidden pitfalls in testing, this may be the deepest. If all appropriate security precautions aren't taken at the right time, no amount of pressure from any source can get the security watchdogs to relent. Many a DOD contractor has come to acceptance test time only to be told by *his own* security people that the test couldn't be run.

"Identify special test tools needed . . . ." Anything the tester doesn't have routinely available should be listed. With respect to tools, the big question is how to install and verify them.

5.1.12 Section 12—Responsibilities

"Identify the groups responsible for managing, designing, preparing, executing, witnessing, checking, and resolving. In addition, identify the groups responsible for providing the test items identified in 3.2.3 [Section 3—Test Items] and the environmental needs identified in 3.2.11 [Section 11—Environmental needs]." In other words, who is on the hook for each of the tasks and items listed in the plan. From this list, the tester or program manager can develop written assignments for all these items.

5.1.13 Section 13—Staffing and Training

"Specify staffing needs by skill level. Identify training options for providing necessary skills." The procedure for computing staffing levels can be found in Chapters 15 (Estimating Test Costs) and 16 (Status Accounting), but a brief discussion is appropriate here.

Each task described in Section 10 of the Test Plan should be analyzed and the amount of effort (in person-months), E, determined. Then the task duration, D, is computed from project schedule or from the task time-line. An estimate of the number of people, P, required for the task is calculated from

$$P = \frac{E}{D}$$

For example, for a task that is estimated as requiring 15 person-months of effort, but that must be completed in 6 calendar months, the Test Manager must assign 15/6 or 2.5 people. (Of course, as Fred Brooks points out so forcefully in his book *The Mythical Man-Month* [Brooks 1975], people and time are *not* interchangeable. But as a first approximation, this calculation is reasonable.) Finally, the test planner decides if each of these people must possess the same skill levels. For most tasks requiring more than one person, a leader is assigned who has some fairly high level of skill or seniority, and the remainder of the staff is filled by more junior individuals. If specific skills (operating system experience, say) aren't available, the tester should identify the method of training the people who will be assigned to the task. If the work is being done for the government, include the level of security clearance required to perform the task.

5.1.14 Section 14—Schedule

"Include test milestones identified in the Software Project Schedule as well as item transmittal events." This requirement can be satisfied by including the event chart (bubble diagram) developed during the planning process. IEEE 829-1983 asks that additional test milestones be included and that the time duration for each task be estimated. All of this information is available in the tester's time line. It may be desirable, though, to change the format of the chart from a Pert-like bubble chart to a more conventional set of time lines (called a Gantt chart or bar chart). If the time line was developed using an automated tool, this kind of conversion is almost certainly available. For a more detailed discussion of scheduling, see Kerzner [1979].

It should go without saying, of course, that the testing schedule presented in the Test Plan should be consistent with the software development schedule presented in the Software Development Plan and with the overall system schedule in the System Management Plan.

5.1.15 Section 15—Risks and Contingencies

"Identify the high risk assumptions of the test plan. Specify contingency plans for each (for example, delayed delivery of test items might require increased night shift scheduling to meed the delivery date)." The essence of management is planning for problems. Anyone can manage when things go according to plan, but what do you do when things go wrong? This section of the plan may be the most important of all because it is here that the beginnings of these plans are developed and presented.

Of course, it's not necessary to list every possible thing that could go wrong, because most of them won't. But it is important to list (a) the things most likely to go wrong, and (b) the things that will have the biggest impact if they do go wrong, regardless of the probability. The tester should go back to the list of test items and the list of environmental needs and ask himself or herself just how important each of these items is and how confident he or she is about the availability dates. If the task plan bubble chart was created using a project scheduling tool, the tool can identify *slack time* available before each of these items is required. If there is little or no slack time or if the consequence of a delay is severe, then a contingency or work-around plan is needed.

In identifying work-arounds, the tester is limited only by his or her creativity. Some, but by no means all, of the possibilities are

- Working nonstandard shifts
- Working overtime (longer days, or weekends, or both)
- Adding additional personnel[6]
- Deferring some test items to later tests—if the test items are late or if the error content in previous ones has been high
- Using simple test drivers rather than sophisticated simulators—if it's the simulator that's late
- Reducing the amount of detail in developed test procedures (using "expert-level" test procedures)—if the test procedures are late or if there is a significant specification change or other event that makes on-time completion of the procedures risky

---

[6] Remember Brooks in *The Mythical Man-Month* [Brooks 1975]: "Adding manpower to a late project only makes it later."

Of course, it is important to state in the plan that no contingency plan will be put into effect without the approval of project management and (probably) the customer or buyer.

5.1.16 Section 16—Approvals

"Specify the names and titles of all persons who must approve this plan. Provide space for the signatures and dates." This is self-explanatory.

5.2 DOD–STD–2167A

DOD–STD–2167A can define the software development process for any software product, but its use is mandated by the Secretary of Defense for all *Mission Critical Computer Resources* (MCCRs). But what is a mission critical computer resource? There is a long, rather involved, official definition which can be found in MIL–HDBK–347 [U.S. Department of Defense 1990],[7] but the best practical definition was given by a wag at a workshop

---

[7] The long, rather involved, official definition follows:

"Title 10, United States Code, Section 2315 (Public Law 97-86) provides legal requirements for the acquisition of computer resources within the DoD. For the purposes of this document, MCCR is defined as follows.

A. Mission-Critical Computer Resources are elements of computer hardware, software, or services whose function, operation or use:
1. involves intelligence activities;
2. involves cryptological activities related to national security;
3. involves the command and control of military forces;
4. involve equipment which is an integral part of a weapon or weapons system; or
5. is critical to the direct fulfillment of military or intelligence missions provided that it does not include automatic data processing equipment used for routine administrative business applications such as payroll, finance, logistics, and personnel management.

B. Computer resources whose function, purpose, or use are critical to the direct fulfillment of military or intelligence missions include, but not be limited to:
1. Warning, surveillance, reconnaissance, and electronic warfare systems;
2. Mission-support systems deployed in combat environments;
3. Classified systems and programs;
4. Strategic and tactical military communications systems;
5. Satellite systems supporting strategic or tactical military missions;
6. Environment monitoring and predictions systems directly supporting military missions (e.g., weather and oceanographic);
7. Locating, positioning, mapping, charting and geodesy systems directly supporting military missions;
8. Maintenance systems which provide direct support to weapons systems and software support facilities;
9. Systems used internally within the Department of Defense for classified analyses, research and development in direct support of military or intelligence missions.

C. Computer resources used primarily for routine administrative and business applications such as payroll, finance, logistics, and personnel management shall not be considered military or intelligence mission-critical."

sponsored by the Software Engineering Institute, a government-funded software research center located at Carnegie Mellon University in Pittsburgh. This individual remarked that "if the software is in something that flies or blows up, then it's an MCCR."

The Test Plan described in this section covers formal, or qualification, testing only. Other aspects of testing and test management are either covered elsewhere or are not addressed at all. For example, integration testing and general system shakedown are described in the Software Development Plan. Other test-related topics, such as risks and contingencies, aren't required. This shouldn't be taken to mean that the test manager needn't think about these things. On the contrary, the test manager should have considerable influence on test-related sections of the Software Development Plan, even if members of the development team (or a separate integration team) are charged with nonformal test tasks. Again, the test manager *must* address the topic of risks and contingencies, even if he or she doesn't include risk material in the test plan. The test manager whose test activities are guided and controlled by DOD–STD–2167A does well to keep a copy of IEEE 829-1983 as an additional reference.

5.2.1 Section 1—Scope

Documents prepared to satisfy DOD–STD–2167A, like those written for other government specifications, will contain a number of more-or-less empty paragraphs. This is one of them. The meat of Section 1 is in its constituent paragraphs, not this outer one. Some contractors will submit documents in which outer paragraphs like this one contain no text; others fill a section like this one with a vacuous statement like "This section defines the scope of this Test Plan." It's a matter of taste.

Paragraph 1.1—identification. "This paragraph . . . shall contain the approved identification number, title, and abbreviation, if applicable, of the system to which this STP [Software Test Plan] applies. It shall also identify CSCIs to which this plan applies. If the STP applies to all CSCIs in the system, this shall be stated. If it applies to selected CSCIs, the applicable CSCIs shall be named by title, abbreviation, and identifier." The U.S. Department of Defense maintains a complicated and comprehensive *nomenclature* system for identifying the systems it buys. This paragraph should supply that nomenclature, if it's known at the time, the official name of the system, and its common name or abbreviation. Since the CSCIs to which the plan applies must be explicitly stated, it is not inappropriate to also include a very high-level *structure diagram* for the system. Note that this structure diagram is not a block diagram, that comes in the next paragraph. A typical entry in this paragraph would read like the following:

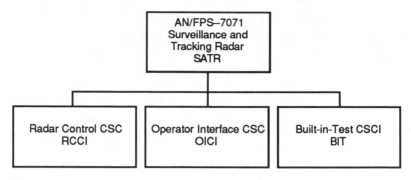

Figure 5.1 A simple CSCI structure chart.

This Software Test Plan, CDRL H005, defines the testing process for the AN/FPS–7071, Surveillance and Track Radar, abbreviated SATR. This Test Plan applies to all Computer Software Configuration Items (CSCIs) included in the SATR, as shown in Figure 1-1, except for the Operating System CSCI, OSCI, which is supplied as commercial off-the-shelf software.

The CSCI structure diagram, referred to in the above paragraph, would appear as shown in Figure 5.1.

Paragraph 1.2—system overview.   This section contains a very brief description of what is going on. That is, what is this new system supposed to accomplish? Most developers have a common paragraph that is used in the system overview section of all documents.

Paragraph 1.3—document overview.   "This paragraph . . . shall summarize the purpose and contents of this document." The best way to fulfill this requirement is to quote the description and purpose of the Test Plan as stated in the DID:

> The Software Test Plan (STP) describes the formal qualification test plans for one or more Computer Software Configuration Items (CSCIs). The STP identifies the software test environment resources required for formal qualification testing (FQT) and provides schedules for FQT activities. In addition, the STP identifies the individual tests that shall be performed during FQT.

If there are any exceptions to the DID (and they should be negotiated with the customer before submitting the plan), they should be stated here. For example: "No test schedule is included in paragraph 4.9.5. Reference is made to the master project schedule contained in the Program Plan submitted as CDRL item A017." This, by the way, is more than an example, it's a good idea. If a separate schedule is carried in the Test Plan, then the plan's author must be very careful to define the order of precedence between the master schedule and the schedule in the Test Plan: redundant information quickly becomes contradictory information.

Paragraph 1.4—relationship to other plans.   "This paragraph shall . . . describe the relationship, if any, of the STP to related project management plans." Really, this means that the tester should discuss the relationship of the tests discussed here with those described in other plans, specifically higher level plans and hardware plans. It's not "plan-to-plan" but "test-to-test."

5.2.2 Section 2—Referenced Documents

The title of this section is "Referenced documents," and it's important to remember that. The tester should not simply supply a project bibliography in this section (unless, of course, that's what the customer expects). Many times a development company's internal Quality Assurance organization or, worse, the customer's auditors check for compliance of action with contract and promise (as stated in submitted documents). Many of those promises are derived from documents listed in Section 2. A tester doesn't want to get hanged for failing to do something that was promised in a reference. But, the reference list is the perfect place to list all those documents which already say those things that reasonably belong in the Test Plan.

5.2.3 Section 3—Software Test Environment

"This section {describes} the plans for implementing and controlling the resources (software, firmware, and hardware) necessary to perform qualification testing." Section 3 addresses the subject of *control,* that is, how does the tester and the customer keep track of what is about to be tested and what has been tested so they don't have to be tested again? A literal reading of the DID will convince the tester that all the government is worried about in this section is *nondevelopmental software (NDS)*[8] and hardware needed to support testing. That's so, but some explicit reference should be made to project configuration management plans, whether expressed in a separate document or as part of company policy, regarding the delivered product. DOD–STD–1467 (AR) [U.S. Department of Defense 1985] defines the proce-

---

[8] Nondevelopmental software (NDS) is any software that is not an end product of the development process, but that is necessary for the creation, testing, or maintenance of the software product. This certainly includes specially developed test software, but it may also include commercial debuggers, utility libraries, the compiler or assembler for the implementation language, the linker used to build the system, and, possibly, the operating system under which all these products function. It's very important that contract software developers have an established definition of NDS and a policy for handling it.

dures for maintaining that portion of NDS needed for the maintenance of software once it becomes operational.

This specific paragraph, that is the outer paragraph, 3, will be vacuous or nearly so, but the control mechanisms should be clearly spelled out in the constituent paragraphs. When writing the Test Plan, the tester should remember that references to other documents, where the same information has already been provided, is encouraged.

Paragraph 3.1—software items.   The author of the Data Item Description (DID) for the Test Plan did a pretty good job of itemizing the kinds of things that should be listed in this paragraph: operating systems, compilers, code auditors, dynamic path analyzers, test drivers, preprocessors, test data generators, and post processors. *Anything* of a software nature that is needed to perform the tests described in the test plan should be included in the list. Additionally, the purpose of each item should be stated. The purpose of most items in the list will be obvious, but by explicitly stating what the support items are used for, the reader will have a basis for choosing alternatives should the need arise.

Ideally, security issues should be discussed in a separate part of a test plan where hardware and software issues can be seen together. However, the DID author has elected to have software and hardware security aspects discussed separately, and this paragraph, 3.1, is where software security and classification is described.

Paragraph 3.2—hardware and firmware items.   What Paragraph 3.1 did for support software, this paragraph does for support hardware and firmware. Again, *anything* necessary to support software testing is listed here, together with its purpose in the test. Examples of hardware support items are the computer to host the tested software, monitoring or test equipment (oscilloscopes, frequency analyzers, calculators, etc.), special interface devices, and simulators, if they can be treated as stand-alone external devices. Hardware security issues are discussed here, too.

Paragraph 3.3—proprietary nature, and government rights.   The subject of proprietary software, licensing, and government (or customer) rights to developed and support software is incredibly large and not well understood. It certainly is beyond most software test managers. The writer of a Test Plan should limit himself or herself to listing those software and hardware items involved in the described tests for which the government (customer) must acquire a license. Operating systems and many configuration management and commercial test support tools fall in this category.

Software developers who produce products for internal use or for commercial sale almost always maintain their own programs, but purchasers of contracted software (custom software developed in accordance with a specification) may elect to have someone other than the original producer take on that task. The U.S. government worries about rights to support software because it also worries about maintenance and enhancement of the developed system. Often, the government itself is involved in maintenance. The government wants to ensure that it has available to it all the support material (or at least equivalent support material) used by the initial software developer.

For the unsure software test manager, it's best to check with the project contract administrator or the company's legal department before completing this section of the Test Plan.

Paragraph 3.4—installation, testing, and control.   "This paragraph . . . shall identify the contractor's plans for installing and testing each item prior to its use. This paragraph shall also describe the contractor's plans for controlling and maintaining each item of the software test environment." It sounds simple, but there are many potential pitfalls in this paragraph.

The last thing a tester wants to do is get involved in testing of commercial software (so-called "Commercial Off–the–Shelf" or COTS). In fact, unless absolutely necessary to convince himself or herself that it's really working, no testing, certainly no formal testing, should be performed on other than the delivered product. But how does one convince a customer that the support items are functioning? A common and useful approach is to state that "Commercial or vendor software will be installed in accordance with vendor instructions [or by a vendor representative]. Successful installation will be taken as evidence of proper operation of the product." This works because it's exactly what a developer does; it is, in effect, verification by certification. Note, though, that because the data bases associated with some support products evolve (and deteriorate) with time, it may be necessary to require reinstallation prior to any formal test.

A similar statement can be made for support hardware: "Commercial or vendor hardware will be installed in accordance with vendor instructions [or by a vendor representative]. Prior to any use of the hardware product in formal verification or validation, vendor-supplied diagnostics will be executed. Successful operation of these diagnostics will be taken as evidence of proper operation of the product." Diagnostic execution prior to a test is necessary, of course, because hardware may eventually wear out.

The tester must also describe how he or she will ensure that the support items, both hardware and software, are the latest releases or are the same as used in previous tests. In other words, how will the *configuration* of the support products be *managed*? Permitting the products to evolve as new releases become available or establishing a baseline release for the duration of testing (and, possibly, product life), are about the only options.

5.2.4 Section 4—Formal Qualification and Test Identification

Section 4 of this Test Plan describes in detail each of the tests that will be run on each Computer Software Configuration Item (CSCI), that is, usually, major subsystem. The meat of this section is in its constituent paragraphs, not this introductory one. Whether or not to include a vacuous introductory statement is, again, a matter of taste.

Paragraph 4.X—(CSCI name and project-unique identifier). Government specification writers seek to cover all possibilities. In this case, they have established a structure which permits a single Test Plan to define the testing requirements for any number of CSCIs. This is a significant cost saver for developers and testers of complex software systems composed of several CSCIs. In the past, a separate Test Plan was required, by standard, for each configuration item. This, of course, resulted in lots of documents, lots of document reviews by both developer and customer, and a great deal of wasted activity. DOD-STD-2167A and the Data Item Description DI-MCCR-80014A, which defines the Test Plan contents, allow for inclusion of all formal testing definitions in a single document. If, for example, there are five CSCIs in a new system, then the Test Plan will contain sections 4.1, 4.2, 4.3, 4.4, and 4.5, each with the subparagraphs as shown in Figure 5.2.

Subparagraph 4.X.1—General Test Requirements. This subparagraph gives the basic ground rules for the test process and establishes the nature of the tests described in components of subparagraph 4.X.4. The contents of this subparagraph serve as guidance to the test procedure writer. The author of the DID has done a good job of giving examples of the kinds of information to be included:

Sub- Section	4.1	4.2	4.3	4.4	4.5
Fixed	*4.1.1*	*4.2.1*	*4.3.1*	*4.4.1*	*4.5.1*
Fixed	*4.1.2*	*4.2.2*	*4.3.2*	*4.4.2*	*4.5.2*
Fixed	*4.1.3*	*4.2.3*	*4.3.3*	*4.4.3*	*4.5.3*
Fixed Intro	*4.1.4*	*4.2.4*	*4.3.4*	*4.4.4*	*4.5.4*
If needed	4.1.4.1	4.2.4.1	4.3.4.1	4.4.4.1	4.5.4.1
If needed	4.1.4.2	4.2.4.2	4.3.4.2	4.4.4.2	4.5.4.2
If needed		4.2.4.3	4.3.4.3		4.5.4.3
If needed		4.2.4.4	4.3.4.4		
If needed		4.2.4.5			
Fixed	*4.1.5*	*4.2.5*	*4.3.5*	*4.4.5*	*4.5.5*

Entries in *italics* are required. Entries in normal type are included as needed. The first (the xx.1) entry is almost always needed.

Figure 5.2 Paragraph numbering progression under DI-MCCR-80014.

1. Requiring size and execution time to be measured;

2. Requiring tests using nominal, maximum, and erroneous data;

3. Requiring testing for error detection and error recovery.

The Test Plan writer should keep in mind, though, that examples given by the author of the DID are just that, *examples*. A standard or a DID cannot impose requirements on a program which are not part of the contract or statement of work (see Chapter 2). Hence, if there are no size or timing requirements on the newly developed software (a very unlikely situation), there should be no size or timing testing required as part of formal verification and validation.[9]

Subparagraph 4.X.2—Test classes.   The categories of formal tests to be executed are defined in this paragraph. This DID lists the following:

1. Stress tests

2. Timing tests

3. Erroneous input tests

4. Maximum capacity tests

But the DID (a) leaves out a test category that is extremely important, and (b) doesn't define what these kinds of tests might be. In the first place, the *functional* test is not mentioned. This is a test (or, more often, a series of tests or test cases) in which the ability of the new software to transform its input into the defined output is tested and verified without regard for performance capabilities. Considering that functional tests will comprise well over half of all formal testing, this is an unfortunate omission. As far as definitions are concerned, the following can be taken as working ones:

> *Stress tests* are test designed to show how the software performs when its environment ceases to comply with the specifications, that is, when there are too many aircraft, or when the number of transactions exceeds the specified maximum, or when data arrives at greater than the speci-fied maximum rate. For software which must undergo stress testing, and most MCCR software must, there is often no specified way for it to operate when its environment goes beyond the specified limits, ex-cept that it must continue to function in a way that permits its operators or users to take some action to relieve the stress. In other words, it can't crash, but must *gracefully degrade*.
>
> *Timing tests* are frequently called *performance tests* or *response tests*.

---

[9] Although the prudent tester will examine the time performance and storage require-ments anyway.

They verify that the software system can perform its functions within the time limits set in the defining specifications.

Erroneous input tests present the software under test with input data which is outside the specified ranges but which might be encountered during actual operation.

Maximum capacity tests verify the software's ability to continue performing in the presence of either the maximum amount of data, or data presented at the maximum rate (this latter being similar to the stress test described above). An air traffic control designed to permit, say, six controllers to handle 50 aircraft each must be tested in the presence of 300 aircraft distributed among the six.

Subparagraph 4.X.3—Test levels. "This paragraph . . . shall describe the levels at which formal qualification testing will be performed." Formal qualification testing means the formal validation of the satisfaction of requirements, called a *sell-off* by many. This really means "Describe how much software must be put together before you begin formal sell-off." DI–MCCR–80014A suggests, with its example, the following levels as possibilities:

1. "CSCI level (CSC or CSU level if necessary)—to evaluate compliance with CSCI requirements." In most software development efforts, a CSCI is a complete subsystem and testing at the CSCI level will be performed on complete subsystems. The CSCI is chosen as an appropriate level for formal testing because this is (usually) the lowest level at which performance requirements (response time, throughput, etc.) are meaningful. Programs involving the development of only a single, self-contained, piece of software may do all of their formal testing at the CSCI level. Note, by the way, the parenthetical comment in the example. The tester should consider formal testing at lower levels, if it's appropriate. Trying to hit all the requirements of a major CSCI in one big test (or series of test cases) at the end of the project puts a lot of strain on developers and testers and leaves the customer or buyer in the dark about what's going on until very late. If build-oriented integration is done (see Chapter 10), then the test manager should consider formal build testing. Such an approach will provide positive evidence of project progress to the customer or buyer and the configuration management overhead necessary to support regression testing as testing progresses from build to build is really minimal.

2. "CSCI to CSCI integration level—to evaluate compliance with CSCI external interface requirements." Individual CSCIs should be tested separately before they are integrated with other CSCIs. That way the tester can ensure that individual functional and performance require-

ments are satisfied and that problems which may arise during the integration process are associated with the interface between CSCIs—one or both of the integrated CSCIs will be mishandling the data flowing between them.

3. "CSCI to HWCI integration level—to evaluate compliance with CSCI external interface requirements." The comment about CSCI to CSCI applies to *any* integration of any type of configuration item to any other type of configuration item. That is, test the individuals separately and then test them in combination.

4. "System level—to evaluate compliance with CSCI requirements not evaluated at other levels." It is perfectly acceptable to defer the formal testing of software requirements to system level testing if that's the most efficient way to do the verification. Some aspects of the software just can't be tested realistically without a full complement of hardware and software.

Subparagraph 4.X.4—Test definitions.   Subparagraph 4.X.4 and its subparagraphs define each of the formal tests or test scenarios to be performed on the Computer Software Configuration Item X. Subparagraph 4.X.4 itself may or may not contain introductory text.

Subparagraph 4.X.4.Y—(Test name and project-unique identifier).   The author of the Test Plan DID has been pretty specific about what is expected in each of these subparagraphs (really subsubparagraphs, to use consistent terminology). In addition to a name and identifier (number), the following information is requested:

1. Test objective—A brief statement of the purpose of the test. For example, "This test shall demonstrate the aircraft tracking capacity of the Radar Processing CSCI of the Kingdom of Argonia Air Traffic Control System."

2. Any special requirements—Anything that might require advance planning. For example, long duration tests generally require that special arrangements be made by participating and witnessing organizations.

3. Test level—The test level to which this test belongs. This should be one of the levels defined in Subparagraph 4.X.3.

4. Test type or class—The category to which this test belongs. This should be one of the classes defined in paragraph 4.X.2.

5. Qualification method as specified in the Software Requirements Specification—Inspection, analysis, or demonstration as defined in the Requirements Specification.[10] The DID implies that only a single method

_____

[10] See Chapter 4, "Planning the Test Process," for a discussion of test and verification methods.

is applicable for a single test, but the tests defined in Subparagraph 4.X.4.Y almost always are long extended scenarios intended to verify compliance with many requirements, with different specified qualification methods. If read naively, the tester might be tempted to list *all possible methods* for every test. What the DID author and all customers really want to see here is a matrix listing all the tested requirements and the method or methods associated with each. This can be part of the cross reference to the SRS and IRS which are also required (see 6 and 7, below).

6. Cross-reference to the CSCI engineering requirements in the Software Requirements Specification addressed by this test—A matrix listing each requirement to be verified by this test and the location in the SRS where it can be found. This matrix will also include IRS requirements and qualification methods.

7. Cross-reference to the CSCI interface requirements in the Interface Requirements Specification addressed by this test—A matrix listing each requirement to be verified by this test and the location in the IRS where it can be found. This matrix will also include SRS requirements and qualification methods.

8. Type of data to be recorded—Depending on the nature of the tests, there may be little specific to include here. If, for example, the software being developed performs essentially straightforward functions with few timing constraints, then most of the requirements will be verified by demonstration, and most of the data recorded will consist of simple "yes" or "no" indications on the test data sheets or in a master copy of the test procedures. If the requirements to be verified include response times and other performance parameters, the recorded data will probably include the results of a number of executions, and some sort of posttest analysis (even if it's only the computation of an average response time) will be necessary. If special recording media are needed (see the discussion of Section 5), here is a place to point that out. Again, this information can be included as part of the testing matrix developed in answer to some of the other DID requirements.

9. Assumptions and constraints—Anything a test witness should know about the test ahead of time. For example, "Test requires version 4.0 or higher of the Operating System to support concurrent system execution and performance monitoring." Or, "During multi-aircraft test scenarios, the trajectory of the test aircraft will be limited to straight line motion."

Subparagraph 4.X.5—Test schedule.   This is pretty much self-explanatory. The section of the activity diagram which includes formal testing is the primary source of schedule information. Generally, a bar, or Gantt, chart is preferred by customers.

5.2.5 Section 5—Data Recording, Reduction, and Analysis

It may not be necessary to say anything at all about data recording, reduction, and analysis, especially if the software system being built is small or straightforward. What customers really want to see in Section 5 of a Test Plan is a list of the algorithms to be used in establishing the correctness, or lack thereof, of the software.

For example, when testing an air traffic control system with accuracy requirements for the tracking and display of aircraft positions, the tester will arrange for the presentation of a number of aircraft to the system (this number is frequently stated in the system's specifications) and the operation of the tracking and display algorithms will be recorded. At the completion of test execution, the recorded data will be recovered and subjected to analysis involving either hand or automated calculations. The data to be recorded will have been stated in the appropriate Paragraph 4.X.4.Y, but the calculations are defined here. If the calculations are to be done by hand, then the equations defining them are listed. If automation is to be used, then the source of the data reduction software and the methods for verifying it are listed.

5.2.6 Section 6—Notes

When software is developed under contract and in accordance with a Department of Defense Standard, such as DOD–STD–2167A, the developed documentation, particularly the documentation which explains how the developer will proceed with the design and implementation of the product, becomes contractually binding. However, it is often useful to include in these documents explanatory or amplifying material which should not be construed as binding. The Notes section is designed for that purpose. Except for a mandatory glossary of acronyms and abbreviations, it has no set format or content and may include anything the Test Plan author wishes. Section 6 is a good place to present the derivation of data reduction algorithms, for example.

5.2.7 Sections 10 and Beyond—Appendices

Unlike Notes, Appendices are an integral and binding part of the Test Plan. What distinguishes the contents of appendices from the main body is that appendices contain information which is, or may be, physically detached from the plan and published separately. Large verification matrices, for example, are often published separately as an appendix to a Test Plan. On projects involving classified information, it is frequently possible to keep the main body of the plan unclassified by gathering and localizing the sensitive information in an appendix which is printed and transmitted using tighter security measures than required for the rest of the document.

REFERENCES

BROOKS, F. P., JR., 1975. *The Mythical Man-Month*. Addison-Wesley, Reading, MA.

IEEE COMPUTER SOCIETY, 1983. ANSI/IEEE 829-1983 "Software Test Documentation."

KERZNER, H., PH.D., 1979. *Project Management: A Systems Approach to Planning, Scheduling and Controlling*. Van Nostrand Reinhold, New York.

U.S. DEPARTMENT OF DEFENSE, 1985. DOD–STD–1467 (AR) "Software Support Environment," Department of the Army, 18 January.

U.S. DEPARTMENT OF DEFENSE, 1988. DOD–STD–2167A "Defense System Software Development (with DIDs)," February.

U.S. DEPARTMENT OF DEFENSE, 1990. MIL–HDBK–347 "Mission Critical Computer Resources Software Support," 22 May.

Chapter 6

Fuzzy Requirements

Before a system can be tested, test cases must be defined, and before test cases can be defined, system requirements must be clearly understood. Unfortunately, most specifications contain at least some requirements that are difficult, if not impossible, to understand. Such requirements are called *fuzzy requirements*. They are so called because their precise meaning isn't clear; either they're improperly stated or they're not completely stated.

6.1 TYPICAL FUZZY REQUIREMENTS

This chapter presents a list of typical fuzzy requirements and identifies possible interpretations of them. Where interpretations are not possible, the reasons for the fuzzy classification are given. Each of the sample requirements is from an actual specification.

Automation shall be extensively employed in all operational and maintenance areas. This requirement is an extraction from a proposal (with the proposal's "will" changed to "shall"); it really shouldn't be in a Software Requirements Specification. But we assume that we're stuck with it. The problem then boils down to the word "extensively." Since the system in question involves software, we can reasonably assume that *something* is being automated; the question is how much. Words like "extensively," in fact, all adverbs, should be flags for testers since they require very precise definition in the context of the system under construction.

> *The system shall . . .*
>
> *. . . provide rapid tasking/reconfiguration capability for various operational configurations.* The questionable terms here are "rapid" and "various." All parties to such a system will be better off if a specific maximum reconfiguration time and the exact conditions under which it must be achieved is inserted into the specification. If more than one operational reconfiguration is possible and if each may require a different maximum, then a table should be provided which shows each possible reconfiguration and the maximum time permitted for it. If the specification does not contain such a table, the test description should.
>
> *. . . perform high-speed Direction Finding operations using the deck and mast antenna elements.* Again, an undefined term: "high speed." The solution is the same as in the previous example, an explicit speed requirement, or, if multiple conditions are possible, a table of speeds.
>
> These last two "requirements" are examples of fuzzy specification of system performance, in this case response time. Response time requirements are subject to interpretation if not carefully worded. Software developers, for example, usually assume (not always explicitly) that an unqualified response time is the nominal or best case response time. System users, on the other hand, will take that unqualified response time as the worst case time. So, in addition to stating exactly what the the response time should be and the amount of tolerance allowed, the specification writer (or the tester reviewing the specification) should be careful to state the conditions under which the response time is to be satisfied. A table is almost always the best way of presenting performance requirements.
>
> *. . . provide the capability to off-line any combination of the below and continue a reduced operational capacity:*
>
> - 1553 Bus
> - HF DF Mast Antenna

The difficult thing about this is the requirement to demonstrate "any combination" of assets in the supplied list as being off-line. In this case, we assume the customer really means "any combination" so we must set up a test for each one. Remember, if there are n objects, then "any combination" means $\sum_{i=1}^{N} \binom{N}{i}$ tests, where $\binom{N}{i}$ is the combination of N things taken i at a time. And remember, $n!$ is the *lower bound* on the number of tests since the system will probably behave differently if the 1553 bus goes down before the HF DF Mast Antenna than it will if the antenna goes off-line first.

. . . *store pertinent intercept data on the streamer at periodic intervals.* This requirement is actually two requirements: (1) store data, and (2) do so at periodic intervals. The definition of "pertinent" may or may not be ambiguous, depending on the surrounding context. The tester (and the system implementers, for that matter) should be aware that the word "periodic" means "at regular intervals" and if that is what is intended, then the interval and the acceptable leeway about that interval should be specified. If "regular intervals" is what is meant, then the intervals, circumstances defining the intervals, and the tolerance on that interval should be explicitly stated. Otherwise, the tester has no option but to measure the interval over successive tests, and if they differ, by even a picosecond, declare a failure. If what is really meant is "whenever available," a common usage of "periodic," then the wording of the specification should be changed.

. . . *provide keyboard editing of all alterable tasking instructions.* This is the same as the "any combination" situation. If the customer really means "all alterable tasking instructions," then a test must be designed for each one. Again, if "all alterable . . ." is meant, then somewhere in the specification there had better be a complete list of the tasking instructions.

. . . *qualify automatically derived track file data to be realistic and report unrealistic data to the operator.* Here the term "realistic" needs to be defined precisely. If this definition involves, as it usually will, several conditions, then a separate test must be developed in which each such condition exhibits an out-of-limits condition. See Chapter 8 for a more thorough discussion of tests for out-of-limits conditions.

. . . *minimize the total number of displays, and avoid dense, hard to interpret displays.* This requirement is another one that came from a proposal, and it's really two requirements, both ambiguous. The first requirement is fuzzy because no one knows that the total number of displays is really the minimum, unless of course there is only one (or none). The second requirement suffers from the undefined phrase "dense, hard to interpret." These two requirements interrelate, of course, since in reducing the number of displays, the risk is that those that remain will be too cluttered to permit easy use by an operator. The correct solution to this dilemma is the inclusion of the displays themselves in the specification.[1]

---

[1] There is a school of testing which holds that not only should the actual displays be included in the specification, but the precise coordinate of *each and every element* in the display should be specified.

. . . permit rapid retrieval and display of active track files text and graphics. Again, a performance requirement without a specific target. The word "rapid" should be replaced with a specific retrieval time.

Built-in-Test/Built-in-Test Equipment (BIT/BITE) malfunctions are not to interfere with intended system performance. This requirement is a time-bomb. If interpreted literally, verification will require measuring system performance during *all combinations* of states, modes, and input presentations while BIT/BITE is functioning correctly[2] (and that has to be verified first), followed by a repeat of that complete test for *each possible* malfunction of BIT/BITE.

The operator, using the keyboard controls of function buttons, textual commands, touch-panel finger-on-glass, and the trackball, shall be able to perform all areas of the AN/SRS–1 [AN/SRS–1 is an existing system] *operation.* Perhaps the biggest problem with specifications is the open-ended requirement. In this case, the difficulty is with the word "all." To actually verify this requirement, it is necessary to identify all areas of AN/SRS–1 operation. Presumably this can be done by examining the specification for that system, but, if that's not the case, then the AN/SRS–1 must be "reverse engineered" in order to produce such a specification.

Numeric ranges and textual wildcards shall be allowed for usage in supplying parametric data for invocation of views. This requirement is ok if it is followed by explanatory material describing what is meant by "numeric ranges" and "textual wildcards." If, however, this is the extent of the specification, then the implementer/designer is left with carte blanche and the tester is doomed to play referee between the customer's visualization of these concepts and the implementer's.

The purpose of the signal acquisition function shall be to provide the ability to detect signal emitters in real time in accordance with operator tasking instructions. It is only possible to verify what something *does*. It is impossible to verify what its purpose is; in fact, its purpose is irrelevant.

The proper alert queues shall be notified. If this requirement is from a customer's specification, then the reference to "alert queues" is probably excessive design detail since function is the proper domain of such a specification. If, however, the term "queues" has been previously defined, then the requirement needs an associated definition of the term "proper."

The operator shall respond with the time of day. If the operator simply folds his or her arms and refuses to enter the time of day, does the software system satisfy the specification? Requirements can only be placed on a system or component under control of the developer, not on any external entity like a human user.

---

[2] This measures against actual performance. It is not at all clear what is meant by "intended."

The self-test phase and amplitude calibration data shall be identical for all ship installations of the system and shall not be changed in the process of ship calibration. The difficult part of this requirement is the term "all ship installations," which needs definition.

These tests are the primary fault detection mechanism of BIT and shall be capable of detecting 96 percent of the equipment failures. This is the classic requirement for built-in-test (BIT) functions and it is ambiguous. Does it mean ". . . shall detect 96 percent of possible equipment failures 100 percent of the time"; or does it mean ". . . shall detect all possible failures 96 percent of the time"? Since it is impossible to identify *all possible* failures, we must assume that the former is the intent because whatever failure we present during testing, the system better detect it. In this case, the customer is presented with a list of failures (presumably the 96 percent or some sample of it) which will be injected into the system. The bit will be exercised for each case. One should be prepared for 100 percent success by the system in detecting the established failures.

But think further about this requirement. As stated, it's really a *system* requirement: It's trying to say that the hardware/software system shall be capable of detecting any possible failure with a 96 percent level of confidence. During the requirements allocation process, the system engineers should determine the test signals which the software should transmit to the equipment and the responses from the equipment which indicate success and failure. System requirements such as this one should never be passed directly to any lower level component, software or hardware.

The BIT software implementing the BIT functions shall be modularly designed and shall make reasonable provisions for the likely growth areas in the system. It's probably possible to prove that software functions are modularly designed since just having modules exist is sufficient. Note, by the way, that this requirement does not mandate modular implementation. The real problem with this requirement is with the undefined terms "reasonable provisions" and "likely growth areas." It is the customer's responsibility to define the nature of these growth areas and to define the degree of expandability required in the resulting system. In lieu of customer definition, a software (or system) test engineer should consult with program management and system engineering personnel to determine acceptable verification methods.

6.2 A CHECKLIST FOR FUZZY REQUIREMENTS

In 1988, the MITRE Corporation of Bedford, Massachusetts, prepared a report for the U.S. Air Force which included a list of keywords and forms to be wary of when preparing or reviewing a specification [Buley, Moore, et al. 1988]. The authors suggest being on the look out for

1. Incomplete lists ending with "etc.," "and/or," and "TBD."
2. Vague words and phrases such as "generally," "normally," "to the greatest extent," and "where practicable."
3. Imprecise verbs such as "supported," "handled," "processed," or "rejected."
4. Implied certainty, flagged by words such as "always," "never," "all," or "every."
5. Passive voice, such as "the counter is set." (By whom or what?)
6. Every pronoun, particularly "it" or "its." Each should have an explicit and unmistakable reference.
7. Comparatives, such as "earliest," "latest," "highest." Words ending in "er" or "est" should be suspect.
8. Words and phrases that cannot be quantified, such as flexible, modular, achievable, efficient, adequate, accomplish, possible (or possibly), correct (or correctly), minimum required, minimum acceptable, better, higher, faster, less, slower, infrequent, to the extent specified, to the extent required, to be compatible, to be associated with.
9. Words and phrases whose meaning can be disputed between developer and customer, such as instantaneous, simultaneous, achievable, complete, finish, degraded, a minimum number of, nominal/normal/average, minimum, steady-state, coincident, adjacent, synchronous.
10. Contractually troublesome phrases:
    a. "Design goal." The developer will spend money and other resources with no guarantee of goal accomplishment.
    b. "To the extent practicable." A decision in the eyes of the developer.
    c. "Where applicable." There are no criteria for judgment.
    d. "Shall be considered." The developer will think about.
    e. "A minimum of X." The developer will provide exactly X.

Most of the difficulty with the fuzzy requirements addressed in this chapter, and with the words and phrases flagged by the MITRE report, arise from the imprecision of the English language as written by most people. Substitutes for prose requirements should be used at every opportunity.[3]

To clarify requirements, the specification author should use any of the following:

1. Equations and logical relations to express constraints and computational requirements.

---

[3] Note the way these imprecise phrases, such as "every opportunity," creep into discussions.

System Mode	Response Times (msec)			
	No Load	Nominal	High Load	Worst Case
Surveillance	500	750	1000	2000
Intelligence	500	1000	1500	2500
Early Warning	500	750	1000	2000
Space Track	500	750	1000	2000
Training	750	1250	2000	3000
Initialization	500	N/A	N/A	N/A

N/A = Not applicable
This table requires careful definition of the terms "No load," "Nominal," "High Load," and "Worst Case."

Figure 6.1 A response time table.

2. Tables to define complex relationships, such as response times as shown in Figure 6.1.

3. Graphs and other illustrations to clarify the intent of prose statements.

4. State transition diagrams like that in Figure 6.2 to express major control changes.

5. Control flow diagrams or flow charts to define complex logic or involved algorithms.

6. Pseudo code to express computational algorithms.

7. Anything else that the author's cleverness can come up with.

6.3 NOTES ON STYLE IN SPECIFICATIONS

Style should never be a consideration when writing a specification—no one gives out prizes for style, only for clarity. Simple, single-verb sentences without extended lists should be the rule. For example, rather than "The system shall do A, B, C, D, and E," say "The system shall do A. The system shall do B. The system shall do C. The system shall do D. The system shall do E." If the order of execution is important, then state that explicitly:

Active Mode	Transition Command					
	Shut Down	Surv Mode	Int. Mode	E.W. Mode	Space Track	Trng. Mode
1. Surveillance	6	E	6	4	4	E
2. Intelligence	6	1	E	3	E	E
3. Early Warning	6	1	E	E	E	E
4. Space Track	6	1	2	3	E	E
5. Training	6	1	2	3	4	E
6. Initialization	STOP	1	3	3	4	5

E = "Error" — A state transition which is not permitted

Figure 6.2 A state transition table.

"The system shall do A. After completing A, the system shall do B. After completing B, the system shall do C. After completing C, the system shall do D. Upon completing D, the system shall do E." If the sequential relationship between tasks A, B, C, D, and E is other than linear, then use a logic diagram: "The system shall perform tasks A, B, C, D, and E as shown in Figure X."

6.4 A WORD ABOUT "TBD"

Finally, a word about the often abused phrase "To Be Determined" or "TBD." TBD is used as a placeholder for requirements that haven't been finalized. TBDs are meant to be conspicuous and easy to spot. They're a message to readers that "there's something missing, but we haven't forgotten it." When used that way, TBDs serve a very useful purpose. Specification reviewers who categorically reject specifications containing TBDS are simply inviting developers to submit specifications with much more subtle TBDs, like the BIT requirement described earlier.

REFERENCES

BULEY, E. R., MOORE, L. J., and OWENS, M. F., 1988. "B5 (SRS/IRS) Specification Guidelines," M88–57, ESD–TR–88–337. MITRE, Bedford, MA, December.

Chapter 7

Software
Fault Tree
Analysis

Before addressing the problem and process of integrating newly developed software elements into a complete, functioning system, it's necessary to give some thought to how a tester decides how to concentrate those resources that may be available for other than requirements validation.

Software Fault Tree Analysis is a technique for analyzing possible failure modes of a software system in order to determine if that software is capable of defending and/or intercepting the failures. The process was thoroughly described by Leveson in 1983 [Leveson and Harvey 1983] and has been revisited several times since [Leveson 1986, Leveson 1991, Leveson, Cha, et al. 1991].

Software Fault Tree Analysis begins by identifying the failure modes of the system that arise from failures of the software. Here, a *failure* is defined as an inability to perform a required function within specified limits. The first category of failures considered are *safety failures*, which are those that lead to casualties or serious consequences. The term "serious consequences" is a bit subjective and needs to be defined by the system designer or the system buyer.

The second category of failures might be termed *mission threatening* in that completely satisfactory operating results are not obtained.

The third category of failures are *minor failures* or *inconsequential failures*. These are failures that do not affect the success or failure of the software operations but that cause inconvenience to the user or operator of the system.

The number of categories may be expanded or changed by the analyst if necessary.[1] The principal reason for establishing the categories is economics. Testing budgets seldom permit the location of all the errors that cause faults, and SRSs seldom differentiate error categories. Hence, we take a top-down approach by concentrating on the most serious of the potential problems first.

Once the failure categories have been defined and the failures of each type listed, we prepare a fault tree diagram for each. The symbols used to build the trees are shown in Figure 7.1; an example is shown in Figure 7.2.

7.1 IDENTIFYING FAILURE MODES

In our more or less continuous example of an air traffic control system, it's possible to identify a number of failure modes. This failure modes list is established by beginning with *system* functions.[2] Some of the failures relating to the loss of an aircraft are:

1. A controller gives invalid commands to an aircraft.
2. A controller gives valid commands to one aircraft that should be given to another.
3. A controller fails to give any commands to an aircraft (possibly a special case of either of the two previous cases).
4. The system fails to communicate with an adjacent control center.

---

[1] DOD-STD-1679A categorizes error, and hence failure, categories as

Priority 1: An error that prevents the accomplishment of an operational or mission essential function;

Priority 2: An error that adversely affects the accomplishment of an operational or mission essential function . . . and for which no alternative work-around solution exists;

Priority 3: An error that adversely affects the accomplishment of an operational or mission essential function . . . and for which there is a reasonable alternative work-around solution;

Priority 4: An error that is an operator inconvenience or annoyance . . . ; and

Priority 5: All other errors.

These could be taken as a starting point for failure mode classification.

[2] It might be possible, of course, to begin the fault analysis starting with the statement of *software* requirements, but the overall failure analysis will be necessary anyway. And, besides, software "faults" or "errors" that don't lead to recognized system failures might more properly be termed "features." Features are characteristics of a software system that, though potential sources of consternation, inconvenience, or even violation of fundamental requirements, are considered part and parcel of its existence.

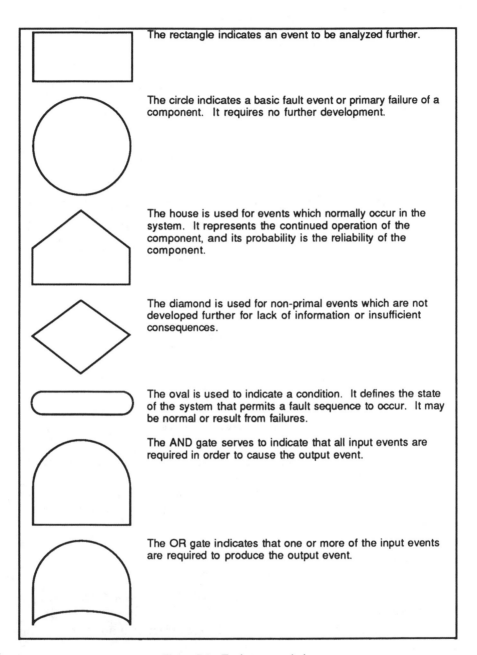

The rectangle indicates an event to be analyzed further.

The circle indicates a basic fault event or primary failure of a component. It requires no further development.

The house is used for events which normally occur in the system. It represents the continued operation of the component, and its probability is the reliability of the component.

The diamond is used for non-primal events which are not developed further for lack of information or insufficient consequences.

The oval is used to indicate a condition. It defines the state of the system that permits a fault sequence to occur. It may be normal or result from failures.

The AND gate serves to indicate that all input events are required in order to cause the output event.

The OR gate indicates that one or more of the input events are required to produce the output event.

Figure 7.1 Fault tree symbols.

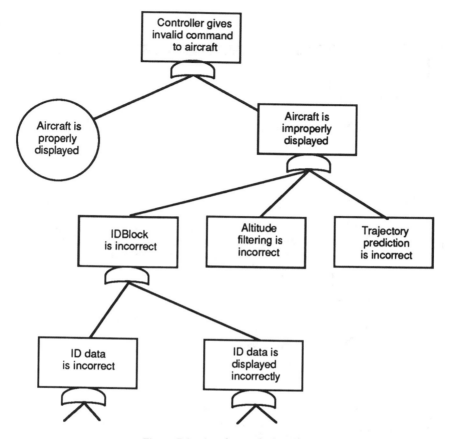

Figure 7.2   A software fault tree.

For a system with the complicated requirements list of an air traffic control system, the list of failure modes will be extensive.

It's important to understand that the list of failure modes will contain system failures that can result from other than software failures. Indeed, the categories of failure cause will include

- Failures resulting from erroneous software.
- Failures resulting from erroneous hardware.
- Failures resulting from hardware faults that were not anticipated by the software design.
- Failures of any of the above types resulting from incomplete or missing requirements.

Once the failure modes list is established, each item on it should be analyzed for its relevance to the software development. In other words, could software execution (or lack thereof) contribute to these failures? Such software contributions could result from:

- The software operating incorrectly;
- The software operating correctly, but ignoring erroneous conditions in hardware;
- The software operating correctly, but confusingly (e.g., so that operators make incorrect decisions).

Note, by the way, that most of this relevance analysis can't be completed until possible causes of the failures have been established.

7.2 FAILURE MODES ANALYSIS

We shall consider some possible failures that could occur in an air traffic control system:

We begin with example 1 of the previous section: An aircraft receives invalid commands from the controller. The fault tree resulting from the analysis of this failure mode is shown in Figure 7.2. We consider the causes of such an invalid command. As with all analyses of this type, it's better to proceed in small steps; that is, as we move from the effect to the cause, we take the smallest logical steps we can so that we don't accidentally omit a potential cause of failure. Hence, we step back from the invalid command to the two choices: human error and system error:

1. Aircraft information is properly presented to the controller who has incorrectly interpreted the data and given a wrong command; or
2. Aircraft information is improperly presented, causing the controller to give the invalid command.[3]

Cause A is a human failure which, while not the direct concern of the software developer or tester, is recognized as a valid failure cause by the Federal Aviation Administration.[4]

Cause B results from a shortcoming of the air traffic control system itself. This cause needs to be examined further. Figure 7.2 gives three possi-

---

[3] We will ignore the complicated case of system failure compounded by human error, that is, where both the system and the controller are at fault. In software testing, we assume that the user performs properly.

[4] Note, however, that improper documentation of software expectations or system actions might lead to inadequate training, which could result in such a human error. Someone in the quality evaluation process should take care to ensure that the documentation accurately describes the software.

ble reasons for incorrect information being presented to a controller (there could be others):

1. The aircraft ID block is incorrect, causing the controller to misidentify the aircraft;
2. The system's altitude filtering is incorrect, causing the aircraft to (a) be displayed at the wrong altitude, or (b) not be displayed at all if the controller has restricted the displayed altitude presentation; or
3. The system has incorrectly extrapolated the aircraft's trajectory causing the controller to miss a potential encounter with another aircraft.

For the purposes of illustration, the fault tree of Figure 7.2 is necessarily abbreviated; each of the above causes can be further analyzed. For simplicity, though, we have shown only the possible causes of reason (1), an incorrect identification block attached to the aircraft's displayed symbol. The reasons for such a fault are either incorrect data or an incorrect display format. In the first case, the developers and testers must investigate the data collection and tracking software (and the external interfaces of that software), while in the second case, the display software (or the display itself) is suspect.

A fault analysis is continued until the developers and testers have satisfied themselves that they have identified all the software failure modes that might result in the software system failing to satisfy its basic mission requirements. This analysis is done independently of any Software Requirements Specification analysis, although the results of all such analyses should be consistent with each other. The test team members will then generate test cases addressing, in addition to the requirements of the SRS, those failure modes that have been identified as critical to overall system success.

7.3 APPLYING FAULT ANALYSIS

When the tester has no insight into the construction of a software system, as happens when evaluating a commercial product, for example, fault analysis is about the only approach to testing available. The tester must answer the following questions:

1. What properties must this software have to satisfy my organization's needs?
2. What undesirable traits might cause this software to prevent that organization from accomplishing its goals?

The first question can be satisfied by preparing a requirements list. But since a requirements list for commercial products is seldom complete because it doesn't address requirements derived from functional ones, we must also answer question 2.

Assume that we're evaluating a word processing system for possible use as the standard word processor in our company. The first thing we do is list the attributes that the product must have:

- It must permit all the usual text processing.[5]
- It must provide dynamically renumbered footnotes.
- It must support dynamically renumbered sections.
- It must support dynamically renumbered figures and tables.
- It must permit creation of a table of contents and an index.

This list of attributes becomes the specification.

In addition, we wish to analyze those negative attributes that might cause us to reject the product, or, worse, might cause us additional expense when they show up unexpectedly. We do this by listing those kinds of failures that we consider unacceptable:[6]

- The product interferes with our existing file structure.
- The product becomes unworkably slow with documents of a size routinely produced by our company.

For each of those characteristics important to us, we'll want to develop at least one, and probably several, nontrivial test cases to ensure that the product we are buying won't surprise us when we least expect it.

Again, when developing test cases and when evaluating designs for complex real-time systems, fault analysis can be useful.

Some of the most difficult errors to analyze are those which are caused by timing problems or by interactions between more-or-less independent processes in a real-time software system. Almost without exception, a series of test cases derived exclusively from the Software Requirements Specification will fail to expose consistently these kinds of problems. The difficulty here arises because the performance of the real-time system consisting of several asynchronous processes is dependent on the interaction of several event time lines—one for each process. In most cases, if all processes are functioning nominally, everything will be fine. But, if one or more begin to crowd their performance limits, unexpected problems can arise.

When evaluating a system design to see if it is liable to suffer from these

---

[5] Don't fall into the trap that we just did for this book. No one will agree on what all the usual text processing capabilities really are: spell them out.

[6] These failure situations could, of course, be positively stated and included in the list of requirements. Conversely, the list of requirements could be negatively stated and listed in with the possible faults.

sorts of intermittent problems, or when attempting to analyze such an error, the tester and developer perform a fault analysis. The software engineer begins with a list of system-level failures which would render the software product unusable, and works through the candidate list of causes. Each of the causes is, in turn, examined for its underlying cause. The process is continued until he or she reaches a set of possible "errors." Each of these candidate errors is analyzed in the light of the software design and of known performance characteristics. Those that can be proven impossible—either because the design precludes the situation[7] or because observed component performance confirms the impossibility—are removed from the list. One of those "errors" that cannot be dismissed as impossible will cause or is causing the failure. This approach is called the Sherlock Holmes technique.[8]

REFERENCES

LEVESON, N. G., 1986. "Software Safety: Why, What, and How," *ACM Computing Surveys,* vol. 18, no. 2, 125–63.

LEVESON, N. G., 1991. "Software Safety in Embedded Computer Systems," *Communications of the ACM,* vol. 34, no. 2, 34–46.

LEVESON, N. G., CHA, S. S., and SHIMEALL, T. J., 1991. "Safety Verification of Ada Programs Using Software Fault Trees," *IEEE Software,* July.

LEVESON N. G., and HARVEY P. R., 1983. "Analyzing Software Safety," *IEEE Transactions on Software Engineering,* vol. SE–9, no. 5, 569–79.

[7] And it will require more than good intentions to really prove that the suspected error can't happen.

[8] In *The Sign of Four* Holmes says to Watson, "When you have eliminated the impossible, whatever remains, *however improbable,* must be the truth."

Chapter 8

Test Case Design

Now that we've done our planning, we'll look at the process of actually creating test cases. In this chapter, we'll limit ourselves to the construction of cases that validate individual requirements[1] or small code units. In the next chapter, "Scenario Generation," we'll see how to combine test cases into continuous and flowing *scenarios*.

Testing strategies fall into two categories: *black box* and *glass box*.

Black box testing ignores program structure and concentrates on the functions performed by the software. In other words, it treats the program unit as a black box.

Glass box testing, on the other hand, ignores the function of the software, to the extent that it can, and concentrates on the structure of the program.[2]

---

[1] Keep in mind that validation is the process of ensuring that the final product, the software in this case, satisfies its original goals, usually a specification or list of requirements. Verification, on the other hand, ensures that the results of each development step, design, code, etc., are consistent with the previous step.

[2] This approach to testing is frequently called *white box* testing. But on the grounds that a white box can be just as opaque as a black box, we've elected to use the term glass box for the testing approach that treats program boundaries as transparent.

Our approach will be to examine each of these strategies to the exclusion of the other. That is, we'll become, first, radical black box testers, then radical glass box testers. It will become clear quickly that neither of these extremes is really practical; in fact, it will be so clear that we'll find ourselves distinctly uncomfortable with these drastic positions. We'll then take a much more pragmatic approach by considering hybrid strategies, those that borrow from each of the two basic game plans.

But first, we need an example to work with. We take as our specification the following:

Write a program module called FACTORIAL(X) which accepts as input an integer, X, in the range

$$1 < X \le 100$$

and computes the factorial function:

$$FACTORIAL(X) = X! = X \times (X\text{-}1) \times (X\text{-}2) \cdots \times 2 \times 1.$$

We'll assume that our target computer has sufficient word length to accommodate 100!. Further, we'll not complete the specification by defining the necessary actions that the module should take if an invalid value of X is presented to it.

There are a number of ways that this specification can be satisfied. We'll examine two. Both are shown in Figure 8.1.

The first method for computing the factorial, Figure 8.1(a), involves recursive computations. That is, the program repeatedly calls upon itself to continue the computation until the terminating condition, $X = 1$, is encoun-

```
function FACTORIAL (X)
if X = 1 then
   FACTORIAL := 1
else
   FACTORIAL := X * FACTORIAL (X - 1)
return
```

(a)

```
function FACTORIAL (X)
data FACTORIAL_TABLE
   /1, 2, 6, 24, 120, ... /
FACTORIAL := FACTORIAL_TABLE (X)
return
```

(b)

Figure 8.1 Two ways to compute the factorial. (a) A recursive solution. (b) A table look-up solution.

tered.[3] When the terminating condition is met, the intermediate results are passed back up the series of calls to the original invocation. A recursive solution such as this takes very little main memory for storage (although it may consume a considerable amount of stack space if the depth of recursion is large) but it will probably be quite slow because of the multiplications and the recursive function calls.

The second method, Figure 8.1(b), uses a table look-up to determine the factorial of the input variable. Assuming, as we have, that the target machine can represent 100! in a single word, this solution is very fast since no calculation is needed, only a direct reference to the precomputed table.[4] But, if the table is large, a lot of memory may be consumed by it.

Both of these methods, recursion and table look-up, are common in the preparation of library functions for general use. The method employed will be determined by the characteristics of the target computer (fast, in which case recursion is the more desirable, or slow with a large memory, where table look-up will be employed).

8.1 BLACK BOX TESTING

Black box testing techniques, *in their extreme,* totally ignore the structure of the program or code unit under test. The software element is considered a black box, hence the name, which, when presented with the input parameters (in the case of our example, X), produces an output ($X!$) which purports to be that defined in the specification. Testing is a comparison of the actual output with the specified output; the method of implementation, whether computer, manual, or anything else, is irrelevant, as shown in Figure 8.2.

But, if we have no knowledge of the way a software component was constructed, then, to be *absolutely sure* that it works, we must prepare a test case for *every possible input condition.* For anything other than a completely trivial program, that is obviously impossible.

But why must we try every possible input case? To answer that question, we'll have to violate the principal rule of black box testing and actually look inside the code.

[3] The case X = 1 is not part of the specified input domain, but needs to be handled because the algorithm chosen uses X = 1 as its terminating condition. We could, of course, have chosen X = 2 as the terminator, but the situation depicted here (a situation that cannot legally be generated externally, but can be produced internally) frequently needs to be considered.

[4] Again, X = 1 is not part of the input domain. For this solution, however, it was included, not because it was necessary for the algorithm, but because it makes the meaning of the table elements more understandable. If we'd begun the table with 2!, then the actual table look-up instruction would have been the somewhat less obvious

```
FACTORIAL := FACTORIAL_TABLE (X-1).
```

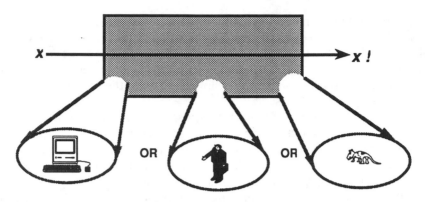

Figure 8.2   The black box concept.

Recall the two possible solutions to our factorial problem illustrated in Figure 8.1. In the recursive case, Figure 8.1(a), there are only two paths through the program:

1. When $X = 1$, which isn't a legal input value according to the specification, and
2. All other values.

If we knew for sure that this was the implementation, we could limit ourselves to a single test case: X somewhere between 2 and 100, inclusive (although, because we're not extremists, most of us would be more comfortable with two or three more).[5-7] The process is similar in concept to the mathematician's proof by induction: first, we test to see that the program functions for its terminating condition $X = 1$, then we test for the general case (namely, any other legal value of X).

But we don't know how the program is constructed. In fact, we've already seen that the solution shown in Figure 8.1(b) is also a legitimate approach to computing factorials. Let's look at Figure 8.1(b) a little more closely.

At first glance, the table look-up solution might appear to also consist of only a single processing path: that each input value is processed exactly the same as every other one. While it is true that there is only a single

[5] Of course, if any checking of input data had been specified, we would need additional cases for the various possible illegal input values.

[6] Note, also, that any test case we select will exercise the $X = 1$ situation required by the algorithm.

[7] The test case X = 1 0 0 is the best choice because, if the implementation is recursive, it invokes all other cases.

```
function FACTORIAL (X)
if X = 1 then
    FACTORIAL := 1
elseif X = 2 then
    FACTORIAL := 2
elseif X = 3 then
    FACTORIAL := 6
elseif
...
return
```

Figure 8.3   The logical equivalent of table look-up.

execution path, keep in mind that every value in the table FACTORIAL_ TABLE has been individually computed. Conceptually, the selection of a particular entry in the table is a revisit to the computation that produced the value stored there. Any one of these computations could be wrong without affecting the validity of the others. The uniqueness of each computational path in the table look-up is much more obvious when we consider that it is logically equivalent to a long string of elseif's like that shown in Figure 8.3. The tester can draw no conclusion about the overall validity of the program from the correctness of a single test case. Just because the program computes 3! to be 6 does not ensure that it will compute 5! to be 120. Hence, we must examine each input possibility.

Of course, there are only 99 values in the input space for our factorial program; we could probably execute that many test cases. But consider the case of an air traffic control program.

An air traffic control program has not one, but a large number of input variables. Some (some operator actions) have only a few possible values, while others (the rest of the operator actions and nearly all of the input variables coming from aircraft in the real world, like speed and altitude) have an essentially infinite number of possible values. It's impossible to prepare, let alone execute, test cases for all possible input values and combinations of values. This leads us to the conclusion that extreme black box testing isn't possible in the real world. But we probably knew that, anyway.

8.2 GLASS BOX TESTING

But is it possible that glass box testing can save us? Let's see.

At its extreme, glass box testing ignores the function of the program under test, and looks only at its code and the structure of that code. As we'll see shortly, glass box testing can't be quite as extreme as black box testing, because the results of some test cases can only be evaluated in the light of the program's intended purpose; but for now, let's try to ignore function.

8.2.1 The Building Inspector Approach

One way to determine the correctness of a program from its structure is to take a "building inspector's" approach. By looking at the construction techniques used to lay bricks, for example, a building inspector can draw some conclusions about the likelihood that those bricks will successfully satisfy the needs of the end user, regardless of whether the original specification was for a stairway or for a chimney. Such things as level and regularly spaced courses, adequate spacing between courses, quality of brick and mortar, and so on, go a long way toward ensuring that the masonry will hang together and contribute to a working product.

In the software world, the analogues to the regularity of courses and the quality of mortar are things like the following:

- *Use of structured constructs* (IF-THEN-ELSE, DO WHILE, etc.). Since Böhm and Jacopini proved that programs can be written using only a small set of control constructs [Böhm and Jacopini 1966], software engineers have promoted the use of languages that make the use of these constructs easy. Limiting program control to a small set of constructs actually means limiting its complexity and enhancing its clarity (see, for example, Dijkstra's paper, "Go To Statement Considered Harmful" [Dijkstra 1968]). It's certainly possible to write incorrect programs using structured techniques, and it's possible to write correct ones that are peppered with gotos, but recent history has shown that use of these methods reduces error tendency. One of the first studies to report on improved correctness when using structured techniques was published by Baker in 1972 [Baker 1972].

- *Meaningful data names.* If a programmer is careful in his or her use of data names, then, at the least, the resulting program will be easier to maintain by another programmer. The tester can take the attitude that if the programmer was conscientious in assigning data names, then he or she was less liable to forget what those variables were for. Also, he or she was probably careful in other areas of the implementation.

- *Extensive use of comments.* Again, the extensive use of *meaningful* comments which appear to be *correct* is generally indicative of care on the part of the implementer.

- *High cohesion.* Cohesion is a measure of the degree to which the components of a software system are single-functioned. Programs in which each module performs a single identifiable function (or perhaps a few closely related functions) are said to be "highly cohesive." Those programs in which modules perform unrelated functions are said to have low cohesion. In examining our single software component for cohesion, we would attempt to determine the number of functions it was performing and their relationship to each other. Cohesion and coupling (below) were first described by Stevens, Constantine, and Myers [Stevens, Myers, et al. 1974]. A complete discussion of these two concepts is found in *Structured Design,* by Yourdon and Constantine [1978]. Highly cohesive software systems are generally thought to have been constructed by giving extensive thought to the functions they must perform. They are also easier to maintain.

- *Loose coupling.* Coupling is a measure of the degree of independence of software components—the degree to which they are isolated from the rest of the software world. If a module requires no information from its caller other than data values (but not flags or command parameters) passed by the calling sequence, then it and its caller are said to be "loosely coupled." The more the module depends on its surrounding environment (as, for example, through Fortran COMMON blocks), the more it and other modules are "tightly coupled." Loose coupling makes for independent components which can be changed or replaced without affecting their logical neighbors. Loose coupling is to be desired.

- *Low complexity.* Most software engineers believe intuitively that the more complex a problem, the more likely that the solution to that problem will be incorrect; that something will have been left out or that some nuance of the problem will have been overlooked. In 1976, McCabe proposed a definition of software complexity [McCabe 1976]. McCabe's technique involved the construction of a *flow graph* for the software component in question. A flow graph is a flow chart where straight line code is compressed into a single point called a *node;* the control flow lines between the nodes are referred to as *edges.* The complexity was then defined as the number of independent paths through that flow graph. For a *proper program,* one with a single entrance and a single exit, the complexity, C, is given by $C = e - n + 2$, where e is the number of edges in the flow graph and n is the number of nodes. McCabe further shows that C can also be computed as $C = P + 1$ where P is the number of *predicates,* the number of decision controlling conditions within the program's structure. McCabe suggests that the complexity of individual components be limited to some small number; others believe that no absolute limit should be set, but that components with the highest complexity be given the most attention in the evaluation and testing process.

- *Use of specific languages.* First, there was machine language, then there was assembly language. After assembly language came an enhanced assembly with macros. At about the same time macro facilities were being developed, the first high-level languages were implemented. Fortran and Cobol were (or are) the prototypical first generation high-level languages; they are procedural and "linear," that is, most control structures and scoping limitations were done by the programmer. The next development was block-structured languages, typified by Algol. Now, the industry is moving toward application-specific and nonprocedural languages. Each improvement and change in philosophy of language was brought about by a desire to bring the language closer to the problem being solved. Fortran, for example, made the implementing of a large class of mathematical expressions easier; Cobol simplified the programming of the file manipulation and data formatting and reformatting common to business applications. By making the language processor (the assembler or compiler) part of the development process, the programmer and software engineer was freer to concentrate on the real problem to be solved. The choice of an appropriate language can be considered an indication of probable quality.

8.2.2 Structure-derived Test Cases

But construction techniques don't ensure that the program actually works; they only increase the probability, based on past experience, that it might work. Given that we're not sure exactly what that program is supposed to do and that we certainly don't know anything about the environment in which it must execute, how might we go about ensuring that it will work?

One thing we can determine from the program code is the number of possible paths through the program and, even more important than the number is the nature or flow of each path. Perhaps we should consider creating test cases that cause each path in the program to be executed. That way, regardless of the data values that might be presented to the program during real operation, we would know the results of executing the path resulting from them.

But, here again, we'll fall victim to the numbers game.

In their book on software engineering, Jensen and Tonies [Jensen and Tonies 1979], present an apparently simple flow diagram which they attribute to Barry Boehm in which the number of independent program paths is approximately 10^{20}). We certainly can't execute 10^{20} test cases. Even with our factorial function, we have 100 possible paths; while that's doable, it's tedious.

So what do we do?

8.3 HYBRID TECHNIQUES

Since we can't implement either pure black box testing or pure glass box testing, we'll have to blend the two approaches. But that's what most testers do naturally. They've learned through experience that mixing strategies is the only way to stay within restrictive budgets and to meet difficult schedules.

The exact mix, that is, the proportion of black box to glass box, used by a particular tester will depend considerably on the software development environment:

1. When working in the contract or custom software world, the emphasis will be on function as stated in the controlling specifications. Testers here will emphasize black box or functional approaches while mixing in enough glass box thinking to keep the numbers game under control;

2. Testers of utility software intended to work in environments determined by, perhaps, unknown users, will concentrate on glass box techniques while using educated guesses about the function in which the software might be employed to identify the most likely execution paths;

3. Testers and evaluators of commercially purchased software whose structure is either unknown or unavailable will rely almost exclusively on black box testing techniques.[8]

In general, the less the tester knows about the environment in which a software component or program will function, the more the testing strategy will tend toward a glass box approach. Conversely, the less one knows about the construction of a component, the more the strategies will incline toward the black box methods.

When developing custom software or when developing a product that has a definite user audience, the mix of black box and glass box techniques will vary with time. During early development and program integration, when components are being examined more or less in isolation and when these components are being joined together, the emphasis will likely be more on the glass box approach. When entire functions become available, and as the system construction nears completion, the tester will slowly shift his or her emphasis toward the black box way of thinking. Formal qualification tests (acceptance tests) intended to validate that the software product satisfies its specifications are almost always black box oriented. In fact, people sometimes speak of "verification testing" when they are referring to testing with a strong glass box emphasis, and "validation testing" when they mean testing that is essentially black box in nature.

---

[8] When faced with the task of evaluating a commercial product, the tester absolutely must begin by enumerating the functions that the product is expected to perform. In effect, a system specification must be written. Then, test cases are developed based on this specification.

TABLE 8.1   Verification Testing Techniques

Black Box Emphasis	Glass Box Emphasis
Equivalence partitioning	Statement coverage
Boundary value analysis	Decision coverage
Cause-effect graphing	Condition coverage
Error guessing	Mutation Testing

8.4 VERIFICATION TESTING

Now we'll take a closer look at some commonly used verification testing techniques.[9] All of these are essentially hybrid because the tester must both know the function of the software under test and have available its design and implementation.

The approaches we'll look at are listed in Table 8.1. They're separated into two categories: those with stronger black box emphasis than glass box, and the complementary group.

8.4.1 Techniques with Black Box Emphasis

Techniques that rely principally on black box approaches to software test design include *equivalence partitioning, boundary analysis, cause-effect graphing, error guessing,* and several others which we won't discuss because they generally require an investment in time and personnel that exceeds the resources of the typical test program.

Equivalence partitioning.   Equivalence partitioning is a test case selection technique in which the tester examines the entire input space defined for the program or software component under test and seeks to find sets of input that are, or should be, processed identically. Such sets of input are called *equivalence classes.*

The input space for a piece of software is the set of *all input situations* that might *possibly* be presented to that software during real operation. Included in the input space are legal situations that have both syntactic and semantic meaning to the program, and illegal situations that are either syntactically or semantically meaningless to it.

The tester partitions the input space because, as we have seen, there is no possible way that he or she can present all possible input values to real-world programs.

---

[9] Here we're using the terms "verification" and "validation" testing as just described. Verification testing is that which is done during integration and program assembly. Validation testing is done to demonstrate compliance with the software's system specification.

Equivalence partitioning can be done in two ways: by examining the program's specification (a basically black box approach) or by inspecting the design and code (a glass box orientation). Developing a complete set of test cases will usually require both approaches.

When the tester examines the program's specifications, he or she will identify very broad categories of input:

1. *Legal input values.* That is, input data[10] which the program expects and is programmed to transform into usable output values;
2. *Illegal input values.* Those kinds of input data that might actually be presented to the program, but that will not produce meaningful output values.

Additionally, the specifications will often identify classes of data within the broader categories. In the tracking software for our air traffic control system, for example, legal input values of aircraft speed will probably include the case of the accelerating aircraft (speeding up or slowing down), the nonaccelerating case (cruising), the case of a turning aircraft, and the cases of increasing and decreasing altitude (ascending and descending). Some of the illegal values that might be specified will include zero speed (objects with zero speed are considered stationary objects by air traffic control systems), zero and negative altitudes,[11] and speeds exceeding a specific threshold.

When the specification has been exhausted, the tester will turn to the program's design and code for further information on how to subdivide the test case categories derived from that external source. The tester will look to see, for example, if all the members of the identified equivalence classes are actually equivalent. That is, does the code actually treat all input values in a particular specified equivalence class the same? At this stage, the test case selection approach becomes similar to that of path coverage (described below) with the important difference that in addition to the program's implementation (derived from the code), the program's intended behavior is examined. For a complete discussion of equivalence partitioning, see Richardson and Clarke [1985].

Once the equivalence classes are identified, at least one test case is selected from each.

---

[10] We use the terms *input data* and *output data* in the very broadest sense. Input data includes all the data values which might be presented to the program under test at any instant coupled with whatever past history or context the program must be prepared to cope with. That is, if a program is required to respond to certain data rates or data densities, then part of a test input data value will be the history that has led up to the current time.

[11] The altitude referred to here is *relative altitude* with respect to the local ground surface.

Boundary-value analysis. Experience has taught the software industry that programs are very liable to fail when processing data that are at the boundaries of their defined ranges. The cases of no aircraft and the maximum number of aircraft are more likely to expose an error in an aircraft tracking program than a test case with the number of aircraft in the middle of the specified range. Consider this requirement: "Linear speed values shall be valid if they consist of signed strings of digits with a numerical value between 0 and 20000, inclusive."

Equivalence partitioning will tell us that we have legal values of speed, S, when the condition exists such that

$$0 \le S \le 20000$$

and that illegal values exist when

$$S < 0 \text{ or } S > 20000.$$

That makes three equivalence classes and, hence, three test cases. In addition, since we're working with strings of digits, we might select test cases to ensure that each of the decimal digits is represented.[12] The following test cases would do that:

$$S = -100, +20, 3427, 18659, 46517.$$

But we shouldn't be too comfortable with those test cases. Experience tells us that, in addition, this program should be tested with the values

$$S = 0 \text{ and } S = 20000$$

because those are values that are most likely to expose an error. The prudent tester will also include the cases $S = -1, +1, 19999,$ and 20001. The values -1 and $+1$ are the integers closest to 0, the low boundary between legal and illegal values; similarly, 19999 and 20001 bracket the upper boundary. All of these cases were selected from the boundaries of the input range defined in the specification.

Cause-effect graphing. Computer programs can be thought of as turning *input conditions* into *output conditions*. In some cases, these input conditions are the values of the data presented to a software component, and the output conditions are the values generated by the software or the error messages produced (if the data is wrong). In other cases, the input conditions are systemwide situations or states and the output conditions are other sys-

---

[12] We should actually ensure that each digit is correctly processed in each possible input position.

tem states. In *The Art of Software Testing* [Myers 1979], Myers describes a technique developed by W. R. Elmendorf of the IBM Systems Development Division for systematically identifying the input conditions for a software product and the output conditions that arise from them.

The technique Myers describes is called *cause-effect graphing;* the class of input conditions are called *causes* and the output conditions *effects*. The process begins by examining the software specification and identifying and listing each cause and each effect, the causes in one column, and the effects in a parallel one. When examining the specification, the tester initially ignores any relation between causes and effects. For example, consider the requirements:

"When the controller depresses the HANDOFF key, the interface software shall determine if an aircraft is currently identified on the controller's console. If no aircraft is identified, the system shall request that one be identified. If an aircraft is identified, the system shall determine if a receiving controller has been established. . . ."

In this situation, the causes and effects are

Causes	Effects
1. Controller depresses HANDOFF key	8. System looks for identified aircraft
2. Aircraft is currently identified	9. System requests an aircraft be identified
3. Receiving controller is established	10. System looks for receiving controller

The causes and effects are next linked graphically using the language of the specification to identify the linkages. Figure 8.4 is the graph for this example. Cause 1 has as an immediate result, effect 8. If cause 2 is satisfied, the result is effect 10; if cause 2 is not satisfied, the result is effect 9. The

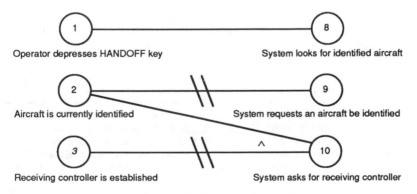

Figure 8.4   A simple cause-effect graph.

process continues until all causes and effects have been examined. In the figure, the double bars on a linkage line indicate that the absence of the associated cause brings about the effect.

From the cause-effect graph, a decision table is created which lists, for each effect, all combinations of causes which can bring it about. This information is entered into a decision table with one column for each possible combination of causes; identical combinations, even if their existence is deduced from different effects, are combined into a single column. The decision table for our example is

	Test Cases		
Cause/Effect	1	2	3
1	1		
2		0	1
3			0
8	1		
9		1	
10			1

The 0's and 1's in the table indicate the presence or absence of the relevant cause or effect. A blank entry means that the status of the associated cause is irrelevant to the effect.

Finally, one test case is generated for each column in the table. In the example, the number of test cases is three and they are very simple. But suppose, as is actually the case in an air traffic control system, that the identification of an aircraft is required for many functions and that only in the hand-off situation does the system proceed to look for a receiving controller. In that case, we have an additional cause, the system is in "hand-off mode," and an additional effect, which may not explicitly be stated in the specification, namely that the system is placed into hand-off mode. The list of causes and effects then is

Causes	Effects
1. Controller depresses HANDOFF key	7. System enters HANDOFF mode
2. System is in HANDOFF mode	8. System looks for identified aircraft
3. Aircraft is currently identified	9. System requests an aircraft be identified
4. Receiving controller is established	10. System looks for receiving controller

The resulting graph shown in Figure 8.5 becomes more complicated as a result and the test case decision table becomes

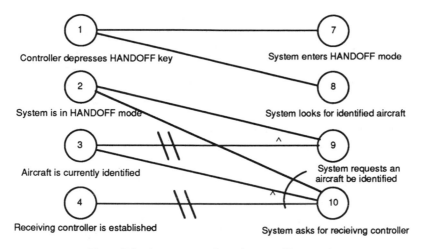

Figure 8.5   A more complicated cause-effect graph.

	Test Cases			
Cause/Effect	1	2	3	4
1	1	1		
2			1	1
3			0	1
4				
7	1			
8		1		
9			1	
10				1

We notice here that the causes for test cases 1 and 2 are the same. Hence, they can be combined into a single test. The number of test cases appears to be the same as the number of effects, but such is not the general case. If causes of a particular effect are related by an "or" condition rather than the "and" in the example, the one case will be necessary for each possible combination of causes.

It's clear that complete cause-effect graphing for a large system is not practical because of the number of input conditions and combinations. Even so, this technique can be useful for low-level testing or when combined with the scenario generation approach of Chapter 9.

Error guessing.   We've noted that the boundary members of an equivalence class are, at least according to experience, more likely to expose errors when part of a test case. Using boundary value analysis, we use a program's specification to identify the boundary members of each of the input data classes associated with the program we're testing.

But there are a lot of input values and conditions that aren't easily identified using formal methods. These are the special values that experienced testers use in project after project. Some examples of such special test cases are

- Time of day passing midnight. This input situation is used to test programs which display the time and those that compute the interval between events;
- Date changing from December 31 to January 1. This situation is similar to the previous one, but the units have been expanded;
- Leap year;
- Nonsensical input such as a negative deposit for a banking program;
- Input cases not identified by the specification such as the situation that arises for interactive graphics programs when several input keys are depressed at the same time or when the user takes an additional action without waiting for the system to respond to a previous one[13]
- Situations where display refresh memory fills or where the display processing time begins to impinge on the central processor time;
- Race conditions, particularly in multiprocess and multiprocessor systems, where the order of completion of two or more asynchronous activities can have a potential (but undesired) effect on the performance of the program;[14]
- No input at all (as opposed to the boundary values of actual input);
- Any other test case that the tester feels has a good chance of exposing an error.

It should be clear that the division between error guessing and boundary value analysis isn't really precise (for example, in the case of null input). But it should be equally clear that error guessing combines well with any other test method the tester employs. In fact, Glenford Myers [Myers 1979] includes, although not by name, error guessing as the fifth of his five rules on equivalence partitioning: "If there is any reason to believe that elements in an equivalence class are not handled in an identical manner by the program, split the equivalence class into smaller equivalence classes." These smaller classes could have a single element in them.

Error guessing differs from boundary analysis in that boundary analysis

---

[13] This one is particularly productive from a tester's point of view since human interfaces are usually very poorly defined, particularly where nonsensical (but generally predictable) user inputs are concerned.

[14] We have more to say about race conditions in Chapter 10.

identifies test cases based on things that are defined in the specification, while error guessing uses experience to identify test cases for things not defined in the specification (but that should be).

8.4.2 Techniques with Glass Box Emphasis

Techniques that rely on the glass box philosophy for test design generally revolve around *statement coverage* or *condition coverage*. That is, they attempt to maximize the number of paths through the program under test which are executed with test data. Most of our discussion in this section will be about this kind of coverage analysis.

The last approach discussed, however, is a bit unique. *Mutation testing* is a way of examining program behavior that was originally only theoretically interesting because the amount of computation resources needed to use it was very large. Subsequent advances in hardware and computational algorithms indicate that this approach indeed has practical applications.

Statement and condition coverage.   Errors in software, manifested as faults and failures (see Chapter 1), are exposed by presenting the software with input conditions it has not previously encountered or by invoking paths through the software not heretofore executed. The black box oriented test design techniques described above are used to minimize the number of situations in which untested combinations of input are presented to the software. The statement and condition coverage methods described here are used to minimize the number of paths not previously run.

The first attempts to ensure complete test coverage required that every statement in the program component under test be executed *at least once* during the test process.[15] It's clear that this requirement is necessary to locate lurking errors. But a little thought makes it equally clear that such a requirement is not at all sufficient.

Consider the procedure, taken from Myers [Myers 1979, page 38]:[16],

```
1 procedure M(A, B, X);

2 if ((A > 1) and (B = 0)) then X := X/A;

3 if ((A = 2) or (X > 1)) then X := X + 1

4 end.
```

---

[15] The Statement of Work for the Cobra Dane radar (AN/FPS-108) built by the Raytheon Company in the early 1970s required that the software developers sign a statement attesting to the fact that every statement in the software had been executed at least once during testing.

[16] This example is from *The Art of Software Testing*, by G. Myers, copyright 1979, John Wiley & Sons, Inc. Reprinted by permission.

For illustration purposes, we hypothesize that the compound connector in statement 2 (the and) is wrong and should actually be or.

The test case (A = 2, B = 0, X = anything) will cause each statement in the procedure to be executed, but will not expose the error because the result of the procedure's execution will be the same regardless of whether the program is correct (contains the or) or is incorrect (contains the and):

- The entry and exit statements, to the extent that they are executed at all, will be invoked by any test case we can devise.
- In our incorrect situation, A = 2 satisfies the A > 1 condition of statement 2; likewise B = 0 for the second part of the compound condition B = 0. Hence, the assignment X := X/A is performed.
- If statement 2 were correct (the conditional connector were or), A = 2 alone would be sufficient to cause the assignment of X := X/A.
- Again, A = 2 by itself will cause the assignment X := X + 1 to be executed in statement 3.

Whether or not the program is correct (has an or connector in statement 2) or is incorrect, executing the test case (A = 2, B = 0, X = anything) causes all statements to be executed, leaves A and B unchanged, and produces the result final X = (original X)/2 + 1. The test case satisfies the statement coverage requirement but can't differentiate between a correct and an incorrect program.

So here we have a test situation that causes each statement in the procedure to be executed, *regardless of whether or not the program is correct*. We need a stronger condition than simple statement coverage.

The procedure above is not a "straight line" piece of code. If it were, statement coverage would have worked as a test case condition. The failure of statement coverage in the above example was clearly caused by the conditional statements. So we proceed to a stronger condition on our test cases. We require that each decision statement in the program take on a true value and a false value at least once during testing. To explore this requirement, we again examine the procedure above. This time, however, we assume that the error is in statement 3 where the condition X > 1 actually should be X < 1. Here, one test case is insufficient, so we invoke the procedure with two cases: (A = 3, B = 0, X = 3) and (A = 3, B = 1, and X = 0). Once again, we satisfy the test coverage condition without exposing the error:

- The combination of A = 3 and B = 0 in the first test case is sufficient to cause the compound condition in statement 2 to take a true value causing X := X/A to be executed, while A = 3 and B = 1 in the second test case cause that condition to be false.

- For the incorrect statement 3, the combination of A = 3 and X = 3 in the first test case causes the i f condition to be true (because of X = 3 satisfying X > 1), while A = 3 and X = 0 in the second case result in a false (because of X = 0 failing X > 1).
- For the correct statement 3, A = 3 and X = 3 bring about a false (A ≠ 2 and X n o t < 1), while A = 3 and X = 0 cause a true condition (because X = 0 satisfies X > 1).[17]

The following table summarizes the result of applying the two test cases to this little procedure.

	Result	
Test Case	X > 1	X < 1
A = 3 , B = 0 , X = 3	statement 1: 3 , 0 , 1 T statement 2: 3 , 0 , 1 F	statement 1: 3 , 0 , 1 T statement 2: 3 , 0 , 1 F
A = 2 , B = 1 , X = 1	statement 1: 2 , 1 , 1 F statement 2: 2 , 1 , 2 T	statement 1: 2 , 1 , 1 F statement 2: 2 , 1 , 2 T

The final state vectors (the value of A, B, and X) at the conclusion of each test case are the same regardless of the status of the problematic condition.

   Here again, we have test coverage requirements that are satisfied without locating the error present in the software.

   The problem with decision coverage arises from the compound nature of the decisions in our test program. By satisfying any one condition of an or, or by failing to satisfy just a single condition in an and, our test cases can cause the execution of certain paths in the program without exploring the remaining conditions. Decision coverage is clearly more thorough than statement coverage, but it is still not sufficient.

   Since compound decisions cannot be tested by decision coverage, we strengthen our test completeness criteria by demanding that *each condition* take on *each possible outcome* at least once during testing. In our example procedure, there are four conditions: A > 1 , B = 0 , A = 2, and either X > 1 or X < 1. Two test cases are needed to cause each condition to be examined. They are (A = 2 , B = 0 , X = 4) and (A = 1 , B = 1 , X = 0). These two cases result in the four decisions taking on the following values:

----

[17] Myers uses (A = 2 , B = 1 , X = 1) as his second test case. But this doesn't fulfill the condition coverage requirement because it causes the incorrect statement 3 to take on a true value for both test cases (because of X = 3 satisfying the erroneous X > 1 in the first case and A = 2 satisfying the A test exactly in the second). This would be OK except that Myers wanted to select two test cases that satisfied the selection criteria and that failed to differentiate between the correct and the incorrect procedures.

	A > 1	B = 0	A = 2	X > 1	X < 1
A = 2, B = 0, X = 4	True	True	True	True	False
A = 1, B = 1, X = 0	False	False	False	False	True

Each condition takes on the two possible values, and the two X conditions do so with different results.

Three observations remain:

First, compound conditions cannot really be tested independently of each other since it is their *combinations* that result in the following statements being executed. Compiler designers cause their products to take advantage of this. In statement 3, above, for example, anytime the A = 2 test succeeds, the X test becomes irrelevant. Most compilers will generate code that will bypass unnecessary tests once the result of the condition becomes known. Hence, the A test can mask the X test. Test case designers must take care to generate cases that not only cause each condition to take on all possible values at least once, but that cause each such condition to be executed at least once.

Second, once we force each condition (that is, each predicate) to take on each possible value, we have, in effect, invoked a requirement for complete path testing [McCabe 1976].

Finally, Cobb and Mills [1990] have shown that test cases derived from coverage criteria, as these have been, are only 1/21 as effective in reducing the operational failure rate of a software product as are test cases derived from the operational profile (see Chapter 7).

Mutation testing.   Mutation testing isn't really a testing technique at all. It's a method for evaluating the adequacy of the test data by examining the ability of those data to differentiate between a correct program and an incorrect one. But because the test data are normally inadequate at the beginning of the process and, at the same time, the program we've written isn't really correct, the process of augmenting the test data and correcting the written program, when the test data actually locates an error, allows us to move toward both a sufficient set of test data and a correct program. Let's look at how this happens.

Mutation testing is based on an underlying premise called the "Competent Programmer Assumption." Richard DeMillo [DeMillo 1983] describes this assumption as follows:

> The Competent Programmer Assumption formalizes an observation of human activity. In this case, the observation is that programmers do not create programs at *random*. Rather, programs that are written by experienced programmers, are written in response to formal or informal understandings of what the program is intended to do. Thus, in response to specifications for a payroll

system, a competent programmer will produce a program that is very much like a correct payroll program. The program produced may be incorrect, inefficient or sloppy, but in the final analysis, it will be more like a correct payroll system than a compiler.

Interestingly, the competent programmer assumption underlies all testing that is other than exhaustive. The only justification we have for terminating testing prior to the presentation of all possible input values or the execution of all paths is the assumption that the designer and implementer have not significantly deviated from a correct solution.

As originally envisioned, the tester evaluating test data adequacy using mutation analysis begins with a correct program and, from it, creates a series of *mutations*. A mutation of a correct program is another program that exhibits differences from the correct one. These differences are inserted to reflect the kinds of errors a competent programmer might make. Often these mutational differences are just referred to as "errors" even though they are, in this case, intentional.

Referring to the example from Myers that was used in the statement coverage discussion, a mutation of statement 2, for example, results when we replace the $>$ symbol in the A test with $<$. Again, in the same statement, a mutation occurs when $X := X / A$ becomes $X := X + A$.

To keep the mutation analysis tractable, the errors inserted into the correct program to create the mutants are restricted to the class of simple ones. Additionally, the mutants are created in such a way that they contain only a single deviation from the correct program.

The "correct" program and the mutations are then subjected to the set of test data being evaluated. If a mutant should pass a test using the candidate data, it (the mutant) is compared to the correct program to ensure that it and the correct one are not *functionally equivalent*. If the mutant is functionally different, then the test data set is enhanced by the addition of a case which will differentiate it from the valid program. The object of the analysis is to augment the data until all the mutants fail when exposed to the test data and the correct program passes.

This is all well and good, but, in practice, the tester isn't sure if the program provided by the developers is correct. In fact, he or she is pretty certain that it's not. So how can mutation testing help? In the brief description of the process in the preceding paragraph, we omitted one possible situation. What happens when the so-called correct program fails when subjected to the test data? If the program is truly correct, this shouldn't happen, so the test data would be corrected by either removing or altering the cases that caused the valid program to fail. But we could, of course, change the program that failed. This is the key to mutation testing.

The newly written program is initially assumed to be correct and mutations of it are created. The candidate program and the mutants are subjected

```
1. Create test data set
2. Create mutants from the program under test
REPEAT
3. Execute program and mutants against test data
4. If a mutant passes the test (and is not functionally
   equivalent to the program under test
      Add a case to different the mutant
5. If the program under test fails and is found to actually be
   incorrect
      Correct it
6. If the program under test fails and is found to be correct
      Alter or remove the test case
7. Return to Step 3
UNTIL ONLY THE PROGRAM UNDER TEST PASSES
```

Figure 8.6   Mutation testing.

to the test data as described above. If a mutant fails, the response of the tester is as before. If, however, the candidate program fails, then it is analyzed. If the program is correct, then the test data is changed, but if the candidate is found to be in error, the test data is left unaltered and the code is changed. The process is then repeated until only the subject program passes the tests. At this point, the candidate program is considered truly correct and the test data is adequate.[18] The process is presented in Figure 8.6.

For a program of even small size, the number of mutants can be quite large. And since each mutant (plus the program under test, of course) must be subjected to the entire test data set each time the data set is altered, the number of test runs is also very large. The availability of computers and computation time to perform a mutation analysis, even one where the kinds of mutant errors are simple, has been a problem for testers desiring to actually implement the process. So great has the computational problem been, in fact, that mutation testing has been considered of only theoretical interest by a large part of the test community.

But research by Richard DeMillo and Eugene Spafford [DeMillo and Spafford 1986a, DeMillo and Spafford 1986b] at the Software Engineering Research Center at Purdue University has shown that by making appropriate assumptions and with appropriate advances in computing technology, a tool can be created that will perform mutation testing and that will locate errors in a candidate program with considerable reliability. The product DeMillo and Spafford have developed is called Mothra.[19]

---

[18] Although it has served its purpose and is no longer needed, except for regression testing during maintenance and enhancements.

[19] Fans of old Japanese science fiction movies will recognize Mothra as the name of a giant moth which terrorized the world in a particularly awful film specimen of the genre. Mothra was a giant, mutant bug.

REFERENCES

BAKER T., 1972. "System Quality Through Structured Programming," in Proceedings of *1972 Fall Joint Computer Conference,* AFIPS Press, Montvale, N.J.

BÖHM, C., AND JACOPINI, G., 1966. "Flow Diagrams, Turing Machines and Languages with Only Two Formation Rules," *Communications of the ACM,* vol. 9, no. 5, 366–71.

COBB R. H., AND MILLS H. D., 1990. "Engineering Software under Statistical Quality Control," *IEEE Software,* vol. 7, no. 6, November.

DEMILLO, R. A., 1983. "Program Mutation: An Approach to Software Testing," GIT–ICS–83/07. School of Information and Computer Science, Georgia Institute of Technology, April.

DEMILLO, R. A., AND SPAFFORD, E., 1986a. "The Mothra Software Testing Environment," in Proceedings of *11th Software Engineering Workshop,* NASA Goddard Space Flight Center.

DEMILLO, R. A., AND SPAFFORD, E., 1986b. "The Mothra Software Testing Environment," SERC–TR–4–P. Software Engineering Research Center, Purdue University, West Lafayette, IN 47907.

DIJKSTRA, E., 1968. "Go To Statement Considered Harmful," *Communications of the ACM,* vol. 11, no. 3, 147–48.

JENSEN, R. W., AND TONIES, C. C., 1979. *Software Engineering.* Prentice Hall, Englewood Cliffs, N.J.

MCCABE, T. J., 1976. "A Complexity Measure," *IEEE Transactions on Software Engineering,* vol. SE–2, December, 308–20.

MYERS, G. J., 1979. *The Art of Software Testing.* Wiley-Interscience, New York.

RICHARDSON, D. J., AND CLARKE, L. A., 1985. "Partition Analysis: A Method Combining Testing and Verification," COINS Technical Report 85–10. University of Massachusetts at Amherst.

STEVENS, W., MYERS, G., AND CONSTANTINE, L., 1974. "Structured Design," *IBM Systems Journal,* vol. 13, no. 2, 115–39.

YOURDON, E., AND CONSTANTINE, L., 1978. *Structured Design.* Yourdon, New York.

Chapter 9

Scenario Generation

This chapter leads the test implementer from individual test cases to complete validation scenarios.

Validation testing concentrates on demonstration of a software system's functions. Commercial software developers frequently develop software demonstrations to assist in selling their product to prospective customers. These demonstrations serve very much the same purpose as the validation scenarios used to qualify software for the government or other contracting agency. The methods used to develop commercial software's demonstrations and custom software's validation scenarios are exactly the same; the only difference between the two is the degree of user involvement required in writing the test procedure (that is, the script).

In developing validation test cases, the test engineer attempts to show the software operating in a realistic fashion. Obviously, some liberties must be taken with reality in order to show all the functions defined in the Software Requirements Specification (since many of them are intended to be invoked only in exceptional conditions), but it's still true that it's difficult to sell a system (and validation testing has a strong salesmanship component) without showing it in as near a realistic environment as possible. The sequence of actions, stimuli, and so on, that is necessary to demonstrate correct software operation is called a *test scenario*.

A software system is designed to satisfy a list of requirements contained in the Software Requirements Specification and the Interface Requirements Specification(s) that define it. While we may be fortunate enough to have software-knowledgeable customer representatives witness our tests, it's often the case that the final system acceptance comes from the user community, which is much more interested in how well the software satisfies the mission as stated in the System Specification.[1] In this case, the test engineer attempts to group SRS requirements according to the system functions they satisfy and then proceeds to demonstrate compliance with these higher requirements. The tester may, in fact, fall back on *implicit* verification—if the system requirements are satisfied, by implication the SRS ones are, too.

9.1 FIRST, AN EXAMPLE

In order to really talk about a functionally oriented scenario, we need a good example of a typical function. The one we'll use comes from the field of air traffic control. Figure 9.1 is a rather stylized map of the northern Atlantic Ocean, and we'll use it to visualize some of the air traffic control activities that take place during a flight from, say, London to Boston.

From the time an aircraft leaves the terminal gate at its point of origin until it parks at a gate at its destination, except for the time it is in transoceanic flight, it is under the supervision of an air traffic controller. From the gate to the take-off runway, *ground control* is in charge. From the point the aircraft is cleared for take-off until it leaves the immediate vicinity of the

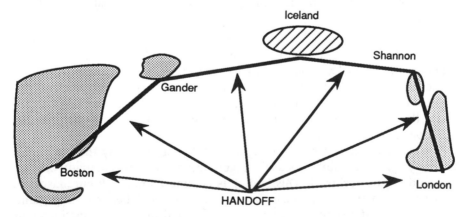

Figure 9.1   From London to Boston.

[1] In the commercial world, the users vote with their checkbooks. And they're very concerned about the ability of the product to solve their problems. In this case, they're comparing the software's capabilities against their own (perhaps unpublicized) specification.

airport, the aircraft is controlled by *departure control*. During most of the flight, one or more *en-route controllers* are in charge. When the plane reaches the vicinity of the destination airport, control is transferred to *approach control;* ground control takes over as soon as the aircraft touches the destination runway.

The transfer of control of an aircraft from one controller to another is called a *hand-off*. The International Civil Aviation Organization (ICAO) has defined a protocol to be followed when handing off an aircraft from one controller to another. Local aviation organizations, such as the U.S. Federal Aviation Agency, place additional restrictions and controls on the process.

In our example, a Flight from London to Boston is handed off as follows:

1. London Ground Control to London Departure Control;
2. London Departure Control to British En-route;
3. As the flight passes Shannon, Ireland, it passes out of official control and into transoceanic flight;
4. As the plane nears Iceland, contact is made with Reykjavik;
5. Nearing Gander, New Foundland, the flight re-enters official control by contacting the Air Traffic Control center at Gander;
6. As the plane leaves the Gander area, it comes under the control of the American en-route system;
7. Nearing Boston, the Boston approach control assumes control, directing the plane to its landing;
8. Upon touchdown, the flight is guided by Boston ground control to its arrival gate.

At any instant, an air traffic controller has under his or her guidance many aircraft. In order to hand control one of these to another controller, he or she must first identify the specific plane to be passed on. Next, the controller must identify to the computer system the controller to receive responsibility for the selected flight. Finally, the receiving controller must actually accept control of the plane.[2]

The U.S. Federal Aviation Agency feels very strongly that any automated system which fails to satisfy the controllers who will actually operate it should not be accepted. This feeling is common among all purchasers of software, but is extremely true in the case of the FAA. It becomes important, then, for the test designer to always keep in mind the actual functions performed by the controllers.

---

[2] By requiring a specific acknowledgment of the hand-off, the aviation procedures minimize the possibility that an aircraft could "fall through the cracks" during hand-off.

9.2 THE THREE STEPS

The three steps in creating test scenarios are as follows:

1. Write a realistic functionally oriented scenario.
2. "Throw" requirements at the scenario(s); 90 percent of the require-ments to be verified will "stick" to one or more scenarios.
3. Adapt existing scenarios or write new ones to pick up the "unstuck" requirements.

9.2.1 Write a Functionally Oriented Scenario

If we return to Chapter 1, "Requirements, Errors, Faults, and Fail-ures," we'll recall that the entire software development process begins with an examination of functionally oriented requirements. By functionally ori-ented, we mean requirements which look at the problem at hand in user terms. For an air traffic control system, for example, functionally oriented requirements describe capabilities of the system that support a controller's actions in terms the controller himself can understand. These would include

- The ability to receive aircraft position from a radar or a radar-interro-gated transponder and to use that position and previous positions to plot the course of the aircraft (track the aircraft).
- The ability to support hand-offs; that is, the ability to permit control of an aircraft to be transferred from one operator to another.
- The ability to receive ICAO-defined transponder codes identifying dis-tressed aircraft and to inform the controller appropriately.
- The ability to provide a list of aircraft about to enter the area of control.
- The ability to reconfigure the display screen's format to accommodate clusters of aircraft.

None of these requirements looks like something a software engineer might be interested in, but they certainly look like things air traffic controllers worry about. In order to get the controllers (as represented by the Federal Aviation Agency) to accept the Air Traffic Control system, the tester will need to orient all of the formal tests and demonstrations toward the control-ler's worries and thoughts; in other words, toward hand-offs, displays, and tracking.

In order to demonstrate the functions of tracking aircraft and displaying their positions, we'll have to provide our system with some aircraft (we'll talk about the mechanics of this later). Initially, we envision a scenario with, say, eight or ten aircraft flying across the system's coverage area. The exact "routes" aren't important except that the individual flights should be scripted in such a way that they are reasonably separated from each other. This separation isn't done for safety, of course, but so the test observers can more easily tell one aircraft from another.

One of the functional requirements we intend to demonstrate is the ability of our air traffic control system to support the hand-off process. This involves two controllers and at least one aircraft. Actually, we'll use two flights since we must show a hand-off being accepted by the receiving controller and one being declined. In order to demonstrate the hand-off capability, the flight paths of our demonstration aircraft (at least the ones involved in the two hand-off attempts) must be something other than totally random: they must pass from the control zone of the first controller into the control zone of the second. If they don't, the risk is that an observer who doesn't understand that the software may not really care if the subject aircraft is in a zone defined only by procedure, may refuse to accept the software because it's not realistic.

Again, we have a requirement for our air traffic control system to accept and properly process the ICAO-defined codes. There are a number of these, but for the purposes of an example, we'll choose the code for "hijack." When an aircraft "squawks" the hijack code, the air traffic control software is expected to initiate an audible signal (to alert the controller) and to cause the hijacked aircraft's symbol on the controller's console to blink (facilitating location of the aircraft on the display). We'll merge this requirement with the hand-off by programming one of our test aircraft as a hijack victim; the controller guiding this aircraft will decline the hand-off of another (presumably because he's busy with the hijack).

A scenario accommodating our thoughts so far is shown in Figure 9.2.

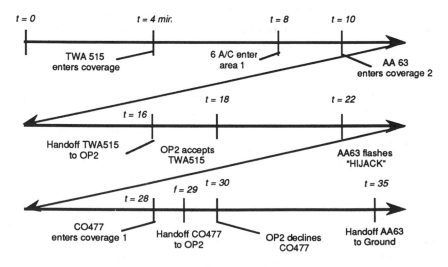

Figure 9.2 A scenario time line.

The diagram shown is called a *time line*. It graphically portrays the key events in the scenario and indicates the times at which they'll occur. Since an air traffic control system is interactive, a large part of the validation scenario will involve a (simulated) controller doing things at a graphics console. It will be important that we leave enough time between required actions to permit the controller to complete each one and to note the results of the action.[3,4]

Included in the scenario in Figure 9.2 are three kinds of events:

1. *General background events*. These are events or activities that provide background to the demonstration and that contribute a great deal to the apparent reality of the scenario. In our case, aircraft entering (and leaving) coverage are examples.

2. *System external events*. These are events or activities that are initiated by systems or objects external to the system under test. In other words, they're events that are beyond the control of the software but to which the software must respond. An aircraft squawking the hijack code is an example of these external events. We differentiate these from external background events (as in the previous category) in that we include system external events for the purpose of showing some capability of the software, not to provide atmosphere or a feel of reality.

3. *System internal events*. Here we mean events and activities that are an integral part of the system's processing activity and that would be meaningless or couldn't happen without the existence of the system. In this case, the initiation of a hand-off from one operator to another is an example of an internal event.

To be sure, the divisions between these categories are a bit nebulous and the categorization of a particular event into one bin or another may be a matter of opinion, but it is useful to recognize the differences. Category 1 events provide reality and context. Category 2 and 3 events are included specifically to permit the demonstration of a function or capability.

Figure 9.3 shows a portion of the test scenario in an *action-response* format. Eventually, we'll want to write a set of test procedures that will be

---

[3] At some point, we may wish to demonstrate the ability of our system to help an overloaded controller by designing a scenario in which events are piled one on the other in such a way that the operator is as stressed as possible (since such situations *can* occur in real life). But our present purpose is to demonstrate that each of the required functions and functional support are present in the air traffic control software. We do this by keeping events separated in time.

[4] It's important, too, to remember that the test executors are human and that they can and will make mistakes in executing the test (and not the intentional ones the test manager has planned). To the extent possible, it's important to leave time between critical actions for the operator to examine his or her input and to correct it if necessary.

Time	Action	Response	✓
t = 4	TWA515 enters coverage of Operator 1	Aircraft ID TWA515 appears on display	
t = 8	6 Aircraft formation enters coverage of Operator 1	6 Aircraft appear on display (verify format)	
t = 16	Begin handoff • Select TWA515 • Depress "HANDOFF" • Enter 2 Operator 2 accepts TWA515	 TWA515 Aircraft ID blinks System asks "Handoff to __" TWA515 ID blinks on console 2 TWA515 stops blinking on all consoles	

Figure 9.3   Action-response test procedures.

in this form. It's useful to begin developing those procedures early in the development cycle. Also, note that we begin noting the specific actions to be taken by the test controller during the validation process. By writing the operational steps, we get an idea of the amount of time required between steps, and will see if there is available time for including *ad hoc* events. Ad hoc events will be type 3 events (above) which are only incidental to the basic story line of our scenario, but which will demonstrate that the software provides other required capabilities. For example, in the case of our air traffic control system, the ability to selectively change the center position of the displayed maps or the colors on the display could be demonstrated while the system is processing the hijack situation since such capabilities are intended to aid controllers in emergency situations by reducing confusion or clarifying displayed information.

"But what about the software requirements?" That's a good question. After all, software validation (ensuring that requirements are met) must necessarily be done against the Software Requirements Specification. In order to address software requirements, we proceed to the next step.

9.2.2 Throw Requirements at the Scenario

Once the details of the functional scenarios have been settled, the tester analyzes each of the requirements enumerated in the software specifications. These are compared to the functional scenarios and correspondences noted. At each step of the validation scenario, one or more software elements will be executing in order to satisfy the functional requirements included in that scenario.

Let's begin by looking at each of the actions and responses in Figure 9.3.

The first action is "TWA515 enters coverage 1"; and the response is "Aircraft ID TWA515 appears on display." The action is generated by our aircraft source. In most cases, air traffic control software is tested using a *simulator*, which inserts the parameters of the aircraft into the software in the form they would have in the real world. The exact nature of the simulator will depend on the test configuration. If the test scenario is being run without any of the external hardware, then the simulation will require that the aircraft data is inserted into the input areas of the software by some specialized software co-resident with that under test or in a processor connected to the input channel which will ultimately receive the data. If the test scenario is run with some or all of the anticipated external hardware present, then the simulator will be inserting the aircraft parameters into the input path at some point external to the operational air traffic control software. In most cases, it's desirable to insert simulated information at a point *as far from the component under test as possible.* By making the insertion point far removed from the software under test, we minimize the amount of interference the simulation itself might have on the operation of the delivered product.[5]

But back to software requirements. To support the air traffic control mission, the software will be required to accept aircraft position and transponder information through its input processes. When we insert the flight parameters associated with TWA515, and all the other aircraft in the scenario, into our system in the format required by the Software Requirements Specification or the associated Interface Specification, we are demonstrating the ability of the software to comply with those requirements.[6]

Similarly, there will be a requirement for the software to display aircraft information in a specific form and in a position on the controller's display which represents its geographic position and altitude. The response to this first procedure step, "Aircraft ID TWA515 appears on display," accommodates these requirements.[7] Again, there will be a performance requirement that the air traffic control software, together with the computer on which it's executing, must cause the aircraft position to be displayed within a specified time interval after the data enters the computer. All these software requirements are validated, at least partially, by the first step in our scenario.

The second action in Figure 9.3 is "6 A/C formation enters coverage 1," and the response is "6 aircraft appear on display." This step is similar to the first, and serves to extend the validation of the input and display requirements; it also provides a number of background aircraft which can be used to support some of the ad hoc actions added to the scenario later as well as to provide some realism.

---

[5] In physics, the Heisenberg Uncertainty Principle holds that by observing an object, we will change it. Unless we're very careful, the same applies to software testing. Test software, whether simulators, recording code, or anything else, has the potential to alter the performance and functional characteristics of the tested programs.

[6] The problem of how we know that the simulated data is in the proper format is discussed in Chapter 12, "Test Tools," since it involves the methods used to validate the simulator.

[7] Of course, the display format requirements will probably require more than a single aircraft in order to cover all the possibilities.

The third action is more complicated and is, actually, composed of several steps, each of which is addressed separately.

We begin the hand-off process: "Select TWA515." Operationally, it's necessary for an air traffic controller to identify a specific aircraft to the software so that special information about it may be requested or because a particular action is about to be taken involving that aircraft. When we select TWA515 to initiate the hand-off sequence, we're actually showing that the software complies with the selection requirement.[8]

The response to the selection of TWA515 is "TWA515 aircraft ID blinks." The Software Requirements Specification will indicate that the display software must acknowledge an aircraft selection by causing the aircraft position symbol and its associated identification to blink. This response will permit validation of the software against that requirement.

Next, the test controller is told to "Depress HAND-OFF" and the response is "System requests 'Hand-off to _____.'" As long as it's clear, the exact text of a system response message is seldom of serious concern to a user. But to provide consistency of wording and format, a good Software Requirements Specification or Interface Requirements Specification will mandate the exact wording and data content of every message displayed by the system to its operator. Here, we validate the software response to two requirements: the text of the system's hand-off initiation message, and, more important, that a specific button, labeled "HAND-OFF" (but, of course, the software can't read the label) actually initiates the hand-off sequence.

After the hand-off is begun, and the software has requested the identity of the receiving controller, the scenario tells the test controller to "Enter '2'" and the the software's response is that the "TWA515 symbol blinks on console 2." When the TWA515 symbol actually blinks, we've also begun verifying that the software can accept and process information from the keyboard. With a data entry action such as this, the test designer can get quite creative. The Software Requirements Specification will define the valid range of numbers for the identity of the receiving controller and, for the scenario to proceed, we'll eventually want to enter a legal value. But before that, we might ask that the test controller enter one or more invalid ones, for example, a nonexistent controller (say "7" if we have a six-controller configuration), or an illegal format (such as an alphabetic), or an existing controller whose console is currently off-line. In each case, we'll have the

---

[8] We can get creative with our scenarios, too. Air traffic control displays are frequently crowded with aircraft symbols. One of the problems that must be addressed by the software, and for which there will be requirements in the Software Requirements specification, has to do with the ability of the controller to select a specific aircraft from among several which are displayed in close proximity. If the simulated trajectories are set up appropriately, we could have TWA515 shown on top of or close beside one or more of the six aircraft that entered the coverage during the previous step.

opportunity to validate the software's compliance with an input validation requirement.

Finally, the scenario excerpt in Figure 9.3 calls for the action "Op 2 accepts TWA515," and indicates that the appropriate response is "TWA515 stops blinking on all consoles." And again, a number of software requirements will be involved: the operator selection of a blinking aircraft identifier, the acceptance of an aircraft hand-off, the termination of the blinking of the identifier, and, if we're thinking, the system response if the receiving operator tries to accept some aircraft other than TWA515.

9.2.3 Adjust Scenarios to Accommodate "Unstuck" Requirements

The majority of the requirements in the Software Requirements Specification will stick to the functionally oriented scenarios we've been discussing. A significant portion of the remaining requirements can be worked into these scenarios by including "mistakes" or other expected but abnormal inputs and commands. But some requirements just won't conveniently work themselves into any kind of realistic scenario.

Most of the leftover requirements will involve exception conditions and combinations of exception conditions which would overwhelm a realistic scenario. Reaction of the software to power failures and emergency restarts, while they might be included in the category of "functionally oriented" requirements, are difficult to include in test scenarios that are centered around normal or nominal operations. Similarly, the abilities of the software to handle potentially disastrous but rare combinations of erroneous input information usually require scenarios of their own for demonstration.

Finally, some software requirements are so far removed from functional operation that they must be validated under laboratory conditions. A good example of these kinds of requirements, and quite appropriate in our air traffic control example, is the accuracy specification placed on the tracking software. Validation of tracking accuracy requires a precise knowledge of the location of the tracked objects (provided by the input to the simulation process) and statistical analysis of the observed or calculated positions of those objects. This analysis can be done after the functional scenario is complete, but usually the kinds of aircraft trajectories needed to validate tracking accuracies are not those that make for truly realistic system operations: large numbers of aircraft flying similar trajectories (straight lines, straight up, straight down, high-G turns, etc.) are not very believable, but they're what the testers use for these kinds of requirements. These requirements are validated in specially generated scenarios that don't pretend to be realistic.

For simple systems, or those with only a single source of input, the scenarios that are developed as we've described are essentially complete and need only to be cast in the form required by the buyer to become complete

test procedures. But for more complex systems, air traffic control or automated teller systems, which may have to process data simultaneously from
several user positions, it's necessary for the tester to ensure coordination
between the test positions.

This coordination is needed so that system responses are repeatable in
case retesting is required and so that correct system response can be predicted prior to the test's execution.

We take the time lines developed for each of the operator positions
and, at least conceptually, lay them side-by-side. We want to ensure that
activities at one input position don't interfere with those at another, either
by causing unpredictable system operation or because one action keeps an
observer from watching the system's response to an activity at another position.[9] Let's think for a moment about each of these.

The bane of testers, and of system developers, is the system that be-
haves one way when events happen in the order A,B, and another when they
happen B,A. When a tester's scenarios uncover software errors, and they
will as they're rehearsed, it will be important to repeat the sequence of events
that led to the error *in the exact order in which they occurred*. If that repetition can't be done, then it's quite probable that the developers won't be able
to diagnoses the error, or even duplicate it. And, if the repetition can't be
done, we won't know if the problem's fixed.

Finally, remember that a principal goal of our scenario based testing is
selling the software: we're trying to convince the buyer that all the software
requirements are satisfied. If an activity at one input position interferes with
the buyer's ability to observe events at another, then that buyer may not
see all the requirements demonstrated and may not, therefore, accept the
software. It's possible to avoid some of this by requesting that the buyer
provide multiple observers, and that's a good idea anyway, but there's often
a lead individual with the authority to override the decisions of any of his or
her subordinates. That person should witness everything.

---

[9] It's also necessary to ensure that the system actually operates while receiving data from
all positions simultaneously. More than one tester has spent so much time preparing a carefully
choreographed scenario designed to show all capabilities that he or she neglected to examine
such simple, and occasionally unstated, requirements as the ability to process simultaneously
data from more than one input channel.

Chapter 10

Integrating
the Software

Sooner or later, someone has to put the software into a workable whole. The process of doing this is called *integration*. On some projects, integration is done by members of the development team; on others, it is done by an independent team; and on still others, it is done by the "test team." In this latter case, the duties of the test team are twofold: (a) locate and eliminate bugs and functional problems, and (b) demonstrate that the software satisfies all the requirements stated in the Software Requirements Specification (SRS).

Reasonable arguments can be made for any of the three approaches toward integration. However, the strategy that seems to be the most efficient is the second, an independent integration team (independent in the sense that different people do the integration than do either the development or the formal testing). The separation of integration from the other tasks permits a more effective division of labor and more flexibility in the acceptable levels of seniority assigned to the various tasks:

- Development can be done by specialists in design and programming. Junior members of the team can be effectively utilized in such an environment and can more quickly become experienced in development;

- The integration can be done by a relatively small number of people experienced in integration of software generally and with the specific problems being solved by the software developers;
- The "test team" can concentrate on requirements validation.

Notwithstanding the above, all members of all teams should communicate with each other frequently. We'll revisit this problem of organization after we've examined the purpose of each of the several types of integration.

10.1 THE PURPOSE OF INTEGRATION

Integration is the process of constructing a software system from its constituent pieces. It involves building something large from a number of small pieces, and in that sense it's always done "bottom-up" regardless of the order in which the pieces are selected. In the discussions that follow, we'll use the term "verify" frequently. In this case, however, we expand the definition of verify to include not only examination of the ability of the software to satisfy explicitly stated requirements, but its ability to satisfy user needs, regardless of whether or not all those needs are stated in the requirements specification.

Here, the tester and the integrator will find himself or herself treading on soft ground, particularly where custom or contracted software is the object of the integration. We certainly don't want to provide more than the customer has paid[1] for; but we also want to ensure that the customer gets what he or she should reasonably expect, regardless of the completeness of the specification.

10.1.1 Unit Testing

Unit testing is normally done by the software developers and is intended to ensure that the software unit—which we have intentionally not defined[2]—satisfies its functional specifications.

---

[1] Or maybe "asked for" is the right term. We don't want to exceed the user's constraints, but, conversely, we want to provide the best system possible consistent with customer funding.

[2] There is considerable disagreement in the software community regarding the definitions of the terms "unit" and "module." Some developers consider modules to be made up of one or more units; others hold that units are composed of one or more modules. Further, there is no consistency regarding the definition of the smaller of these two entities (whether unit or module); that is, some require each procedure, subroutine, or function to be defined as a unit (or module) while others claim that a unit (or module) may consist of more than one compilable entity so long as the unit (or module) itself performs a single function. This book is generally with the school which holds that modules are composed of one or more units and that each unit may consist of as many procedures, subroutines, or functions as are needed to solve the one problem assigned to that unit.

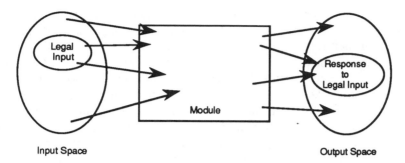

Figure 10.1   Unit testing.

Units can be thought of as translation entities:

$$\textbf{Output} = \textbf{UNIT(Input)}$$

This situation can be seen in Figure 10.1. Unit testing explores the behavior of the unit when presented with values of **Input** which are both inside and outside the defined legal input space. The strategies for selecting the values, particularly equivalence partitioning, boundary-value analysis, and error guessing, presented to the units are discussed in Chapter 8 and in other books on testing.[3] When selecting the legal and illegal values to be presented to the unit, it's important that the developers (or whoever actually does the testing) explore any situation that could realistically be presented to the unit in operation. The question will arise, however, as to what exactly is *possible* input. Figure 10.2 depicts the connection of four units (involved in unit-to-unit integration, see below). Each of the four units, identified as M1, M2, M3, and M4, has an input space. The input space of M1 is external to the control of any of the units. The input spaces for M2 and M3 are, together, the output of M1:

$$\textbf{Output}_1 = \textbf{Input}_2 \cup \textbf{Input}_3$$

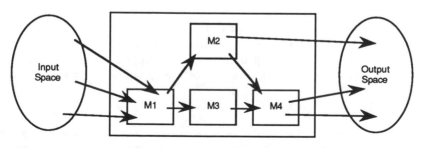

Figure 10.2   Unit-to-Unit integration.

[3] Myers, for example, gives a list of five rules to be used in selecting test cases.

If M1 properly transforms the defined legal values of its input space into output, and if it correctly filters out or corrects the illegal ones, then, *in this application,* neither M2 nor M3 will see illegal input values and, hence, it may not be necessary to explore the operation of them in that situation. Indeed, it's quite permissible to design these two units as though such input were impossible. (Don't stop reading here, though, see the next subsection).

When considering unit testing, keep in mind that some authorities, including Mills and Cobb [Cobb and Mills 1990] consider unit testing generally to be misdirected. They suggest that rather than giving equal emphasis to all functions, no matter how unlikely they are to be used in real life, testing should be oriented toward the functions and groups of functions most likely to be invoked by the software's operational environment. This is an attitude that is consistent with failure-based testing (see Chapter 7).

10.1.2 Unit-to-Unit Integration

Groups of units are often called *modules*, so this phase of the integration and test process is frequently called *module testing.*[4] Unit-to-unit integration verifies input-to-output transformations of *groups of units* or modules. This is the first stage of true integration. This activity of integration is similar to unit testing in that it concentrates on the transformation of specified input into specified output. In fact, the development team frequently performs this task.

The goal of unit-to-unit integration is to ensure that "blocks" of units function correctly when presented with legal and illegal values from the input space of the block.

Emphasis during unit-to-unit integration is on three things: correct transformation of input to output, defense of the group of units against errors in the input stream, and module-to-module interface operations.

Correct transformation of input to output.   In this sense, unit-to-unit integration is very similar to unit testing except that the focus is on groups of units. The group is treated as a sort of "super unit" as shown in Figure 10.2. The input space for the group is defined as the union of the input spaces of all the units in the group that can accept information from the outside. In Figure 10.2, the input space of the group is the same as that of unit M1.

---

[4] We can get into a considerable discussion regarding the definition of a unit and a module. Generally, we define a unit as a small, single-functioned, separately compilable entity. Modules are entities that are individually controlled using the developing organization's configuration management procedures. It's important that the Software Development Plan or the Software Test Plan carefully define these terms.

Defense of the group against errors in the input stream. In this case, considerations are very much the same as those involved in unit testing. The response of a group of units to errors, that is, illegal inputs, that can realistically be presented to that group should be examined as soon as the group is assembled or linked from its constituents. However, input sequences that can't realistically be presented should be ignored during this phase of testing.

Module-to-module interface operations Perhaps the greatest single source of errors in the entire software development process is misunderstandings in interface definitions. We've alluded a number of times in this and the previous sections to the fact that units and groups need not be tested for proper operation in the face of erroneous or illegal input that cannot possibly happen. The problem occurs when we attempt to determine what's possible and what isn't. The task of the tester and the integration team at the unit-to-unit integration level is assuring that what one development group understood as impossible input is either truly impossible or prevented by the design of the group providing the driving unit.

10.1.3 Process Integration

As used in this book, a process is a group of units that implements one (usually) or more (occasionally) software-level functions. For development organizations operating under DOD–STD–2167A, a process is often a high-level computer software component (CSC).[5] Process integration verifies process-to-process communication. As groups of units become reliable (in the dictionary sense rather than that of Chapter 14), the integration begins to assemble them into *processes* which perform complete and identifiable functions. Figure 10.3 shows a system consisting of four separate processes which happen to reside in four separate processors. Process integration can occur even if all processes are resident in a single processor.

The focus during this stage of integration is on process-to-process communication since the interfaces between processes is particularly trouble prone. The nature of the communication between processes will be defined in one or more Interface Requirements Specifications (which might be included with the Software Requirements Specifications or which might be in the System Specification).

Individual processes are usually developed by single individuals or by small teams which have an understanding of their immediate assignment because they communicate every day. Problems arise because the teams assigned to different processes communicate only briefly and, usually, at

[5] Under DOD-STD-2167 (no suffix "A"), the term would be Top-Level CSC or TLCSC.

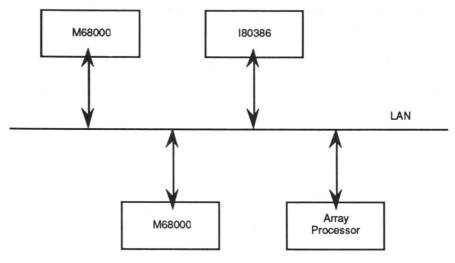

Figure 10.3 Process integration.

unpredictable intervals—often only when problems occur. Frequent team-to-team communication is necessary for error-free interfaces.

10.1.4 Subsystem Integration

The difference between a process and a subsystem will depend on the size of the software system being developed and its design. A subsystem is usually a separately executable entity. Frequently, the term "program" is used. In government terminology, a subsystem is often a CSC from the top tier of the software hierarchy or a complete Computer Software Configuration Item (CSCI).

Subsystem integration verifies subsystem functioning and performance. Once a complete subsystem—not yet defined, but including all the components necessary to transform externally generated input into externally used output—is available, performance can be examined. Hence, subsystem integration focuses on two types of requirements: functional and performance.

The comment made about process integration being susceptible to interface problems between components is also pertinent to subsystems. Indeed, the larger the software components being integrated become, the more likely that errors will be present in the implemented interfaces between them. Sloppy definition is the usual cause (see, for example, Chapter 6, "Fuzzy Requirements," for discussion of poorly defined requirements for software).

Functional requirements, or long strings of them, define input-to-output transformations. Since complete subsystems are frequently executable in a

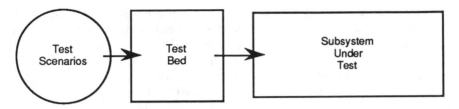

Figure 10.4   Subsystem integration and testing.

stand-alone fashion (that is, they are frequently independent programs), they can often be tested by using an external test bed such as a *simulator*[6] as shown in Figure 10.4.

Performance requirements define how well the subsystem or system operates. These requirements define such things as *how fast, how many,* and *volume* (that is, how fast do the inputs come and for how long).

The tester or integration team member assigned to verifying performance at this level needs to give a great deal of thought to the manner in which performance requirements will be confirmed.

Speed and response requirements.   The techniques used to verify speed and response requirements will depend, to a great extent, on the precision identified in the software specifications and on the size of the time units involved. Obviously, one uses a different method to check a required 5-second response time than a 5-millisecond one. In the former case, a stop watch will often suffice if the bracketing events are visible to the integrators and testers; in the second, some sort of electronic assistance such as a frequency counter or an oscilloscope will be necessary.

The stated precision will determine the number of test executions necessary to verify software performance. As a rule of thumb, the number of successful executions (or the number of data points needed) is determined by the number of significant fractional zeros in the requirement as stated:

$$N = 10^{n+1}$$

where N is the required number of executions, and n is the number of significant fractional zeros.

Thus, if the required response time is 5 seconds (stated with no fractional zeros), the number of successful test executions needed is 10 or 10^1. If the required response time were 5.0 seconds, then the number of executions would be 10^2 or 100.

Quantity requirements.   Quantity requirements define "how many" things a system must be able to keep track of. Quantity requirements gener-

[6] See Chapter 12, "Test Tools."

ally say nothing about the rate at which data is presented to the program (for then they would be volume requirements) but may define the total number of items to be processed (as in "The Cross Reference System shall provide for a library of 200,000 books") or the number of items that must be processed at one particular time (as in "The Air Traffic Control System shall be capable of simultaneously tracking 500 aircraft"). Test cases which explore the ability of the software to meet quantity requirements require the generation of large quantities of valid test data that are realistic and not overly repetitious (200,000 different book titles or 500 aircraft flying different realistic trajectories). These test cases generally present the data to the program in a continuous stream over some period of time, although it may be necessary for the large quantity of data to be made available instantaneously. In the air space around most air traffic control systems, the number of aircraft in view changes slowly over time; seldom do large quantities of aircraft appear at exactly the same time. However, when the air traffic control system is first started it will detect a large number of aircraft, perhaps a quantity near the specified maximum, very quickly.

Volume requirements.   Volume requirements define the rate at which data are presented to the software (as in "The Automated Teller System shall be capable of handling user transactions at a peak rate of 100 per minute and at an average rate of 50 per minute for periods of 2 hours"). Test cases that probe the software's compliance with volume requirements must be capable of presenting data to the software rapidly. The mechanism that does the data presentation must be at least as fast as the software being tested (when executing in its target computer).

Finding "race" conditions.   Whenever more than one independent process operates in a software system, testers worry about the sharing of resources between and among these processes. "Resources," in this case, includes external and internal data stores, hardware and software service entities, the processor in which the processes reside, and the input and output pathways within the software. Several unfortunate interactions can arise among processes:

1. Deadlock, in which two processes are each waiting on the other to release a resource;

2. Starvation, in which a process is prevented from executing even though it may not be waiting for a resource other than processor time; and

3. Critical race, in which the correct operation of the software relies on the deterministic access to resources by two or more processes when, in fact, the access is not deterministic [Karam and Buhr 1990].

All of these conditions have, at one time or another, been referred to as *race* conditions because they often arise from the unpredictable timing of the operation of one process with respect to that of another. In other words, the processes race each other to the desired resource.

Searching for Deadlock.   Deadlock arises when two processes are each waiting for the other to release a needed resource. Perhaps the most common cause of deadlock is inconsistent allocation of resources to requesting processes. For example, assume two processes P_1 and P_2 which each require access to the resources A and B. If P_1 and P_2 make their requests in the order shown in the accompanying table, the following could happen:

P_1	P_2
Requests A then B	Requests B then A

P_1 requests and receives exclusive use of A. Before P_1 can make its request for B, P_2 requests and receives exclusive access to B. At this point we have a deadlock: P_1 cannot gain access to B and P_2 is excluded from the use of A.

Testing for this kind of deadlock is best accomplished by examining the design of the various processes. A mutual exclusion of processes from resource access can be avoided if all processes request the needed resources in the same sequence. If a consistent sequence of request is not possible, then each requesting process should be designed to release assets already allocated if the entire set cannot be obtained. In this case, the best form of testing is design and code inspection.

Identifying Starvation.   Starvation occurs when a process is prohibited from executing even though it has available to it all necessary resources (except, of course, the central processor).

Starvation may occur if task execution priorities are not set properly, or if a priority aging scheme (in which even low priority tasks eventually execute because their priorities are periodically adjusted upward by the operating system or the executive) is not implemented.

Karam and Buhr [1990] discuss the use of automation to detect starvation in a design or implementation, and suggest the use of "livelock analysis" to show the absence of starvation states. Livelock analysis can be done manually, but is a time-consuming endeavor.

Identifying Critical Race Conditions.   According to Karam and Buhr [1990], "A race condition exists when two or more tasks non-deterministically access, either implicitly or explicitly, some shared function (such as modifying a variable). A critical race condition exists when the outcome of a race incorrectly assumes some deterministic behavior."

Critical races are the most difficult problems to find precisely because the outcome of the race is nondeterministic. Each test situation is different from the preceding ones, and the result may very likely be different. It may not be possible to obtain enough instances of failure because of a suspected critical race to permit analysis by the developers.

Karam and Buhr discuss the automation of the identification of nondeterministic accesses to shared functions. They have developed a tool and process for actually identifying such situations in Ada designs and programs. The tool cannot ascertain if deterministic behavior is assumed, but it can locate situations in which such determinism is definitely not present. Given the list of such situations, a software engineer can then make a judgment about underlying assumptions.

If the Karam and Buhr tool is not available, or if the software system is not implemented in Ada, the integrator or test engineer must carefully examine the software design to identify multiple access to shared functions. Global set-use matrices provided by some compilers and by some case tools are useful here. Ultimately, though, the experience of the designers, integrators, and testers is the best means of identifying races.

10.1.5 System Integration

The software system is the complete set of software to be delivered to the developer's customer. Software system integration verifies *system functions* and *performance*.

The first phase of system integration begins when two or more subsystems are brought together (see Figure 10.5). Again, the emphasis is on interfaces.

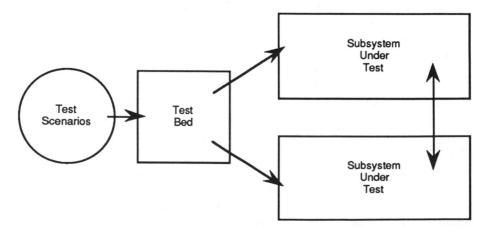

Figure 10.5 Software system integration and testing.

If the previous stages of integration have been done properly, a great deal of system integration can be done using an external test bed possibly coupled with a "listening device" attached to one or more of the inter-subsystem interfaces to ensure that information is flowing properly between the various system components.

10.2 PICKING AN INTEGRATION STRATEGY

Integration is the process of systematically adding newly developed compo-nents to an evolving system. Prior to beginning the integration procedure, the tester must determine the order of selection of components. There are several strategies, each with advantages and disadvantages.

10.2.1 Big-Bang Integration

When we link all the components at once, and test the resulting com-plete system as an entity without considering the correctness of individual pieces, we're doing *big-bang* integration. Big-bang integration is almost uni-versally condemned, and it should be when it's used for large systems.

The essence of integration and testing is the *scientific method:* we make a small change to the system (usually by adding a new component or changing an existing one), devise a series of test cases for the resulting product, predict the response of the modified system to those test cases, and only then do we actually execute the test. If the system fails to satisfy the test cases by not producing the predicted results, we've found an error and we have some idea where the problem is. Specifically, the added or modified component must be involved somehow, either directly or by some interaction with other com-ponents.

If all components are integrated simultaneously, errors are difficult or impossible to diagnose.

However, there are times when small numbers of components can be integrated simultaneously. The tester should compare the relative cost of adding each of the components individually to the cost of "mini-bang" test-ing the set and then trying to analyze the resulting functional and interface problems. It often happens that when the new components are very closely related (that is, they are all associated with a single well-defined function of the final system), the economics of the situation lean toward integrating the group.

10.2.2 Top-Down Integration

The control structure of a software process or program can be presented graphically using a *structure chart* similar to the one shown in Figure 10.6. If integration is done by incorporating the components that reside at the top

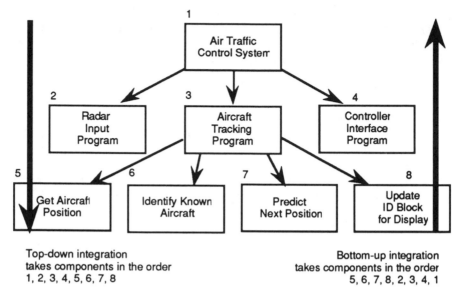

Top-down integration   Bottom-up integration
takes components in the order   takes components in the order
1, 2, 3, 4, 5, 6, 7, 8   5, 6, 7, 8, 2, 3, 4, 1

Figure 10.6 Selecting integration strategy from the program structure chart.

of the chart before those lower down, then it is said to be done *top-down*. Portions of the software that have not been integrated are replaced by *stubs*.

The software community is in almost universal agreement that top-down analysis and design are the most effective ways to approach the problem of system construction. They're not nearly so solid in their opinion of top-down integration.

Top-down integration will permit the tester to create a skeleton version of the program very quickly. This skeleton will often contain most of the basic control logic and may even support some of the user interface. Having such a skeleton early permits the evolving system to act as a test harness for some of the future test cases. It also permits the early demonstration of the partial system to the end user (if the software is being developed in the contract environment) and to management.[7] Working with the evolving skeleton program permits the testing of the basic software architecture.

But top-down integration has some drawbacks that many development organizations consider fatal. One of the most severe problems for developers

---

[7] Often one of the tester's most important duties may be the preparation of software demonstrations. These are used to convince the management of the developer and the user that progress is being made and that the project should continue. It often happens, unfortunately, that the tester becomes so oriented toward demonstrations that he or she is diverted from the real purpose of testing, the search for errors and the proof that the software satisfies its specifications.

of embedded hardware/software systems concerns the nature of the elements at the bottom of the structure chart. For systems with newly developed hardware that must be mated with the software, the input-output drivers for that equipment are often at the bottom of the structure. Because of the nature of top-down integration, these elements will be tested last (or at least late). But the interface between new components (hardware and software, here) is always a fruitful source of errors, and delaying the location of those errors represents risk to the overall development effort. A principal goal of management is the minimization of risk. That means the hardware-software interfaces should be tested first, not last.[8]

A second difficulty with top-down testing is that of creating stubs that can realistically respond to the higher level structure while at the same time supporting test cases that examine the detailed workings of the software's control logic. The problem with creating such stubs has been discussed in Chapter 4.

10.2.3 Bottom-Up Integration

What's good about top-down is a drawback for bottom-up integration and vice versa. Critical modules are addressed very early in the test process. This permits the redesign of interface details to be done before the project has reached a stage where the expense of that redesign is prohibitive. Also, while test drivers (which substitute for the missing program superstructure) are often large and complicated, they have the advantage of being in total control of the elements being tested. Hence, they can control certain test cases, which would be impossible using stubs.[9]

Unfortunately, with bottom-up integration there is no complete software system until the very end of testing. This may mean that flaws in the basic software architecture aren't found until late. A change to the basic software architecture at such a time can be very expensive.

10.2.4 Build Integration

The difficulties with both top-down and bottom-up integration have led many developers to take a hybrid approach. Perhaps the most common is *build testing*, sometimes called *phased integration, functional integration,*

---

[8] Of course, some of the risk can be reduced by navigating individual legs of the structure chart as early as possible in order to get down to the high-risk modules.

[9] It has been suggested that the total amount of test software needed for a large project will be about the same whether the product is tested top-down or bottom-up. In the top-down case, the tester will need a large number of relatively small stubs; in the bottom-up case, a small number of large test drivers.

or *thread integration.*[10] The approach is to use the Software Requirements Specification or, if possible, the System Specification to identify as many complete functions as possible. A characteristic of these functions is that for each there is a complete input-to-output transformation. Each of these input-to-output functions is called a *thread.*

These threads are grouped according to the categories assigned when the Verification Cross Reference Index was created. Groups of threads are called *strings.* Strings that are grouped by user-recognizable function are called *builds.* These groupings will differ for different systems and different user applications. They might be, for example, "graphic, computational, control," or they might be "operational, training, maintenance." A typical build sequence for an air traffic control system might be

Build 1—Basic System Control. All functions associated with basic resource control are integrated during Build 1. This would include the operating system, mode-switching software (needed, for example, to transfer between normal operation, training, and maintenance), and basic keyboard and display functions.

Build 2—Radar Input to Display Output. Those functions necessary to accept a radar/transponder signal from an aircraft and display it at the correct point on a controller display. At this time, the tester is concerned only with the correct positioning of the displayed data and the correct display of data contained in the signal (such as altitude and distress status).

Build 3—Object Tracking. Those components needed to analyze aircraft motion and to predict where the aircraft will be when next detected by the radar equipment are integrated next. Some of the tests performed during Build 3 will use the previously established ability of the software to correctly display object positions.

Build 4—Local Communications. With Build 4, the functions that permit a controller to communicate with others in the same control center (and do a hand-off as described in Chapter 9) are added to the system.

Build 5—External Communications. After local communications have been integrated, the next functions to be added are those that permit the control center to talk to other centers (for the interchange of flight plans).

Of course, the sequence of integration must be consistent with the order of development; after all, we can't test what we don't have. And

---

[10] The taxonomy of software testing is by no means standardized. Each of these terms has been used to mean other things.

the sequence should be considered changeable when circumstances warrant.[11]

Because build integration works with complete end-to-end functions, it leads to useable, if not complete, systems early in the integration process. Schedule pressure in the custom software world may be alleviated by delivering these partial systems.[12] These functioning, if incomplete, systems provide the same morale boost that comes in top-down testing.

Additionally, by concentrating on complete functions, those that are associated with risky components (interfaces with new hardware, for example) can be integrated first. This provides the risk-reduction advantage of bottom-up integration.

Build integration has some potential pitfalls, though. In particular, build integration requires more discipline in the configuration management used to support it. This is because some components (module 1 in Figure 10.7, for example) may be involved in more than one build. When new functions are added during later builds, all these "pivot" components must be identified and the functions that they supported in the earlier builds need to be thoroughly regression tested.

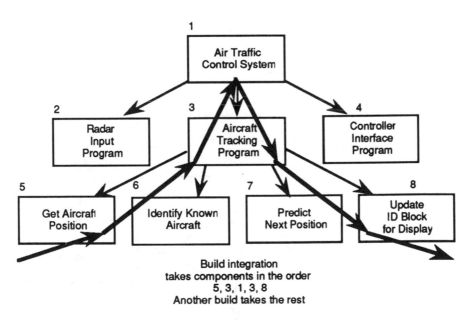

Build integration
takes components in the order
5, 3, 1, 3, 8
Another build takes the rest

Figure 10.7   Build integration.

[11] When the allocation of functions to particular builds is changed, the tester must remember to reallocate the resources (including time and money) consistently.

[12] This is strictly an emergency procedure. It's generally a sign of bad management to get into a situation where partial deliveries are necessary.

10.3 USE THE FORMAL TEST PROCEDURES TO GUIDE INTEGRATION TESTING

When the system development process requires a formal acceptance test, as most custom developments do, the individuals responsible for the acceptance test will prepare test procedures which will be submitted to the buying agency for approval. Those test procedures will require "testing" and "debugging" just as does the software. The best people to do the procedure evaluation are the integrators. Why? Because they have the evolving software system available to them, and the software is the best test vehicle for test procedures.

But using the test procedures is a benefit for the integration team, too. After all, someone has to think up the integration test cases. Why not start with the ones devised by the formal testers and go from there? The process of mutually testing software and test procedures is shown in Figure 10.8.

One caution is needed when concurrently testing software and procedures. When there is a mismatch—the results of software execution aren't as predicted by the procedures—the temptation is to change the procedures

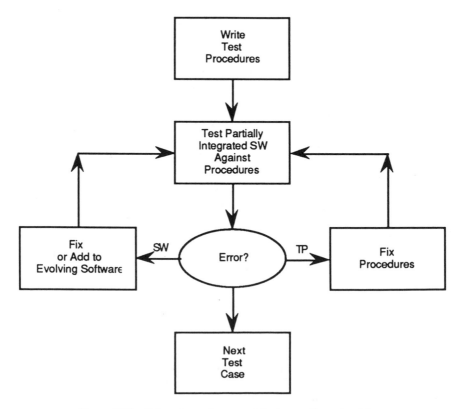

Figure 10.8 Debugging software and test procedures together.

to agree with the software. That's wrong. The correct procedure is to compare both software and procedure to the specification and then to change whichever is incorrect.[13]

REFERENCES

COBB, R. H., AND MILLS, H. D., 1990. "Engineering Software under Statistical Quality Control," *IEEE Software,* vol. 7, no. 6, November.

KARAM, G. M., AND BUHR, R. J. A., 1990. "Starvation and Critical Race Analyzers for Ada," *IEEE Transactions on Software Engineering,* vol. 16, no. 8, 829–43.

[13] This means that when the software fails to satisfy the procedures, we shouldn't rush to change the software either.

Chapter 11

Formal
Demonstrations

Demonstrations are the events that sell a system. The degree of formality varies depending on the development environment. While commercial software developers often conduct formal demonstrations, they have considerable control over the format of their demonstrations, and the amount of formality can be adjusted according to the size and degree of technical sophistication of the customer audience. The custom software developer has less flexibility: demonstrations are strictly controlled, and the amount of latitude for deviation from preplanned procedures is usually small. The most rigorously formal demonstrations are those conducted for government agencies. This chapter is written with government-style demonstrations in mind. Readers of this chapter should evaluate their own situations and approach the material accordingly.

Formal demonstrations may be known by several names:

- Acceptance Test
- Formal Qualification Test
- Sell-off

An acceptance test is oriented to generating final acceptance of the software by the buying agency; the result of a formal qualification test is approval for the software to move on to the next phase of product development (which may be customer acceptance, but which might only be hardware-software integration).

The characteristics that differentiate a formal demonstration from any other kind of test are

1. The customer is present; and
2. The procedures used for the test (that is, the script) have been previously submitted to the customer and approved.

In other words, the key word is "customer."

With the customer in attendance at a formal demonstration, and with acceptance of the software on the line, it should be clear that we're not looking for errors. That is, the last thing we want is a surprise from our system.

To ensure a surprise-free and successful demonstration, the software tester must make appropriate preparations prior to the actual test[1] and must conduct the test according to previously determined protocols. This chapter addresses pretest and test conduct.

11.1 PREDEMONSTRATION ACTIVITIES

Prior to the conduct of a demonstration, the test conductor will want to ensure that the software system is indeed functioning correctly. This will involve exercising the software with a set of test cases designed to expose the errors which almost certainly exist in the product as it first comes from the developers.

At the same time, the tester will want to prepare a set of test procedures that convincingly demonstrate that the software complies with the requirements for it set down in the Software Requirements Specification and that instill in the customer a degree of confidence that the software will satisfactorily solve the user's problem.

We've covered the development of test scenarios in Chapter 9. The integration of software components and the use of the candidate test procedures as a basis for error detection is described in Chapter 10.

11.2 THE TEST READINESS REVIEW

The Test Readiness Review (the TRR) was first described in DOD–STD–2167 (no suffix A). It was conceived as a review of the results of test activity that take place in a developer's facility before a formal test

---

[1] To avoid repeating the word "demonstration" too much, we'll use the word "test" as an alternative. Readers should keep in mind that this equivalence is strictly for readability purposes and applies only to this chapter.

or demonstration is conducted. Historically, the buyer was at the mercy of the developer. When the contractor sent the notification letter that formal testing was to begin, the buyer had to show up or be prepared to pay for contract delays.

But the buyer has a limited budget, too. Too many trips with too many people can be expensive. Also, too often the demonstrations were unsatisfactory in depth or the software failed to perform as expected and as claimed.

So the government decided that before any formal testing was to take place, the results of all internal testing by a contractor would be subject to a mandated review similar in scope to the Critical Design Review. The Military Standard, MIL–STD–1521B, defines the subject matter of the TRR. Some of this is considered here because the results of the TRR discussions will affect the formal demonstrations and, particularly, the pretest meeting that precedes it. What follows, by the way, is not a complete repeat of MIL–STD–1521B, but only a description of those aspects of the TRR which the Test Manager should be absolutely certain the buyer understands prior to the commencement of formal testing.

Commercial software developers aren't necessarily required to submit themselves to a Test Readiness Review (unless, of course, their corporate standards require one), but a smart Test Manager will mentally submit his or her project to the considerations listed in MIL–STD–1521B before notifying management or, riskier still, the press, that a capability demonstration or an external release is to take place.

11.2.1 Changes to System Baselines

Baseline changes include any changes to the requirements or design of the system since the last time those items were publicly presented and discussed. If there are substantive changes to any of the baselines, they should have been discussed with the customer prior to the formal TRR.

Requirements changes.   If the requirements levied on the software system are different from those in effect at the Critical Design Review (or even at the last technical interchange meeting), then the differences need to be explicitly stated. The reason should be obvious: the software will reflect the latest understanding on requirements while the test procedures and, possibly, the specification may reflect an earlier agreement. Any possible source of disagreement or misunderstanding should be brought out during the TRR since the buyer's concurrence here will be effective approval of the discussed changes.

Design changes.   Not only are requirements changes of interest to the software buyer; changes to the product design are as well. Again, the reasons are fairly straightforward: at previous reviews, the customer agreed that the design as presented was responsive to the agreed-to requirements. If the design has subsequently changed, he or she will want to review the changes to ensure that the design as implemented still addresses all requirements.

As a practical matter, software designs are usually quite stable by the time of the TRR, and this part of the discussion normally results in few surprises.

Test plan changes.   If there have been changes to the Software Test Plan since it was last presented to the customer, those changes are discussed at the TRR. Of particular interest are the reasons for changes. If the test manager has elected to implement work-arounds because assumptions in the original test plan have not been satisfied, that should be stated and the risks associated with the work-around presented.

Again, if certain test activities which were presented as part of the original test plan have been deferred to later phases of testing, the reasons for the deferral need to be addressed.

Test procedure changes.   The test procedures are the basis for formal testing and, as such, are approved by the buyer prior to the actual conduct of the tests. The submittal and approval process requires a fair amount of time, and during that time, the last stages of software integration and informal testing are performed. These tests normally include several "dry runs" of the upcoming formal tests and they often identify areas in the test procedures that aren't completely optimal. That is, parts of the test procedures may not really show what they were intended to show, or they may not be workable.

Major errors in the test procedures will require a resubmittal, but minor flaws can usually be handled in a less formal way. When minor flaws in the test procedures are noted, the best approach is to record them for presentation at the TRR and to correct the working procedures using a "red-line" process.

The TRR can be the occasion for the submittal of changes to the test procedures.[2] Each of the alterations is described and the reason for the change is presented.

11.2.2 Integration Procedures and Integration Results

Of particular interest to the buyer is the kind of testing performed during software integration. Most buyers realize that simply testing or demonstrating a real-time software product against the specification's "shall's," as is

---

[2] Accompanied, of course, by the necessary contractual material to make the submittal official.

done during a Formal Qualification Test, is not sufficient to ensure that obscure timing errors and race conditions do not exist.

The software development organization, including the integration and test teams, uses the TRR to describe the kinds of tests performed during the software integration process. Note that integration testing need not be limited to product evaluations which require software execution. If, for example, the test team has subjected the product design to a race condition analysis (as described in Chapter 10), that is an appropriate topic for the TRR.

The purpose of this review of integration testing is to ensure that the development group (again, including the testers and integrators), has subjected the software product to more than a superficial requirements-driven evaluation. The kinds of test performed during integration testing will have been documented in the Software Development Plan (for government contracts) or in the Software Test Plan.

11.2.3 Software Problems

At the TRR, most customers are principally interested in the kinds of problems or errors that have been detected in the software and the progress that has been made in correcting those problems. Almost all customers know that errors will have been found, and few are so naive as to think that all errors have been removed by the time of the TRR.

The easiest way to approach the discussion of software problems is simply to present a list of all detected problems and the current status of them. Specifically, the integration and test team should present, for each detected problem.[3]

1. The symptoms;
2. The severity of the problem. DOD–STD–2167A suggests the following categories of severity:
   a. Priority 1 problems, which jeopardize personnel safety or endanger an essential mission capability,
   b. Priority 2 problems, which seriously degrade the software's ability to accomplish its mission,
   c. Priority 3 problems, which degrade the software's ability to accomplish its mission, but for which a work-around exists,

---

[3] The point at which recording and counting of problems is begun requires some thought. If the counting is begun too early, an artificially high error count may be reported at the TRR even though most have been closed. Conversely, initiating the count too late may lead to such a low count that the thoroughness of testing is put in doubt. The best time to initiate recording and problem counting for a software component (whether CSU, CSC, or something else) is when the component is placed under the first of the developer's configuration management procedures.

    d. Priority 4 problems, which result in inconveniences to the user but which do not endanger the accomplishment of the product mission, and

    e. Priority 5 problems, which cover all other cases.

3. The underlying cause of the problem (if known);

4. The nature of the correction (again, if known; if not known, the presenter can use his or her best judgment as to whether speculation is warranted);

5. The status of the problem analysis and correction.

The customer will, of course, be most interested in open problems, and, for the sake of saving time, the presenter may restrict the actual discussion to just the open problems (although a record of all problems should be included in the back-up documentation).

Occasionally, a software contractor for the U.S. government has delayed the recording of software problems until after the TRR so that a presentation like the one just described could be avoided. The reason was a misguided belief that a discussion of discovered problems would lead to a failure of the TRR or to a desire on the buyer's part to defer the FQT until more informal testing has been done. The presentation of problem and error status may, of course, result in just such a request by the buyer, but a failure to present any problems will probably result in even more serious consequences.

11.3 PARTS OF THE DEMONSTRATION

A formal software demonstration (an FQT, say) consists of four parts, two of which precede the conduct of the test, and one of which precedes the actual gathering of participants:

1. The customer notification, which is a formal and contractual communication to the buyer that the contractor believes the software is ready for the demonstration and that, in fact, the demonstration will take place;

2. The pretest meeting, during which all witnesses to the demonstration are briefed on what will happen during the test;

3. The demonstration itself; and

4. The posttest meeting, during which the witnesses discuss and agree on what happened during the test.

11.3.1 Customer Notification

Before a formal demonstration can be conducted, the customer must be notified. The precise rules for notification will be spelled out in the contract or its Statement of Work (SOW).

Most customers require 30 days' notice before the start of any test. This is reasonable because the user and others interested in the system and the results of the test may not reside near the developer's facility; travel and lodging arrangements need to be made.

Customers will also require some statement of software status. This status will include the number and nature of outstanding problem reports. Testers are often surprised to learn that most customers are willing to witness formal tests of software that has known deficiencies. The statement of deficiencies may not accompany the contractual notification letter, but at least should be made verbally at the time of notification.

11.3.2 Pretest Meeting

Each formal demonstration is preceded by a pretest briefing. Broadly, this meeting introduces the participants and witnesses and informs each of the events that will take place during the test. The most fundamental and unbreakable rule during formal demonstrations is "Do not surprise the customer."

To avoid surprise, it's necessary to discuss with the customer all aspects of the test with which he or she may not be familiar and even some that are familiar. This will include the status of the software, the status of the hardware on which the test will be run, basic ground rules regarding ad hoc testing, and anything else the Test Manager thinks might be of interest or importance. Some of this material will be a repeat, and an update, of the TRR discussions.

To be consistent with the philosophy of not surprising the customer, most of the information presented at the pretest meeting should have been communicated to the buyer prior to the actual meeting.

Purpose of the test. The purpose of the test is demonstration that the software configuration item (or system or component or module or unit) complies with its defining requirements as stated in the appropriate Software Requirements Specification.

At this time, the Test Manager will identify the software under test by its official title and configuration management identification (as established during predemonstration activities) and will list each component of that software (also with official identification) and the active version number. This formal identification is important in establishing the precise program *baseline* that exists when the test is successfully completed.

Status of the software.   Particularly if the software development activity has been under way for some time, trouble reports will have been written against one or more of the components of the software under test. One purpose of the pretest briefing prior to a formal demonstration is identification of the exact status of the software. Although both contractor and customer can expect the software to be reasonably error free, it is permissible for *some* discrepancies to exist.

At the pretest briefing, the Test Manager will inform the customer of the total number of trouble reports that have been written and the number of these that are still open. Each of the open reports will be briefly described. Those that affect the software under test will be discussed in detail and the effect of their resolution on the validity of the test will be presented. The goals of the presentation are

1. Determination that the deficiencies documented in the trouble reports will have little or no significant effect on the overall goals of the current test;
2. Determination that correction of the documented deficiencies will not invalidate the results of the current test; and
3. Determination that validation of the correction of these deficiencies can be conveniently done at some later time.

If any of these items can't be established, then the formal demonstration will have to be rescheduled.

Although formal tests can be, and are, conducted on software with unresolved problem reports, the buyer representative must agree to the proceedings. This being the case, any potentially controversial trouble reports should be discussed with the customer representative prior to formal test notification.

Status of the procedures.   Test procedures are normally submitted to the customer 30 to 60 days prior to the actual execution of the formal test. Between the time the procedures are submitted and the time the test is run, a considerable amount of software testing (and error correction) takes place. Because the procedures usually define carefully scripted demonstrations, any change to the software under test potentially will require a change to the procedures themselves. Frequently, also, the submitted procedures themselves are found to be in error either because the test engineers misinterpreted the specification or because the software evolved after the procedures were originally written.

In any case, program schedules generally make it impractical to resubmit the procedures (only to find that even the new ones are wrong . . .) so the test engineers employ a process called *red-lining*. Red-lining involves making manual (pen and ink) changes to a master copy of the test procedures as testing and correction continues following procedure submittal.

When the customer arrives at the contractor's facility for the formal software demonstration, it's necessary to describe each manual change to the approved procedures and to get customer concurrence with those changes. If the customer doesn't agree to the red-lines, then the test must be run against the approved procedures *as submitted* and it's a sure bet that the test will fail.

11.3.3 Test Conduct

Following the Pretest Meeting, the witnesses and testers adjourn to the test location. The specifics of this location vary, of course, with the nature of the software system being developed. For small, PC-based systems, the test may take place in the same room as the Pretest Meeting; for complex real-time systems, the test may take place in a laboratory full of computers and support hardware, or even in the target installation.

Creating the executable software.   Very few software developers actually "cook" a test by using software specifically programmed to pass the individual test cases. There is often, however, some question regarding traceability from the controlled source code to the executable instructions in the processors. The best way for the Test Manager to handle this potential trouble spot is to compile and link the software product from the deliverable source code as the first step in the test.

Creation of the executable program from source code can take a long time and the temptation during qualification test dry runs is to bypass the creation step. The tester who skips any step that is part of the formal activity is asking for Murphy's law to be invoked!

Number of test witnesses.   Testers are well-advised to keep the number of participants in a test to a minimum. It's difficult to tell a customer that some of his associates can't witness the test (and, in fact, it may be contractually impossible), but it's often necessary. Too many participants cause confusion. At the very least, some will have difficulty seeing the results of test cases. Also, the more participants, the more likely the case that some are not particularly knowledgeable of the system and that means that there is risk of much discussion and explanation concurrently with test execution. This discussion may severely disturb whatever choreography may have been built into the test scenarios.

Problems encountered during the test.   It's best to keep a large quantity of Problem Report Forms near the test location. During the formal test, *any question* as to the proper operation of the software should be considered a potential trouble report and should be written up as such. The time spent in dispositioning these "anomalies" during the test will only disrupt the careful choreography of the test and probably create hard feelings between developer and witness when the former informs the latter that he or she "doesn't understand software." The proper place to disposition problem reports is the posttest meeting.

11.3.4 Posttest Meeting

At the conclusion of the test, all the participants and witnesses reconvene to assess the results. The goal of the posttest meeting is not the determination of success or failure, but agreement on what actually happened.

Each of the problem or discrepancy reports is evaluated and its impact on the test and, more important, on future testing and system delivery is determined.

Problem disposition.   The first task of the posttest meeting is a discussion of each of the discrepancy reports generated during the conduct of the test. Each report should be categorized as

1. No problem, software performed in accordance with specification. This will be a frequent disposition if the philosophy of recording any questionable performance of the software is followed.
2. No problem, software performed in accordance with the specification, but a change in the software is desirable for mission or operational reasons. Reports in this category are treated contractually like the previous category, but they may be included in a list of changes or enhancements to be incorporated after software qualification.
3. Software did not perform in accordance with the specifications. This is the category of true errors. For each problem report with this disposition, a priority or severity classification should be attached.
4. Test procedures are in error. There are two subsets to this category. In the first, the software is considered correct, and in the second, the software status is not clear. For the case of correct software, an after the fact red-line can be generated (assuming the procedure correction is that simple) to correct the test procedures. The results of the red-line can then be incorporated in the posttest document submission. If the compliance of the software with the SRS is unclear because of the test procedure error, a red-line may still be possible, but a retest of the software will be necessary.

A copy of each problem report which documents a true error is transmitted to the development group for analysis.

All reports, regardless of disposition, are included in the Test Report.

Planning for retesting.   Eventually, for each of the problem reports documenting "true" errors, a correction or fix to the software will be provided by the development group. It will be necessary to (a) determine if the formal test just completed must be re-executed, or (b) incorporate a demonstration of the correct operation of the fixed software into another test event. For the case of deficient test procedures, the software can be declared instantaneously "fixed" and the same two retest possibilities are considered.

The decision to retest or to include fix verification in a later test will depend on the severity of the errors and, to a great extent, on the nature of the fixes. During the posttest meeting, the test team and the buyer will only be able to make recommendations based on the observed discrepancies and some educated guesses as to the nature of the upcoming changes. As a general rule, the existence of problems classed as Priority 1 (endangering personnel safety or mission success) or Priority 2 (severely reducing the effectiveness of the software) will require a re-execution of the formal demonstration; the existence of problems classed as Priorities 3, 4, or 5 will not necessarily do so.

Agreeing on what happened.   The senior representatives of the buyer and the developer (often the Test Manager) should sign the official log of the test to certify that the log accurately documents the events that occurred during the conduct of the test. This log is often a copy of the test procedures, including all relevant data sheets and trouble reports, exactly as they were executed, meaning any deviations from the original procedures are marked.

The signing of the test log in no way commits the buyer to the acceptance of the software. It only attests to the accuracy of the log. Final acceptance or rejection of the software will come after the signed log and the test report have been reviewed.

11.3.5 The Test Report

Agreement on what happened is developed at the posttest meeting; the documentation of that agreement is the Test Report. The format of a Test Report will depend on project circumstances and on buyer preferences, but it will contain

1. *The as-executed test procedures.* A copy of the approved test procedures with any red-line modifications that were made during the test, accompanied by all test data sheets or a hard copy of electronically recorded data makes up the bulk of the test report.

2. *All problem reports.* A copy of every problem report generated during

the test, regardless of disposition, and the agreed-to disposition is included in the test report.

3. *Recommendations for retesting.* The Test Manager, the Software Development Manager, and the senior Buyer Representative will suggest a retesting strategy to demonstrate that the legitimate problems reported during the test are solved. These recommendations could be for a complete repeat of the just finished test, or for the inclusion of some form of problem retesting as part of a future formal test activity (for example, hardware/software testing).

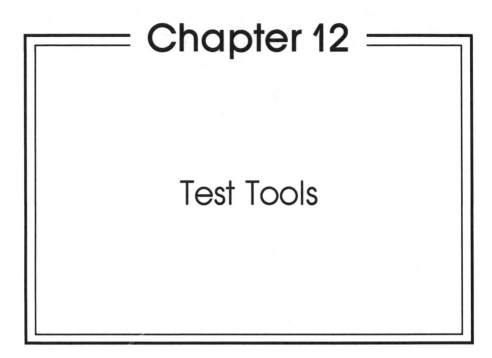

Chapter 12

Test Tools

The last people to automate their activities are the ones who provide automation to the rest of the world: the software developers. And the last of the software people to automate are the testers. But there are tools available.

This chapter discusses test support tools that are available to assist the software tester in completing his or her task.

12.1 HOST/TARGET PROBLEM

In the early days of software engineering, the software was developed on the same computer on which it was designed to execute. That meant that development and testing were done on the same computer platform. Whatever problems there might have been in scheduling computer time, there was, at least, a consistency in the target instruction set. Things aren't so simple these days.

Modern embedded systems execute on computer platforms dedicated to the problem to be solved, called the *target* computer. Primarily, that means that the target computer has attached to it only those peripherals necessary to implement the designed solution. That usually means that there are only limited means for injecting controlled input data or for recording intermediate software outputs; most testing is done on the system used for development, the so-called *host* system.

12.2 LOW-LEVEL TOOLS

Low-level tools are those that are closest to the implemented code and the farthest from the final system. By this definition, many low-level tools are supplied by the computer vendor or the development language vendor; they're very generic. Many of these tools aren't so much test tools as analyzers and evaluators which can help locate doubtful constructs and questionable implementation practices.

Low-level tools are very source language specific or they're very computer platform specific. This means they are usable in a variety of applications, but they aren't much good for testing a complete system.

12.2.1 Syntax Analyzers

Syntax analyzers read source code and evaluate it against a predefined set of quality characteristics. While some of the tasks performed by these analyzers duplicate those done by a high-order language compiler, the analyzers can often be more extensive in scope and, in some cases, more specific to a given application. Some of the things done by syntax analyzers include

- Examination of each source statement for valid syntax,
- Examination for use of doubtful or impermissible constructs (GO TOs, for example),
- Location of variables that are referenced before they are set,
- Location of variables that are never referenced,
- Identification of code that can never be reached.

12.2.2 Complexity Analyzers

Complexity analyzers could actually be classed with the syntax analyzers (above) since they read source code. There is no set definition of complexity, but the term is usually used to mean the extent of the computation being performed by the subject component. Since a highly complex problem may be difficult to comprehend in all aspects, the most complex entities are more liable to contain errors. The McCabe cyclomatic complexity [McCabe 1976] is the most usually implemented complexity metric.

12.2.3 Debuggers

Debuggers are basically analysis tools for use by developers in locating the source of a software fault that has been uncovered during actual testing.[1] Debuggers work with machine object code and, often, the matching source code and permit the examination of computer memory as the software unit or module executes (and after execution is complete).

Even though they are primarily analysis tools, debuggers can be used for testing since they normally permit the controlled starting and stopping of code execution and the examination and changing of memory. Tests can be defined in which the debugger is used to establish an input situation (perhaps by inserting the appropriate values into a set of variables), execute the code (by directing control to the component under test), and examine the results (using the debugger's memory read facilities).

12.3 INTERMEDIATE-LEVEL TOOLS

Intermediate-level tools aren't language or platform specific and they aren't application specific. That means they may not be much good at detailed debugging and they may not help in testing a complete system. They are, however, well suited to supporting the software integration process.

12.3.1 Source Code Control and Build/Make

Often, the most frustrating problem for the tester is keeping track of the latest version(s) of the software components. Even if integration and testing were done after all the software was coded and unit tested, changes would still occur in response to errors and shortcomings detected during the shakedown process. The normal situation, though, is that integration testing begins while a significant amount of development is uncompleted. As a consequence, changes come, not only in response to detected errors, but as code and unit tests are completed. In a large system with many components and modules, configuration management bookkeeping is impossible without the help of automation.

The Source Code Control System (SCCS) in the UNIX™ environment provides version control for software components and, in conjunction with the MAKE utility, provides for the creation of a software system using only the latest available versions (or, if tester declines the latest version for some reason, any specifically identified one). Further, MAKE permits consistent

---

[1] Testing and debugging are not the same thing. Testing determines the presence of bugs, debugging removes them (occasionally by inserting different ones).

compilation and linkage of even very complex software systems. Utilities similar to SCCS and MAKE exist for most operating systems.

12.3.2 Test Data Generators

One of the goals of testing is to "put some miles" on the product, that is, present the new system with a broad sample of the input situations that may arise in actual operation. This "seasoning" serves to give the developer, tester, and buyer some confidence that the product can survive the real world. But to get the mileage, the tester needs a large supply of valid data. And we mean a *large* supply because most modern software systems must execute continually for many hours, in some cases, for days or weeks without cessation. The test process should create situations which approximate a typical operational duration.

The manual generation of large quantities of test data is slow, tedious, and error-prone. Here, we use error-prone in the sense that the test data actually contain errors rather than valid information. Automation is clearly the key.

One enterprising U.S. government contractor constructed a test data generator which permitted the user to describe the syntax of incoming information[2] using Backus-Normal Form (or Backus-Naur Form, if Peter Naur is acknowledged as one of the developers of Algol).[3] BNF permits the description of input message in a recursive form that simplifies input message parsing, which is what compilers do, and message generation, which is what these test data generators do. For example, some of the input to an air traffic control system might be described as

```
<Aircraft>        := <ACID> <Transponder code> <Altitude>

                     <Heading> <Aircraft type>

<ACID>            := <Airline prefix> <Numeric suffix>

<Airline prefix> := <Alpha character> | <Airline prefix>

                     <Alpha character>⁴
```

The analysis of the BNF input description proved fairly straightforward to

---

[2] In this case, the application was a communication message processor stimulated by ASCII messages. However, the concept here can easily be extended to any input message basis.

[3] See Naur [1963].

[4] This is neither a complete example nor a completely correct one. It is intended only to show that BNF can be used to describe syntaxes which receive "messages" that are composed of smaller component messages (which might occur more than once in the course of a single input stream).

implement. The contractor's data generator would read the BNF description and generate a prespecified number of messages of that type and insert them into a message script that could be played back later during the test process.

No general tool exists which can support all test situations, but the creation of a test data generator like the one described here is well within the ability of most developers. Indeed, by creating a custom version, a developer can ensure that the test data generator creates data streams consistent with the specific application.

12.3.3 Regression Analyzers

Whenever software is changed, not only does the tester need to verify that the new or changed code works, but that the so-called "unchanged code" continues to work properly. This process of searching for unintended side effects is called *regression testing*, and it isn't easy. The reason that regression testing isn't easy is the complicated interconnection between pieces of software that are seemingly unrelated. At least three kinds of interconnections are possible:

1. *Data connections* in which the pieces both work with the same data. Set-use matrices can be used to identify the most straightforward form of data connection, the use of the same variable. But more subtle connections, say the simultaneous use of the same dynamic memory area by two software components, can't be detected so directly.

2. *Timing connections* in which the performance of one piece affects the operation of the other. The most common timing connection occurs when two or more, as a group, must perform a function or set of functions, within a stated time interval. An increase in the amount of time taken by one component affects the amount of time the others may take.

3. *Requirements connections* in which one component is involved in the support or satisfaction of more than one SRS requirement, say R_1 and R_2. When that component is altered to accommodate a change in R_1, its ability to satisfy R_2 is endangered.

Keeping track of all types of interconnections is difficult in a complex system. Tools that assist in the difficult bookkeeping involved are regression analyzers. The design structure of the software is described to the analyzer. Henceforth, whenever a change is made to any of the analyzed code, the analyzer produces a list of those components that must be retested or those requirements that must be reverified.

12.4 HIGH-LEVEL TOOLS

High-level tools work with the entire software product, taking a black-box approach to testing and validation. These tools provide input situations to the product and, in many cases, intercept and analyze the response. Such tools are called *simulators* because they attempt to simulate the entire environment in which the software must operate. Some have said that simulators are sort of a super combination "stub-driver."

The thoroughness of the simulation varies from situation to situation, but the basic idea of a simulator is as shown in Figure 12.1. In this figure, the software under test is surrounded by the simulator product. The simulator provides input to the subject software and receives the responses. For most simulators, the test stimulus is determined by a *scenario* or *script* which is prepared ahead of time.

For so-called real-time simulations, the platform on which the simulation software runs must be fast enough to feed all scripted data to the software under test (on whatever platform it's executing) and simultaneously receive and process the responses.

Commercial simulators tend to be generic and specialize in one or a few types of input channel. Their primary application is for keyboard or keystroke simulation. More comprehensive simulators are developed specifically for the target application. It's not unusual to find the simulation development effort equal to or larger than that associated with the end pro(

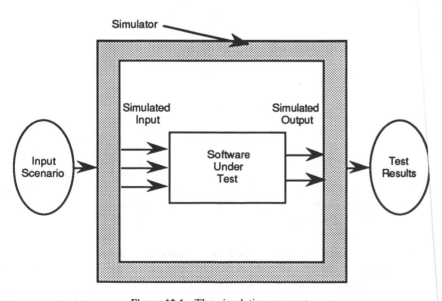

Figure 12.1   The simulation concept.

12.5 VERIFYING THE TOOLS

You don't connect a hospital patient to unverified diagnostic equipment. You don't give a lie detector test using an uncalibrated polygraph. You don't test your car's emission system using detection equipment that hasn't been certified. And you don't test software with untested or unverified tools. Verifying and testing the tools can be a big job for the test manager, especially if the tools have been specifically developed for the job at hand.

If the test tool is a commercial product, it's usually enough to put the product under configuration control, install it as described by the vendor (or have the vendor install it), and then take its Commercial Off-the-Shelf (COTS) status as prima facie evidence that it works as advertised.

On the other hand, a specially developed tools package may require a test and validation effort every bit as big as that needed for the end product.

If a tool is to be used as part of a Formal Qualification or Acceptance test, the requirements for validation and configuration management can be severe since buyers are hesitant to let one contractor black box check out another. If the tool is to be used for internal or informal testing, the degree of control is essentially a function of the trust the user has in it.

12.6 CHECKLIST FOR TOOL ACQUISITION

When contemplating the purchase of acceptance of test tools, the test manager needs to consider several things about the tool vendor and the tool itself. The following material presents a number of questions which must be asked about the product and its maker. There is no fixed answer for any question, but an answer should be available for each.

12.6.1 Questions About the Tool Vendor

The test tool vendor may be called upon to support its product. It's important to evaluate the vendor's capacity to provide that support.

Verify the quality of the vendor's product support.   If the support of the vendor in solving problems with the tool will be important to the tester (and it will), the quality of the vendor's product support must be verified. The best way to do that is to obtain a list of other users of the tool. Any vendor unwilling to provide such a list should be avoided.

Verify the quality of the documentation.   Even more important than the quality of the product support will be the quality of the documentation provided with the tool. The documentation will be the principal source of information about how the tool is implemented. As with product support, other users of the tool can provide insight into the quality of the manuals and on-line help.

The test manager is cautioned against being misled by the weight of the documentation. The tool documents must be used by the testers. The best evaluators of the documentation are the eventual users of it. The test manager should give the actual testers copies of the manuals and let them decide.

Verify the variety and quality of training.   It is sometimes necessary to train the testers in the use of a tool. If the test manager feels that this is the case for his or her system, then the quality of the vendor's training program must be determined. Once again, other users will provide information.

The test manager should determine if all members of the test team must be formally trained or if it will be sufficient to educate a single (or a few) individual who can then train the rest.

12.6.2 Questions About the Tool

If the vendor of a candidate tool generally measures up, the tester should move on to evaluating the tool itself.

Verify the ability of the tool to support large projects.   If an automated test tool has limitations, they will show up when testing large projects. Software projects involving large numbers of requirements, lots of modules, or large numbers of input situations will often bring a test tool, and almost all microcomputer-based tools, to their knees due to lack of compute power.

There are no absolute thresholds for defining the term "large," but one might use the following guidelines:

A project involving more than 1,000 requirements qualifies as large.

A project composed of more than 100 modules (however defined) qualifies as large.

A project implemented with more than 50,000 to 100,000 lines of source code qualifies as large (100,000 for sure).

As a related subject, the speed of the tool must be compared to the speed of the product under test. When considering speed, the compute platforms of both the product and the tool are involved, but the general rule is that the tool and its processor must possess adequate compute speed to keep up with the product being tested. Even better, the tool and its processor must have sufficient reserves to ensure that *no* response of the software product and its processor will be missed.

Verify the extensibility of the tool.   If a test tool is useful for a particular configuration of the tested product, one needs to consider whether a significant change in product configuration (upgrading an operating system, say) will necessitate a concomitant change in the tool.

Verify the robustness of the tool.   As with other software products, the term robustness is not completely defined. Generally, though, it means the ability of the product to survive its operational environment and to give useful results. Other users of the candidate tool can provide evaluations about the robustness of the tool under consideration.

Verify the usability of the tool.   If the selected tool requires a Ph.D. in Computer Science with a speciality in Data Structures to use, and if the members of the test team possess only Bachelor's degrees, the tool will probably prove unsatisfactory. The test manager should know this. A product evaluation period coupled with conversations with other tool users will usually expose this kind of situation.

12.7 CODE INSTRUMENTATION

Not all test tools are purchased nor do all tools act independently. One of the most common forms of test tool is instrumented code. This is code that physically resides in the product under test and that is compiled and linked with it. The purpose of the instrumentation is the examination of internal variables and conditions to ensure that they are as the software specification and design intends them to be.

A familiar form of instrumentation is the PRINT or WRITE statement inserted into an evolving program to assist the author in debugging the code. But instrumentation can be more than PRINT statements. Assertion statements built into a program to verify that the conditions for its execution are satisfied are another form of instrumentation. So are breakpoints. And so are special variables which hold the results of intermediate computations. In fact, any code that is not directly related to solving the user's problem, but that aids in demonstrating that the problem is solved, qualifies for the term instrumentation.

Code instrumentation is a legitimate and efficient technique for testing software. But, and it's a big "but," once the instrumentation has been inserted into the software product, *it can't be removed*. If the instrumentation is removed after testing, then the executable image (the thing that actually solves the user's problem) isn't the same image as the one that was tested. Instrumentation logic in a program is generally benign in that it doesn't affect the functioning of the product, but it does alter its performance (at the very least, the instrumentation increases the memory requirements of the software). Consider the case of two processes, A and B, in a real-time system. It may be that so long as A always finishes operating before B the system works well. But if the execution of instrumentation code in B is what causes B to always finish second, removal of that instrumentation will change the results of the race, and may result in a software failure.

In those situations where the removal of instrumentation code is actually necessary, the test manager should plan on some form of retest or regression test after the removal to verify that the software still functions properly.

REFERENCES

McCabe, T. J., 1976. "A Complexity Measure," *IEEE Transactions on Software Engineering,* vol. SE–2, December, 308–20.

Naur, Peter (ed.), 1963. "Revised Report on the Algorithmic Language Algol 60," *Communications of the ACM,* vol. 6, January, 1–17.

Chapter 13

Testing
AI Software

A somewhat cynical software development manager once observed that "The difference between conventional and AI software development is that developers of conventional software pretend they know what they're going to build, while developers of AI software admit that they don't."

In the case of conventional software, a developer is presented with a system specification that is a statement of a problem to be solved and some idea of what a solution to that problem might be. Implicit in such a specification is a functional statement of the system behavior under a number of real or envisioned situations.

The ability to specify functional behavior implies that the problem to be solved is well enough understood that high-level execution details of the resulting solution are known. Problems that are approached using Artificial Intelligence (AI) methods or require some form of AI solution are frequently so ill-defined or open-ended that no such solution statement can be formulated.[1] Specifications still exist in the AI world, but they tend to be problem

---

[1] One can argue that the reason for *most* software development problems, whether AI or not, is the inability of customer or developer to adequately define either the problem or any form of solution. The term *unprecedented system* has been coined to describe those that have no precursor.

statements without much of a hint as to what an acceptable solution might be.

As they proceed from the problem statement, AI software developers often enlist the aid of "experts" to guide them in the direction of an acceptable solution. This permits the generation of a system which displays some approximation of this expert's idea of solution behavior. Because testers desire independence from the development team and because the number of experts is limited (occasionally to a single individual), a similar approach in the preparation of test procedures may be unavailable to the test team. Indeed, even if a different expert is available to assist in the development of the test process, the potential exists for disagreement with the other expert. The question then becomes one of determining the "right answer." In this case, unlike that of conventional software development, the customer is a doubtful arbiter because of the fuzziness of the original problem.

Even presuming that some approach toward generation of agreed-to test procedures can be found, additional problems plague those charged with testing the AI system:

- For knowledge-based systems, does the system *correctly* reflect the knowledge given it?
- For knowledge-based systems, is the knowledge given the system *correct?* Who decides? Systems can be envisioned where this may not matter, at least not in the same way as conventional software, since the product may be self-correcting.[2] In this case, the question may become "When the system discovers that it is incorrect, does it move toward correctness by an acceptable amount?" Again, who decides?

It has been suggested that AI software acquisition proceeds through three identifiable phases, as opposed to seven for conventional software. These three phases are:

1. *System Definition*, which is characterized by a high degree of iteration and prototyping as incrementally developed software is examined for acceptability.
2. *System Implementation*, during which the final prototype is transformed (not by modification, but by means of design, code, and test) into a final system.
3. *System Operation.*

The key difference between AI software development and conventional development is in the area of requirements determination or system defini-

---

[2] A quick review of current literature indicates that self-correcting software is *not* a common occurrence.

tion. In conventional systems, as has been alluded to above, the problem being attacked is well enough understood that an enumerated list of requirements can be prepared prior to any design activity. In the AI world, the problem understanding is such that requirements definition is performed in conjunction with the initial system design. This process is known as *prototyping*. The "right answer" to the customer problem is, consequently, a far more rapidly moving target than most developers are accustomed to.

But regardless of how different the AI situation is, the software tester must, eventually come up with an approach. A large fraction of the AI software developed for deliverable products falls into the category of so-called "expert" systems:

> Expert systems, concentrating on the organization and thought processes of the human mind, comes under the artificial intelligence umbrella. In recent years, business has given expert systems the most attention. Because of the attention, expert system technology is beginning to take on its own identity. To some this means that AI *is* expert systems. To others, it means expert systems no longer belong to AI. [Laswell 1989]

Fortunately, this means that there is also strategy for testing expert systems. It has been described by Laswell in [Laswell 1989].

13.1 STEP 1: TEST CASE SELECTION

The basic approach to testing is to devise a test case, define the system response, then see if the system reacts as predicted. The difficulty, because of the fuzziness of the problem to be solved, is defining the correct response. In the absence of a specification, the tester needs some other standard of performance.

"The best standard available for expert system measurement is the past performance of human decision makers" [Laswell 1989]. That's the starting point: compare the response of the expert system to the previous response of a human expert. To do this, though, the tester needs a large base of test cases for which the human response is known. These cases should be real ones that are or have been handled by humans in the normal course of business. In the early stages of system evaluation, the tester won't make any attempt to second guess the human—that can come later when actual evaluation is done.

13.2 STEP 2: ESTABLISH THE CONFUSION MATRIX

The basic evaluation mechanism for each test case is the *confusion matrix*, which is nothing more than a list of actual system responses and a comparison of those responses to each of the possible ones:

	Y List all possible outcomes ⟶					
	0					
		0				
			0			
				0		
					0	
						0

X ⟵Actual Output

The elements of the confusion matrix $C = [c_{xy}]$ are the cost of responding x when the best decision, as defined by an expert or panel of experts, is y.

In the case of a game program, for example, there will generally be a number of moves available in each situation. The confusion matrix establishes the risk associated with each move. The risk, or cost, values are established by experts or, in some cases (the buying and selling of securities, for example), by actual calculation.

During testing, the normal case would be to bring about each outcome in the matrix, but that generally will not be possible. We attempt to find a representative set of test cases, as defined by the system's operational profile, that maximizes the number of output cases covered.

13.3 STEP 3: REVIEW TEST CASES FOR BEST RESULTS

An expert system should provide an optimum for any situation, consequently each of the test cases selected by the test manager or the test manager in conjunction with the evaluation expert is reviewed for the best result. For any system with a large number of test cases, which is any nontrivial one, this a large and labor intensive task; it's often the place where AI testing falls down.

13.4 STEP 4: RUN AND ENUMERATE THE TESTS

The test cases are executed and the system response is recorded in a *results matrix*. The results matrix has the same dimensions as the confusion matrix. In this case, though, the elements of the results matrix $R = [r_{xy}]$ count the number of times the system responded x when the best answer was y.

The best result for each is usually the one with the lowest cost. However, when considered in an operational context, the lowest cost result may not be the overall best result, because of consequences which may occur later in execution. We can see this, for example, in a chess playing program where a material sacrifice may bring about winning chances at a cost.[3]

13.5 STEP 5: COMPUTE THE CONFUSION COST

The confusion cost for each individual (x,y) is computed:

$$T_{xy} = c_{xy}r_{xy}, \text{ for all x, y}$$

This is simply the cost of responding x when the best response is y, weighted by the number of times that situation arose during testing.

13.6 STEP 6: COMPUTE THE CONFUSION FOR EACH RESPONSE AND FOR THE SYSTEM

The next step is to sum the confusion factors associated with each possible recommendation:

$$C_y = \sum_x C_{xy}.$$

If the best response was always chosen (c_{yy}, for all y), c_y would take on its minimum value, probably zero or close to it.

Then compute the total confusion factor for the system:

$$C = \sum_y C_y$$

13.7 STEP 7: COMPUTE THE WORST POSSIBLE RESULTS

For each recommendation, compute the worst the system could possibly do, given the ratings for each response:

$$_{worst}C_y = \sum_x (\text{total \# of } x\text{'s} \times \text{worst } x)$$

The total confusion for the entire system is, then

[3] A good specification, of course, will identify the cost of losing positional or temporal (time) advantages, which are the only appropriate reasons for losing material in a chess game.

$$\text{worst}C = \sum_y \text{worst}C_y$$

This is the system confusion factor for the worst possible system result and we can compare system response to this worst case. Laswell, however, claims that it is better to compare the system's actual response, as reflected in its confusion factor C, against random response. He says this because even the real world (without the new system) won't respond in the worst way; rather it will act in a more random fashion:

$$\text{random}C_y = \frac{\sum_x (\text{maximum } \# \text{ of } x\text{'s} \times \text{worst } x)}{\text{maximum } \# \text{ of } x\text{'s}}$$

and

$$\text{random}C = \sum_y \text{random}C_y$$

13.8 STEP 8: COMPUTE THE SYSTEM RATING

The system rating is a function of the system's actual response and the random response:

$$R_{\text{system}} = \left[1 - \frac{C}{\text{random}C} \right]$$

The sign convention for R_{system} is such that the closer R_{system} is to unity, the more "correct" the system is. If, for some reason, the system responds in a manner that is worse than random, R_{system} may become negative.

A minimum acceptable threshold for R_{system} can, and should, be included in the software specification.

REFERENCES

LASWELL, L. K., 1989. *Collision: Theory vs. Reality in Expert Systems,* QED Information Sciences, Inc., Wellesley, MA.

Chapter 14

Software
Reliability

"Software reliability" is a hot topic in the software engineering community. But before we can discuss measuring software reliability, we have to tackle an even more fundamental problem: what is it?

Simply stated, software reliability "is the probability of failure-free operation of a computer program for a specified time in a specified environment." This definition is taken from Musa [Musa, Iannino, et al. 1987] and is consistent with the older one for hardware systems (where we need only substitute the word "system" for "computer program").

Using the above definition, it's important to note the word "probability." The reliability of any system cannot be measured absolutely. Any particular copy of a system might run for years, even with a low reliability figure, or it might fail tomorrow even with an extremely high reliability. We'll see shortly that statistics play a large part in the prediction and estimation of software (or any other kind of) reliability.

In the hardware world, reliability has traditionally been expressed in terms of the *mean time between failures,* or *MTBF,* since most users are really interested in how long they can operate a system without it failing.[1]

---

[1] We have, of course, been ignoring the question of what constitutes a failure. We'll come back to that, but for now refer to Chapter 1, "Requirements, Errors, Faults, and Failures."

This concern stems from the fact that parts wear out. That is, even a well-designed system will eventually fail. The MTBF measures this tendency of the finished product to deteriorate with time. Consistent with this concern is the customary position that failures which result from design errors do not count against the MTBF. This idea is based on the presumption that a design error, once discovered, will be corrected and will never again result in a system failure. For reasonably simple systems, even simple software systems, this is a valid assumption. But in complex software systems, that's all there are: design errors and implementation errors. Software doesn't wear out.

It's been suggested, of course, that some software systems deteriorate with time. That is, their performance degrades until they become virtually unusable. Anyone working with software as memory or disk space fragments has seen this phenomenon. But these kinds of problems are actually symptoms of design and/or implementation deficiencies or limitations.

Also, the probability of failure (or success to use the strict definition of software reliability) is a function of the input data stream (in the broadest sense), to a far greater extent than is true in hardware. Hardware will eventually wear out if power is applied for a sufficiently long time. The same isn't true for software. A program can run in its idle loop forever.[2] Only when input data triggers the incorrectly designed or improperly implemented sections of code will a software failure result. In other words, the successful operation of software is much more dependent than is hardware on the specific *mission* or *operational profile* being executed. A very shaky system in a benign environment has a high probability of successful mission completion while even a robust system in a pathological environment has a low probability.

In fact, many software systems will not see pathological or stressful environments until very late in their lifetimes. This is because most systems are built to accommodate a considerable amount of growth in that environment and when the capacities of the system are approached, a new system is acquired.

All of the above not withstanding, what happens when we're told (or contracted) to build a reliable software system? Just what do we measure or calculate? And, how do we combine whatever we come up with and the traditionally computed hardware reliability or MTBF?

One school of software reliability thought holds that it is possible to compute for a computer program something similar to a hardware MTBF and that the two parameters can be combined using standard techniques of reliability theory.

A second school says that software really is different from hardware and that failures resulting from design and implementation errors are not the

---

[2] Providing, of course, that the computer system on which it runs has a reliability of 1.0.

same as wear-out or usage failures. Members of this school believe that software engineers and testers are better off keeping records of identified errors and estimating the number of remaining errors in the software.

A third group claims that for systems containing hardware and software some sort of probability of mission success should be calculated. Note, by the way, that these three schools are by no means mutually exclusive.

At this time, those believing that software failures from design and implementation errors can be counted as system failures and that an overall software MTBF can be computed or measured are in the majority. This arises partly because users are concerned with the reliability of *complete systems* and aren't really interested in the cause of a failure. Users are pressing acquisition agencies and designers for a system reliability or MTBF which includes figures for both hardware and software.

This attitude has caused some consternation in the hardware community because consistency demands that if design and implementation errors can count against software reliability, then they must likewise count against hardware reliability.

14.1 WHAT'S INVOLVED IN RELIABILITY CALCULATIONS?

There's a great deal more to software reliability than calculating something called an MTBF. For a complete reliability program, three tasks are performed:

1. Predict the reliability of the product before it's built;
2. Estimate the reliability of the product as it's being built; and
3. Measure the reliability of the product after it's operational.

We'll look at each task as it will be performed during the software life cycle. At this time, we won't spend too much time discussing the methods, but we'll look at the reasons for each step.

14.1.1 Predict the Reliability of the Product Before It's Built

Customers don't make reliability requirements just for the sake of having a software MTBF in the specification.[3] They state an MTBF for software because they want an overall reliability for the system they're buying and they realize that software is an integral part of that system.

---

[3] At least, they shouldn't do that. These days, though, one might just find an occasional MTBF or reliability requirement included as a hedge against "poor quality" software.

Developers should also realize that the software is a part of the complete system and, even more important, that the reliability requirement is just as important as any functional requirement. That means that as the software is designed, the reliability of the system that will result from that design should be continually predicted. How else can the developers have confidence that the stated reliability will be met? Too, predicted software reliability figures can be important discriminants in deciding between alternative design approaches.

The techniques for predicting reliability are based on past experience. If a similar product has been built in the past, then the reliability of a new product can be expected to be similar to the old. If a developer is entering new territory, industrywide experience can be used [McCall, Randall, et al. 1987].

14.1.2 Estimate the Reliability of the Product as It's Being Built

As the software construction proceeds, the developers, and the customer, must ask the question "Are we achieving our design goals?" One way to determine that is by estimating the reliability of the product based on what we've seen as the system is put together. The developer who waits until the end of the job to find out that he didn't get where he was going has wasted a lot of time and money.

Even if it appears that the required reliability will be attained, the continuing estimation will permit the developer to decide when it's time to transition from development testing to product acceptance.

The techniques for estimating reliability are based on observed errors (even if they've been fixed) and test coverage.

14.1.3 Calculate the Reliability of the Product after It's Operational

Once the software product is operational, the developer gathers data on its actual reliability so that more accurate predictions can be made in the future.

14.2 PREDICTION

When it is proposed to design a system which includes computers to perform a complex and demanding job, it is assumed that the required investment will be justified according to the perfection by which the job is performed or by the large number of times which the system can do the job. This assumption cannot be justified when a system fails to perform upon demand or fails to perform repeatedly. Thus the reliability of a system is critical to its cost effectiveness. [McCall, Randall, et al. 1987]

Prediction is the process of attempting to determine the reliability of the software product before it exists. The characteristics used in the determination are, therefore, external to the software itself. The U.S. Air Force attempts to predict the reliability of systems by considering the application, the method of design and implementation, and the group doing the development. The Air Force prediction procedure will be of interest even to developers of commercial, nondefense software. A summary of the method follows.

The reliability (expressed as a probability of successful operation) for a complete system is given by

$$R = R_H \times R_S \times R_X$$

where R_H is the reliability of the hardware in the system, R_S the reliability of the software, and R_X the reliability associated with other things.[4] If $R \geq 0.95$, then the reliability equation can be approximated by

$$PF = PF_H + PF_S + PF_X$$

where PF is the *probability of failure* and is computed from

$$R = (1 - PF)$$

The reliability of any part of a system, the software in our case, is a function of its components. In predicting the reliability of the software, whether expressed as a probability of success or a probability of failure, the first step is to *establish the components to be covered by the prediction.* Since there are established ways of combining the reliability factors of components, we need to know exactly which components are to be included in the prediction and how they are connected.

In addition to the connectivity of the software components, it's important to know rough frequency of execution of each (a faulty component that seldom executes contributes very little to the probability of system failure). The Air Force suggests the following categories: *routinely, irregularly, conditionally, exceptionally* (exception handlers), *on demand* (for example, in response to operator actions).

Finally, it's necessary to develop a reliability prediction model for each of the components.

At project initiation, the fault density of each component is predicted from

---

[4] Included in R_X, for example, is the probability that a software failure is caused by a hardware fault or interruption.

$$F = A \times D \times S_I$$

where A is a reliability predictor in units of faults/loc (loc = line of code) based on the application category in which the software product fits, D is a multiplier that is a function of the development environment, and S_I is another multiplier that is a function of the requirements and design representation (that is, the development methodology). At this point, we calculate fault density rather than failure rate because most historical data is kept in those terms. Eventually, we'll convert the computed fault density to failure rate by either examining the software design and comparing that to the operational environment (the preferred way) or by applying a transformation factor based on the performance of similar systems.

The recognized application categories, the associated value of the fault density estimator, A, and the suggested fault density to failure rate conversion factors are shown in Table 14.1.

TABLE 14.1 Fault Density Prediction by Application Category

Application Category	Base Fault Density (A)	Failure Rate Transform
Airborne Manned spacecraft Unmanned spacecraft Mil-Spec avionics Commercial avionics	.0128	6.2
Strategic C^3I Strategic C^2 Indications & Warning Communications	.0092	1.2
Tactical Tactical C^2 Tactical MIS Mobile EW/ECM/ECCM	.0078	13.8
Process Control Industrial Process Control	.0018	3.8
Production Center MIS Decision Aids Inventory Control Scientific	.0085	23.0
Developmental SW Development Tools Simulation Test Beds Training	.0123	Not Available

Fault density in faults per line of code; failure rates in failures per CPU hour.

The Air Force recognizes the same three types of development environment described by Boehm [Boehm 1981]:

1. *Organic*, in which the development group is responsible for the overall application (for example, flight control software designed and implemented by the product development or manufacturing organization).
2. *Semi-Detached*, in which the software is developed by individuals with specialized knowledge of the application area, but who are not a part of the sponsoring organization.
3. *Embedded*, in which the software is developed (a) by software specialists who are not directly connected with application, and (b) in accordance with a written specification.

Most contracted software is developed in an embedded or, at best, a semi-detached environment; commercial software tends to be developed using either organic or semi-detached organizations. The fault density multiplier, *D*, used by the Air Force is shown in Table 14.2.

The Air Force has also observed that some development techniques seem to produce higher quality software than do others. The multiplier S_I is a function of methodology and is calculated from

$$S_I = S_A \times S_T \times S_Q$$

where S_A depends on the way data anomalies in the software are handled, S_T on the rigor of requirements traceability, and S_Q on the results of a quality review.

The anomaly management multiplier is in the range $0.9 \leq S_A \leq 1.1$ depending on how well the inputs are defined (reasonableness values, tolerances, etc.) and on the complexities involved in the software detecting and correcting data anomalies automatically.

The requirements traceability multiplier, S_T, has a value of 1.0 if 90 percent or more of the specification requirements are explicitly addressed by the software design; it has a value of 1.1 if fewer than 90 percent of the requirements are addressed by the design.

The quality review multiplier, S_Q, has a value of 1.0 if the ratio of the

TABLE 14.2 Effect of Development
Environment on Fault Density

Environment	Multiplier
Organic	0.76
Semi-detached	1.00
Embedded	1.30

number of requirements and design discrepancies to the number of requirements is less than 0.5, and is 1.1 otherwise.

During the coding phase, additional factors are considered when predicting software fault density. The fault density, F, is computed by

$$F = A \times D \times S_I \times S_2$$

where A, D, and S_I are as described above and S_2 is determined by implementation techniques:

$$S_2 = S_L \times S_M \times S_X \times S_R$$

The multiplier S_L is a function of the language used for development
and is calculated from the total number of delivered source instructions,
$SLOC$, the number of high-level source instructions, $HLOC$, and the number
of assembly language instructions, $ALOC$, as

$$S_L = \frac{HLOC}{SLOC} + 1.4\left(\frac{ALOC}{SLOC}\right)$$

S_M is determined by the modularity of the software as

$$S_M = \frac{0.9u + w + 2x}{N_M}$$

where N_M is the total number of modules in the system, u is the number with
fewer than 200 lines of code, w is the number with a size between 200 and
3,000, and x is the number larger than 3,000 lines of code. Note that $N_M = u + w + x$.

The multiplier S_X comes from the software's complexity:

$$S_X = \frac{1.4a + b + 0.8c}{N_M}$$

where a is the number of modules with a McCabe cyclomatic complexity
[McCabe 1976] greater than 20, b is the number with a complexity between
7 and 20, and c the number with complexity less than 7, as above. N_M is the
total number of modules and, this time, is equal to $a + b + c$.

Finally, the multiplier S_R is determined by a standards review. S_R has
a value of 1.5 if more than half the modules in the system fail to comply with
accepted coding standards. The value of S_R is 0.75 if fewer than 25 percent
exhibit standards deviations, and the value is 1.0 for the in-between case.

Once the fault density of the component is known, the next problem is
converting it to a failure rate, $\mathcal{F}$, that is, the number of expected failures per
second of operating time:

$$\mathcal{F} = \mathcal{F}(F).$$

The problem here is determining the nature of this function $\mathcal{F}$. The most straightforward, but probably least accurate, approach is to use the Failure Rate Transforms in Table 14.1.

$$\mathcal{F} = F \times R_F$$

where R_F is the transform.

If the software engineer has available an execution model for the software product, he or she can use that to calculate a predicted failure rate which accommodates the actual software design.

If the software component is predicted to have size s, then the software engineer can anticipate that it contains Fs faults. Since the component doesn't actually exist, the software engineer must assume the faults are equally distributed throughout.

Now, if the execution model predicts that the component will execute at a rate r, we have a failure rate of

$$\mathcal{F} = \text{Faults} \times \text{rate} = Fsr$$

First, failure rate at time t, $\mathcal{F}_t$, is converted to reliability, R:

$$R = e^{-\mathcal{F}_t}$$

Next, the reliability values for individual components are combined using standard reliability techniques [U.S. Department of Defense 1984]. Figure 14.1 shows the combination of computed reliabilities for two simple cases.

The reliability predicted by this method is the worst case since it assumes the component contains no loops or branches. It further makes the optimistic assumption that the input data will always expose the faults.

14.3 ESTIMATION

Once the software implementation and integration phases begin, the development team should continually estimate the reliability of the software as it is assembled and tested. This is necessary for two reasons. First, it's important to know if the predicted reliability of the software system is actually being achieved; if not, modifications in design may be required. Second, if the required reliability is being approached, the developers will want to know when they get there so that they can move the development effort to the next phase, usually hardware/software testing or acceptance testing.

John Musa et al. [Musa, Iannino, et al. 1987] have advocated one approach to reliability estimation while James McCall [McCall, Randall, et al. 1987] suggests another.

The Musa approach calls for calculating a failure density function by

$$f(t) = L_0 e^{-L0t}$$

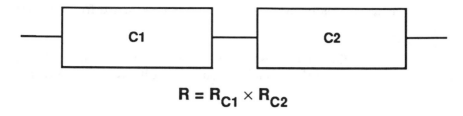

$$R = R_{C1} \times R_{C2}$$

(a) Components executing in series

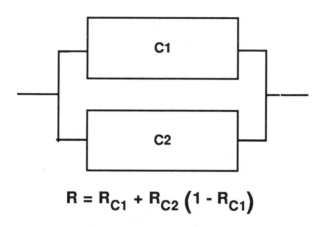

$$R = R_{C1} + R_{C2}\left(1 - R_{C1}\right)$$

(b) Components executing in parallel

Figure 14.1 Combining reliability values.

where L_0 is the observed instantaneous failure rate (sometimes called the hazard function). It is initially estimated as with the prediction techniques above or established from past history and project-specific metrics. t is the total amount of test time for the program expressed in terms of computer processor utilization (e.g., CPU hours). The area under the curve $f(t)$ between 0 and t represents the probability of failure by time t.

McCall computes a failure rate using either

$$F = \mathscr{F}_{T_1} \times T_1 = 0.2T$$

or

$$F = \mathscr{F}_{T_2} \times T_2 = 0.14T$$

where $\mathscr{F}_{T_1}$ is the average observed failure rate, $\mathscr{F}_{T_2}$ is the failure rate at the end of testing, and T is given by

$$T = T_E \times T_M \times T_C$$

where T_E is a function of the test effort and is determined from the ratio $\dfrac{\text{Test hours}}{\text{Total hours}}$.

T_M is a function of the test methodology and is determined by the guidebook [Presson, 1984]. T_C is a function of the test coverage and is given by

$$T_C = \frac{1}{V_S}$$

where

$$\begin{cases} V_{S_1} = V_{S_1} \text{ for CSC testing,} \\ V_{S_2} \text{ for CSC integration testing,} \\ V_{S_3} \text{ for CSCI testing} \end{cases}$$

and

$$V_{S_1} = \frac{\text{Paths tested}}{\text{Total paths}} + \frac{\text{Inputs tested}}{\text{Total inputs}}$$

$$V_{S_2} = \frac{\text{Modules tested}}{\text{Total modules}} + \frac{\text{Module interfaces tested}}{\text{Total module interfaces}}$$

and

$$V_{S_3} = \frac{\text{Requirements tested}}{\text{Total requirements}}$$

Also

$$F_{T_2} = \frac{\text{Total discrepancy reports during testing}}{\text{Total test time}}$$

and

$$F_{T_2} = \frac{\text{Discrepancy reports during last 3 periods of CSCI testing}}{\text{Total test time}}$$

Finally, the total failure rate is estimated from

$$F = F_{T_2} \times T_2 \times E$$

where E is a function of project stress as measured by input variability and workload.

Finally, the tester should keep two thoughts in mind when implementing a software reliability program:

1. Reliability is indeed a statistical metric. One-of-a-kind software systems are, by themselves, an insufficient sample size for the drawing of valid conclusions. During development, even systems such as commercial

word processors, which will be sold by the thousands (it's hoped), exist only as a single entity. Hence, when design or implementation errors are discovered during testing, their removal means that they truly will not be seen again. The number of samples necessary for a meaningful statistical estimate is attained by executing a large number of test runs with input data which closely approximates what the software might see in the real world, the *operational profile*.

2. As with all testing, the *scientific method* defines the process. That is, predict first, then measure. Do not measure and then decide if the product is "good enough." Define "good enough" first.

REFERENCES

BOEHM, B., 1981. *Software Engineering Economics*. Prentice Hall, Englewood Cliffs, N.J.

McCABE, T. J., 1976. "A Complexity Measure," *IEEE Transactions on Software Engineering,* vol. SE–2, December, 308–20.

McCALL, J., ET AL., 1987. "Methodology for Software Reliability Prediction," Technical Report RADC–TR–87–171. Rome Air Development Center, November.

MUSA, J. D., IANNINO, A., AND OKUMOTO, K., 1987. *Software Reliability*. McGraw-Hill, New York.

PRESSON, E., 1984. "Software Test Handbook," Technical Report RADC-TR-84-53. Rome Air Development Center, March.

U.S. DEPARTMENT OF DEFENSE, 1984. MIL–HDBK–338, Vol. II "Electronic Reliability Design Handbook, Vol. II of II," 15 October.

Chapter 15

Estimating Test Costs

One of the first things a tester is asked is "How much will the testing cost?" When told, the questioner usually responds with "That much! What can we do to cut that a figure?" It's not the place of this book to discuss the costing and pricing strategies of software organizations, but it is its place to discuss costs and contributors to testing costs. After all, one can't be a good manager without a plan, and a plan includes a budget.

15.1 COST DRIVERS

When we set out to estimate testing costs, the first thing we need to understand are the factors that contribute to those costs. These factors are called *cost drivers*. To maintain some amount of precision, we'll define a *test cost driver* as any measurable quantity whose value can be shown to have a positive coefficient of correlation with testing costs and that has some apparent *causal* connection with them. Table 15.1 is a list of frequently suggested parameters (metrics). The column labels in Table 15.1 categorize some of these metrics as size metrics, that is as parameters associated with the size of the program, and as complexity metrics, those associated with how com-

TABLE 15.1   Some Test Cost Drivers

Size Metrics	Complexity Metrics
Lines of code	Interfaces
Modules (units)	Interface traffic
CSCs	Application
CSCIs	Number of requirements

plicated the program is. Each is examined more closely in the sections that follow.

15.1.1 Size Metrics

The size of a software product obviously correlates with the cost of development, but does it also correlate with the test cost? And if there is a correlation, what metric do we use to actually figure size?

Lines of code.   Everyone knows about lines of code. At least they think they do. And it's almost certainly true that the number of lines of code in a project correlates directly and positively to the total testing cost for that project: Big programs require more testing than small ones. But lines of code is difficult to apply consistently.

The first problem with lines of code as a metric is one of definition. Exactly what is a line of code. In the "old days" when programs were written in machine language, the definition was easy: each instruction counted as one line of code.

After the advent of assembly language (at least early ones), things were almost as easy: each statement, usually excluding comments and assembler directives, was a line of code. The only area of contention had to do with data declarations and comments: do they count or not? Then came macros, single statements which are expanded by the assembler into many, sometimes hundreds of, instructions. Some developers argued that each expanded instruction counted, while others held that only those actually written by the program's author counted (meaning that expanded macros could count, at most, once, when initially defined). The latter prevailed.

The first higher level languages were much like the nonmacro assembly languages. The number of lines of code in a Fortran program, for example, could be determined by counting the number of cards (or card-images) in the source program that were not comments (that is, didn't have a "C" in column 1).

Counting wasn't too difficult until two things happened. First, software engineers[1] decided that a single language was too limiting for solving some

---

[1] This early in the history of software development, the term "software engineer" hadn't been thought of. In fact, "computer science" was uncommon. Most people who designed and implemented software were included in the single category "programmer."

```
BEGIN
   IF (Alpha <= Beta AND NOT (End_of_file)) THEN
      BEGIN
         FOR i=1 TO 47 DO
            BEGIN
                        .
                        .
                        .
            END
          x = Beta + Number_of_records;
      END
   ELSE
      BEGIN
                 .
      [Equally complex sequence]
                 .
      END
   ENDIF
END;
```

Figure 15.1 Problems in code counting.

of the problems that were being attacked with computers. Assembly language was best for some parts of the problem, like talking to the hardware, while higher level languages were better, or easier, for other parts, like doing coordinate transformations and orbital calculations. When languages were combined, the question that arose was one of merging lines of code counts. How many lines of assembly language were equal to how many lines of Fortran? Most software engineers today, but by no means all, consider each instruction written by a programmer as a line of code, regardless of the language. That's why higher order languages are more productive than assembly language. They get more done with fewer statements.

The second thing that happened wasn't a discrete event but a process, and it presented a far more difficult problem. Higher level languages continued to evolve and language designers developed concepts that made counting lines difficult. One of the first languages to cause difficulties was Algol [Naur 1963]. Algol was the first widely used "block structured" language, that is, a language that permitted compound statements as a normal part of the syntax. Today, block structured languages are common, but the problem of counting lines of code remains: how many lines of code are there in the code fragment in Figure 15.1? In this case, it's not even clear how many statements there are. There are tools for counting, but there is no industrywide consensus as to exactly what constitutes a line of code.

Number of modules. The more modules (or units or small components) there are in a system, the more it should cost to test. After all, each of these modules must be integrated and the interfaces to the remaining software must be exercised. One might be tempted to predict a strong linear relationship between the number of modules and the testing cost. And there actually is such a relationship for unit and integration testing. But the number of modules doesn't always correlate to the cost of system testing because, while closely related to the number of derived functions necessary to implement the software, the number of modules isn't really related to the number of *system functions* being supported by the software, and system testing is mostly concerned with these.

Large components and programs.   What was said about the number of modules can also be said about the number of large components (CSCs) and programs (e.g., CSCIs, although they may not be exactly the same thing). The more of these there are in a software system, the more interfaces there are to be tested. And, particularly with these larger entities, the more early testing must be done. Unlike the number of modules, the number of large elements does tend to correlate well with the number of system functions. The drawback with these measures is granularity. The larger the entity we select to count, the fewer there will be for a given project. Hence, a mistake in estimating the number of large components or programs by a small absolute number (and we can't have fractional programs) means a large relative error in the cost estimate.

15.1.2 Specification and Design Metrics

While size metrics generally correlate with testing cost, are there others that might lead to a more reliable estimate of testing cost? There are attributes of a software system that relate to the intricacies of the problem being solved and the complexity of the offered solution.

Interfaces.   The number of external interfaces defines the number of different sources of input to the software system and, hence, has a direct effect on the number of input-to-output transformations that must be performed by it; the number of internal interfaces is indicative of the internal complexity of the proposed solution. Interfaces are always a source of misunderstanding between development groups.

Interfaces are defined in Interface Requirements Specifications (IRSs) and the definitions must be extremely precise. In particular, the boundaries (or edges) of each input value must be clearly stated. If they're not, the development groups will evolve their own interpretations.[2] And, the more

---

[2] In a software system developed by one Defense contractor, the specifications stated that "the system shall be capable of tracking and uniquely identifying up to one hundred targets." The design specifications for the software satisfying this requirement specified that the target identifier would be an integer, but was no more specific than that. The development teams

complex the nature of the variables in the IRS, the more lengthy will be the testing process.[3]

Application.   The U.S. Air Force Rome Air Development Center has a large quantity of cost data which clearly supports the idea that some applications are more error prone (and, hence, more costly to test) than others [McCall, Randall et al. 1987]. Some of this cost comes from the nature of the problem itself (some aspects of signal processing are less well understood than compiler development, for example), and some comes from the needs of the users (if human safety could be affected by software operation, more testing will be demanded by the users).

Requirements.   The number of requirements contained in a software system's defining specifications, the Software Requirements Specification and Interface Requirements Specification(s), has a great effect on the cost of testing because sooner or later at least one test case must be generated for each one. Some testers are prone to saying that the number of requirements is the principal determinant of testing costs for the custom (contract) software developer. And this may actually be the case.

The problem with requirements, though, is that not all requirements are equal. To be sure, the custom developer's contract will require a formal demonstration of compliance with every requirement in the specifications. But the degree of rigor associated with that demonstration and the risk to final delivery for noncompliance varies from requirement to requirement. For example, the Software Requirements Specification for an air traffic control system will include requirements to

1. Display aircraft position with a stated precision and accuracy;
2. Extrapolate the aircraft position in order to predict where it will be in the near future;
3. Perform built-in-test functions at stated intervals;

came up with three different interpretations for target identifier, abbreviated here as I D:

$$0 \le ID \le 99,$$

$$1 \le ID \le 100, \text{ and}$$

$$0 \le ID \le 100.$$

The latter solution is clearly incorrect because it accommodates 101 targets but it is the only one that can accept data from the components adhering to the other two definitions.

[3] Interfaces are notoriously undertested in the software world. To thoroughly test an interface requires a very detailed exploration of the behavior of all the software in the face of all realistically possible variations of the data flowing across it. That often takes more time and money than the tester has available.

4. Display the current date and time of day at a controller-selectable position on the display.

Each of these requirements is important and each has been included in the specification for a particular reason. However, it should be fairly obvious that requirements 1 and 2, which involve the examination of the displayed positions of many simulated aircraft and a statistical analysis of the measurements, are more difficult to test than requirement 3, which only requires an observation and an interval measurement (or measurements).[4] Further, requirement 3 is more difficult to test than number 4, which merely needs an observation. Also, since requirements 1 and 2 relate to the position of planes in the air, they can be considered safety-related and, hence, deserving of more rigorous testing.

So, in order to use requirements as a cost determination metric, the tester must have an established categorization scheme for requirements and must analyze the software specifications and carefully classify each requirement contained in them.

Function points. In 1979, Allan J. Albrecht of IBM suggested that rather than worry about how big a software system was or how many requirements statements were contained in its specifications, developers (and testers) would be better off estimating what he called "work-effort" by determining what the software actually did [Albrecht 1979]. The technique described by Albrecht involved the analysis of the amount of data the program would receive and produce. The result of the analysis was expressed as *function points,* a weighted sum of the number of inputs, outputs, master files, and inquiries provided to or generated by the software. Albrecht and Gaffney [1983] have demonstrated the correlation between function points and development effort (and, presumably, the test effort).

From a purely practical point of view, function points may be a more workable measure for the tester because they provide a measure "information space" with which the program must work and a measure of the number of data transformations that must be performed. This may more accurately reflect the number of actual test cases that must be developed than other metrics, notably the size metrics.

The use of function points as a test effort metric has the same difficulty as the use of requirements, though. In the function point analysis, a subjective complexity value is used as a weighting factor. In other words, the estimator must determine the difficulty associated with developing the software that implements the function point. This estimate is necessarily subject to error and individual bias.

---

[4] There will be additional requirements associated with these built-in-test functions. The ability of the software to satisfy each of these will, of course, have to be tested.

The parameters used in computing function points do not, unfortunately, include many of the attributes associated with complicated real-time systems. Indeed, the results of one U.S. Navy study indicate that no attribute factors associated with typical Navy applications are statistically significant for computing program size (or, by implication, the internal complexity of the software) other than the chosen language [Laranjeira 1990].

15.2 COST ESTIMATION MODELS

Assuming that we can identify a reliable set of cost drivers, it would be nice if there was a simple formula into which we could plug the determined values for them and which would, as a result, provide an estimate of the testing cost. Well, there really aren't any that could be termed reliable. The problem, as we'll see, is that they all must be calibrated to an organization's way of working. We will, however, look at three of the more popular estimation models. Keep in mind that these three models estimate the total software development cost, not specifically the testing cost. If an organization's cost history can't separate testing costs from other development costs, then the best rule of thumb is that the total testing cost (including unit, integration, and qualification testing) will be between 40 percent and 50 percent of the total development cost:

$$Testing\ Cost \approx 0.5 \times (Development\ Cost)$$

15.2.1 Empirical Estimation

The general formula for empirical cost models derived from a single cost driver is

$$Cost = c_1\ (Cost\ Driver\ Value)^{c_2}.$$

where c_1 and c_2 are derived from the historical data. Here the term "Cost" is used in its broadest sense to mean expenditure of some resource (a term used by Pressman [1987]). As quoted by Pressman, Walston and Felix give five single driver empirical models based on historical data from 60 software development projects of varying sizes:

$$E = 5.2 \times L^{0.91}$$
$$D = 4.1 \times L^{0..36}$$
$$D = 2.47 \times E^{0.35}$$
$$S = 0.54 \times E^{0.06}$$
$$DOC = 4.9 \times L^{1.01}$$

where E is effort (in person-months), D is project duration, S is staff size,

DOC is lines of software documentation, and *L* is the number of source lines of code (in thousands).[5]

If different models are used for different parts of the development effort, the total cost of the project is found, naturally enough, by summing the individual values:

$$Total\ Cost = \sum_i Cost_i$$

It is interesting to note that the relations determined by Walston and Felix are not linear in the independent variable, yet most software practitioners assume that they are. It's common, for example, to hear software engineers talk of development productivities in terms of lines-of-code per (person-)day. Walston's and Felix's equation for effort, assuming the exponent of *L* to be unity, works out to about 9.6 lines of code per person-day.[6]

15.2.2 Boehm's COCOMO Model

In 1981, Barry Boehm described a comprehensive model for the estimation of software development activity [Boehm 1981]. Boehm's Constructive Cost Model (COCOMO)[7] predicts the amount of effort required for development and the total development time for the project. The primary independent variable in the COCOMO is the estimated (or actual) number of delivered lines of code; in the basic model it is the only one, in the intermediate and advanced models, other parameters can modify the effect of program size.

The prediction equations for basic COCOMO are

$$E = a_b(KLOC)e^b b \text{ and } D = C_b(E)_e{}^d b$$

where *E* is the effort in person-months, *D* is the duration in calendar months, *KLOC* is the estimated number of delivered lines of code (in thousands). The parameters a_b, b_b, c_b, and d_b are determined by the development environment as shown in Table 15.2.

Boehm, and the U.S. Air Force Rome Air Development Center, recognize three substantially different development environments:

[5] Walston, C., Felix, C., "A Method for Programming Measurement and Estimation," *IBM Systems Journal*, vol. 16, no. 1, 1977, pp. 54–73 as quoted by Pressman.

[6] As this is written, the quoted productivity for the U.S. Defense Industry is somewhere between 6 and 8 lines of code per day. The lower value for defense contractors is usually attributed to the additional documentation requirements of the government.

[7] Tables and text from Barry W. Boehm, *Software Engineering Economics*, © 1981. Reprinted by permission of Prentice Hall, Englewood Cliffs, New Jersey.

TABLE 15.2 Basic COCOMO Development Environment
Parameters

Development Environment	a_b	b_b	c_b	d_b
Organic	2.4	1.05	2.5	0.38
Semi-detached	3.0	1.12	2.5	0.35
Embedded	3.6	1.20	2.5	0.32

Organic mode, in which the software is designed and implemented by software engineers who are part of the using community. Essentially, this is an environment in which the developers are completely familiar with the most subtle nuances of the application.

Semi-detached mode, in which the development team is composed of engineers who are not part of the using community but who are familiar with the application area.

Embedded mode, in which the designers and implementers are software engineering specialists who are not necessarily familiar with all aspects of the application area.

Boehm defines organic, semi-detached, and embedded in terms of the overall size and complexity of the problem being approached. In Boehm's terms organic mode applies to relatively small projects, semi-detached to intermediate projects, and embedded mode to large ones. Boehm and the Air Force don't use the same words in their definitions, but the definitions are consistent because of the logistics of software development.

Boehm extends the basic COCOMO model by considering a set of "cost driver attributes":

1. *Product Attributes* encompassing the required software reliability, the size of the application data base, and the overall complexity of the product.
2. *Hardware Attributes* including run-time performance constraints, memory constraints, the volatility of the virtual memory environment, and the required turnaround time.
3. *Personnel Attributes* composed of analyst capability, software engineering capability, applications experience, virtual machine (i.e., platform) experience, programming language experience.
4. *Project Attributes* addressing the use of software tools, application of (modern) software engineering methods, and the required development schedule.

Each of the components making up the above attributes is rated by the COCOMO user on a six-point scale that ranges from "very low" in

TABLE 15.3 Intermediate COCOMO
Development Environment Parameters

Development Environment	a_i	b_i
Organic	2.4	1.05
Semi-detached	3.0	1.12
Embedded	3.6	1.20

applicability to "extra high." The values assigned to the attribute components are combined according to tables provided by Boehm into an "effort adjustment factor" (EAF). This extended model, known as *Intermediate COCOMO,* then estimates the project effort by

$$E = a_i(KLOC)e^{b}i \times EAF$$

where a_i and b_i are as given in Table 15.3 and EAF ranges, typically, from 0.9 to 1.4.

As with any estimation technique that depends on lines of code estimates and the user's judgment of, among other things, complexity, the resulting value for effort is only as good as the data provided the model. Testers and other software engineers should avoid the trap of "backing into the right answer" by, in effect, solving the COCOMO equations for the proper value of KLOC.

15.2.3 Putnam's Estimation Model

In 1978 Putnam [1978] published an estimation model which characterized software development effort as a Rayleigh distribution. That is, staff level increases fairly rapidly, but not instantaneously, as the task begins, reaches a peak, and then tails off less rapidly than it began (as shown in Figure 15.2). Putnam's equation for the effort, K (in staff years) for a software project is

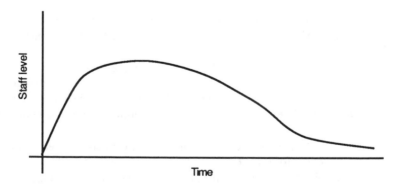

Figure 15.2 A generic Rayleigh effort curve used by Putnam.

$$K = \frac{L^3}{C_k{}^3 t_d{}^4}$$

where L is the number of delivered lines of source code, t_d is the development time in years, and C_k is a constant reflecting the development environment. C_k ranges from 2,000 for a poor software development environment to 11,000 or higher for an excellent environment.

Again, though, the Putnam model doesn't actually give an estimate for the testing effort. It estimates the total development effort.

15.3 ESTABLISHING A COST DATA BASE

Each published cost estimation model relies on cost-driver data collected from many projects by many developers or from projects in the developer's experience. They aren't specific to other organizations. And most models don't specifically address testing costs.

Which brings us to the question of just how much it does cost to test. At the beginning of the previous section, it was suggested that

$$Testing\ Cost \approx 0.5 \times (Development\ Cost)$$

But that's only a rule of thumb. Every development group is a little different. Each of the parameters in the chosen model must be established for the specific development organization and development environment.

This calibration is done by accumulating cost, size, complexity, and other data from completed projects developed under similar circumstances. These data are saved in a cost data base. From this data base, individual project estimates are done on a project-by-project basis.

REFERENCES

ALBRECHT, A. J., 1979."Measuring applicaton development productivity," in Proceedings of *IBM Applications Development Symposium*. GUIDE Int. and SHARE, Inc., IBM Corp., Monterey, CA.

ALBRECHT, A. J., AND GAFFNEY, J. E., JR., 1983."Software Function, Source Lines of Code, and Development Effort Prediction: A Software Science Validation," *IEEE Transactions on Software Engineering*, vol. 9, no. 6, 639–48.

BOEHM, B., 1981. *Software Engineering Economics*. Prentice Hall, Englewood Cliffs, N.J.

LARANJEIRA, L. A., 1990."Software Size Estimation of Object-Oriented Systems," *IEEE Transactions on Software Engineering*, vol. 16, no. 5, 510–22.

McCALL, J., ET AL. 1987. "Methodology for Software Reliability Prediction," Technical Report RADC–TR–87–171. Rome Air Development Center, November.

NAUR, P., ED., 1963. "Revised Report on the Algorithmic Language Algol 60," *Communications of the ACM,* vol. 6, January, 1–17.

PRESSMAN, R. S., 1987. *Software Engineering: A Practitioner's Approach,* 1-567. McGraw-Hill, Singapore.

PUTNAM, L., 1978. "A General Empirical Solution to the Macro Software Sizing and Estimating Problem," *IEEE Transactions on Software Engineering,* vol. SE–4, no. 4, 345–61.

Chapter 16

Status Accounting

Every engineer is an optimist and has infinite faith in his or her ability to get a job done and to get it done as quickly and as efficiently as possible. Unfortunately, the engineer's faith frequently exceeds his or her capabilities or external circumstances and he or she begins to fall behind the set schedule. The first indication of a problem may be nothing more than a feeling of frustration; then the inability to get a small piece of the software to compile; then a fight with another group about hardware availability. And pretty soon there's a serious problem. How did this come about? One day at a time.

Most managers recognize this fallibility and ask for regular status reports. They do this so they can detect the first signs of problems and can take corrective action as quickly as possible. This chapter describes a method of status reporting and accounting that is used regularly in the defense contracting business and that is based on the concept of *earned value*.

16.1 PLANNING A TASK

Before any status information can be collected, it is necessary to know what has to be done. There are two stages in planning: initial planning, in which the job is outlined, and task planning, in which detailed resource assignments are made and measurement criteria are determined.

16.1.1 Initial Planning

Initial planning is the process of understanding the project or program. The engineer must review the contract, including the statement of work, the documentation requirements, and all specifications, and decide on the most expeditious path for accomplishing his or her task. The process of planning a software test program is described in Chapter 4.

16.1.2 Task Planning

Task planning is the process of estimating required resources and deciding on progress measurement techniques. The steps involved are

1. Preparing task descriptions;
2. Estimating and scheduling the tasks; and
3. Establishing measurement criteria.

Each of these is described briefly below.

Task descriptions.   Task descriptions describe in considerable detail the work to be done. When doing task planning, each task identified in the sequence diagram[1] for which the test engineer is responsible should be described. Each task description names the task, states its general purpose, defines a nominal period of performance, defines specific requirements of the task, estimates the manpower necessary to accomplish the task, and gives some rationale for that estimate. Figure 16.1 shows a sample task description.

Scheduling and estimating.   When individual tasks have been defined and descriptions written, a schedule is generated and a staffing plan is generated.

A schedule, like that shown in Figure 16.2, shows the job to be performed as a set of time lines with each identified task presented separately. Key dates for the project are given to put the task schedules in context and dependencies between tasks are indicated either with dotted lines or with footnotes. An important part of the schedule for each task is the indication of any required deliverables or other milestones that can be used for monitoring progress.

A staffing plan is a sort of numerical schedule in which the number of people required to accomplish each task is shown. Like the schedule, each task is presented on a separate line. An estimate of the staffing requirement for a task is determined by

[1] See Chapter 4, "Planning the Test Process."

TASK DESCRIPTION

PROJECT: Firebird   DATE: 11/19/83
WBS TITLE: Project Management   WBS: XYZAA

1.0   <u>PURPOSE</u>
      To provide a centralized Program Management
      Function for total program coordination and con-
      trol.

2.0   <u>PERIOD OF PERFORMANCE</u>
      Full time Month 1 through Month 18 then part time
      to Month 33.

3.0   <u>TASK DESCRIPTION</u>
      3.1   Establish PMO and program organization struc-
            ture.
      3.2   Establish program control functions.
      3.3   Interpret customer management requirements,
            reconcile company policy and establish con-
            sistent program plans, procedures and direc-
            tives.

4.0   <u>BASIS FOR BID</u>
      This element is a LOE with consideration given to
      program size, complexity, customer, CDRL require-
      ments, and dollar volume.

5.0   <u>SUMMARY OF DIRECT LABOR</u>
      One senior engineer (labor code BAEENG) full time
      from the start of contract through completion of
      prototype and .01 M/M per month through the product
      support period (Month 33).

6.0   <u>HISTORICAL REFERENCE</u>
      This element is supported on the basis of compari-
      son to four (4) programs similar to this completed
      by the division within the last three (3) years.
      See Historical Reference File in the Contract
      Administration Proposal file.

Figure 16.1 Sample task description.

$$Staff = \frac{Effort}{Duration}$$

This is as good as we can do initially, but it directly violates the dictum of
Brooks [1975] that people and time are not interchangeable. Effort is defined
in the task description and is the effort required to accomplish the task. The
proposed duration is also defined in the task description, and the planned
duration, which is usually the same, is shown on the schedule. Staffing requirements are calculated using the planned duration. When preparing a

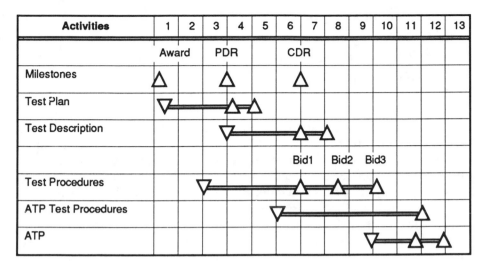

Figure 16.2 Sample schedule.

staffing plan, a good rule is to always round the calculated requirement upward to the nearest half person. This upward rounding will compensate slightly for the fact that no one actually works with 100 percent efficiency.

If the staffing is presented in such a way that the desired job categories and labor grades are stated, then the staffing plan becomes a budget since it is only necessary to multiply the manpower by the appropriate pay rates to determine the dollar value of the task.

Establishing measurement criteria.   As a final step in the task planning process, each identified task is assigned a method of measurement that will be used to determine progress.

Three parameters calculated from the project status information can be used to monitor progress. These are the budgeted cost of work scheduled *(BCWS)*, the actual cost of work performed *(ACWP)*, and the budgeted cost of work performed *(BCWP)*.

BCWS, the value of work scheduled to date, represents the amount of work that should have been been done; *ACWP*, the actual cost, is the amount of money spent doing whatever work has actually been done; and *BCWP*, the cost of work performed or completed, represents the value of the work that has actually been accomplished. Each parameter is expressed in dollars so that direct comparisons can be made between them. The rules for translating work scheduled and work accomplished into dollars are established during the task planning stage by defining a measurement method, and they remain constant throughout the duration of the project.

The common methods for determining *BCWP* are

1. Level of Effort (LOE)
2. 50–50
3. Value Milestone (Quantitative Output)
4. Objective Indicator
5. 0–100

Level of effort is an appropriate measurement technique for those tasks that have no discrete milestones. Management and support tasks are measured this way since the effort required for them is generally a function of program length rather than tangible output. Using this method, the task is assumed always to be on schedule; *BCWP* is always equal to *BCWS*.

The *50–50* method is used for tasks of moderate duration, up to three accounting (or review) periods. These tasks usually have a single milestone, the end product. In this method, 50 percent of the maximum possible *BCWP* is earned when the task is started and the remainder is earned when the task is finished.

The *value milestone* measurement technique is applied to long tasks with many repetitive events (such as test case design). *BCWP* is calculated by dividing the number of events completed by the total number in the task and multiplying the ratio by the total task budget.

The *objective indicator* method of measurement is used for tasks that exceed three accounting periods in duration and that include closely spaced discrete events with tangible outputs. An example of such a task might be one for test plan generation where the discrete events could be draft preparation, draft submittal, final preparation, final submittal, and customer approval. Values are assigned to each event and *BCWP* is set equal to *BCWS* for the period in which the indicator is completed.

For extremely short tasks, say one accounting period, the *0–100* method can be used. No value is earned for the task until it is completed, at which time 100 percent of its value is assigned.

16.2 STATUSING A TASK AND DETERMINING VARIANCES

With budgets and measurement criteria established, it is a relatively simple matter to determine the status of a job. Each task within the job is examined and *BCWP* is determined in accordance with the rules established during planning. This *BCWP*, together with the *BCWS* determined from the plan and the *ACWP* resulting from charges to the task, is used to determine the task's status.

Variances are deviations from a plan. Detecting a variance early and analyzing its causes are the first steps in getting back in line with the plan.

This section discusses the method for calculating variances and then addresses their causes and suggests some corrective actions that can be taken.

16.2.1 Calculating Variances

After a task has been statused, *ACWP, BCWP,* and *BCWS* are calculated to determine where the project is and where it should be. From these, cost and schedule variances are determined.

Schedule variance.   A schedule variance, *vs,* exists when the amount of work performed differs from that which was originally scheduled, regardless of how much or how little it has cost. The schedule variance is calculated from *BCWP* and *BCWS* by

$$vs = BCWP - BCWS$$

It is clear from this formula that *vs* can be either negative or positive. A negative *vs* means that the work accomplished, *BCWP,* is less than the work scheduled, *BCWS,* and, therefore, the program is behind schedule. A positive *vs* means that the value of the work performed exceeds that which was scheduled and, hence, the project is ahead of its plan. Figure 16.3 is a plot of *BCWP* and *BCWS* showing both negative and positive schedule variances.

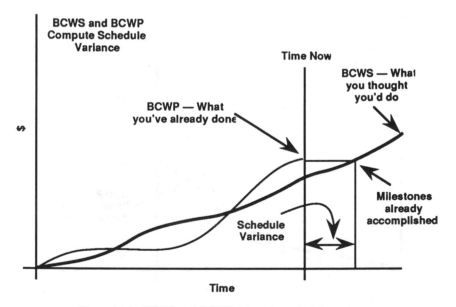

Figure 16.3   BCWS and BCWP determine schedule variance.

At job completion, *vs* is zero since all work initially planned has been performed. That is

$$BCWP = BCWS$$

The schedule variance for any part of a program or project is the sum of the schedule variances of its constituent pieces.

Cost variance.   A cost variance, *vc,* exists when the amount of money spent differs from the amount that was planned for accomplishing the work, regardless of how much time it took. The cost variance is calculated from *BCWP* and *ACWP* by

$$vc = BCWP - ACWP$$

As with a schedule variance, a cost variance can have either sign. A negative *vc* means that the amount of money spent on a task, *ACWP,* exceeds the amount the plan says the task is worth, *BCWP,* and, therefore, the project is overrunning its budget. A positive *vc* means that the amount spent is less than expected and, hence, the project is underrunning its budget. Figure 16.4 shows both overrun and underrun situations.

Unlike the schedule case, the cost variance does not necessarily go to zero at project completion.

The cost variance of any part of a program or project is the sum of the cost variances of its constituent pieces.

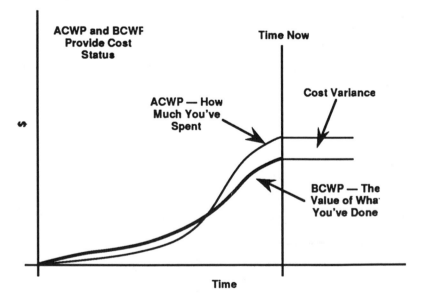

Figure 16.4   ACWP and BCWP provide cost status.

Performance indices.   In addition to the schedule and cost variances, *vs* and *vc*, which are essentially instantaneous measures of the project, there are a number of performance prediction parameters which can be calculated from *BCWS, BCWP,* and *ACWP*. These are the *cost performance index*, the *estimate at complete* or *EAC predictor*, and the *verification index*.

The cost performance index or *CPI* is an efficiency indicator and is defined as

$$CPI = \frac{BCWP}{ACWP}$$

The *CPI* is a measure of how much "bang" the project is getting for each "buck" spent. A *CPI* less than unity indicates inefficiency; that is, less is being returned than is being invested.

The *estimate at complete* predictor or *EAC Predictor* is calculated from the *CPI* and the budget at complete or *BAC* according to

$$EAC\ Predictor = \frac{BAC}{CPI}$$

This calculation assumes that the efficiency demonstrated to date will continue unchanged. This may or may not be a valid assumption since there are two types of variations: *proportional variations* which result from inherent efficiencies or inefficiencies in the way of working and *one-time* or *impulse variations* which result from unexpected perturbations in cost or schedule over which the development or test engineers have essentially no control. If the apparent cost variation is the result of a one-time occurrence or if the engineer expects an improvement (or reduction) in efficiency, the EAC that is actually reported may be different from the EAC predictor.

The *verification index* looks at the effort remaining in a task and relates it to the amount of money remaining to accomplish it. The *verification index* is calculated according to

$$Verification\ Index = \frac{BAC - BCWP}{BAC - ACWP}$$

The numerator, *BAC − BCWP*, defines the amount of work remaining: the budget at complete, BAC, is the value of the total task, and *BCWP* is the value of the work already accomplished. The denominator, *BAC − ACWP*, defines the amount of money remaining to perform the task: the budget to complete; *ACWP* is the amount used for whatever has been accomplished. A verification index greater than 1.0 implies more work to be performed than there is money for it. The verification index calculation disregards past performance efficiency and assumes a return to budgeted performance levels. If the denominator is changed to *EAC − ACWP*, the exhibited project efficiency is taken into account:

$$Alternate\ Verification\ Index = \frac{BAC - BCWP}{EAC - ACWP}$$

The indices described above are merely checks and should not be accepted at face value without follow-up analysis. However, the tester should strive to understand any deviation from planned performance which they may seem to indicate.

16.3 EXPLAINING WHAT HAPPENED

It's not possible to meet every plan precisely, and small deviations shouldn't be of concern. However, medium to large variances, especially when they appear repeatedly or show a trend, require investigation.

Most projects set threshold values for vs and vc. When the threshold is exceeded, explanation and corrective action are required. A typical threshold value is 10 percent. That is, as long as

$$\left| \frac{vc}{BCWP} \right| < 0.1 \text{ and } \left| \frac{vs}{BCWS} \right| < 0.1$$

no explanation is necessary. As a project progresses, the thresholds are usually reduced since it is assumed that larger variations due to start-up, and so on, have settled out and the program should be close to its initial plan. A typical mid-project threshold is 7 percent with 5 percent not uncommon late in the program.

But what causes variances and what problems, if any, are they indicating?

16.3.1 Cost Variance

A cost variance means that the wrong amount of money has been invested in getting a job done. If the variance is negative, that is, if the project is overrunning its budget, then too much money has been spent. This can happen for any of several reasons:

1. The personnel assigned to the project aren't very efficient or don't understand the problem.
2. The personnel assigned to the project are more senior than had initially been planned. This reason can be a subtle one to detect since the number of hours invested may be correct or even less than planned, but the pay rate compensates and makes for an unfavorable dollar variance.
3. Too many people are assigned to the job and they're getting in each other's way.

4. More people than originally estimated have been assigned to the program because the scope of the project was underestimated.

A positive cost variance is usually a good thing, but it needs to be
understood before that favorable opinion is voiced too loudly. The reasons
for such a variance are generally the inverse of those above:

1. Personnel assigned are working very efficiently, probably because they
have come "up to speed" faster than predicted.
2. The staff is less senior than predicted, but they're still getting the job
done.

Some other conditions may contribute to a positive cost variance,
though, and they aren't always obvious until the schedule situation is also
examined:

1. Personnel have yet to be assigned to the program or are diverted to
other, more pressing, activities. This situation will show as a positive
cost variance (because the project isn't spending any money) coupled
with a faltering or negative schedule variance (because the staff isn't
getting anything done). This is particularly troublesome on level of
effort tasks (such as management), where there are no schedule milestones to report against, because the lack of activity may mean that
some other task may soon go awry.
2. Costs that should be charged to this task are actually assigned to another. Mischarges can be corrected by administrative personnel, but
are indicative of a lack of understanding of task definitions.

16.3.2 Schedule Variance

A schedule variance means that the work isn't getting done at the predicted rate. As stated earlier, there are two categories of variances: proportional and linear.

Proportional variances.   Proportional variances are due to inefficiencies within the organization and are usually coupled with weak cost
performance: people just aren't working as well as expected. In these cases,
the responsible engineer or tester needs to take action within his or her group
to accelerate progress.

In the case of testing, proportional variances can occur if the software
under test is particularly buggy. In this case, it's not the testers, but the
developers who are working inefficiently.

Linear variances.   Linear variances are generally due to outside influences such as

1. Failure of the customer to respond to requests for information or to approve critical documents.
2. Delay by another part of the project staff in delivering necessary hardware or software (you can't test it if you don't have it).

The software test engineer may not be directly responsible for linear variations in schedule, but he or she must still decide on corrective action or a "work-around plan." Remember: "Just because it's not your fault doesn't mean you don't have to do something about it."

REFERENCES

BROOKS, F. P., JR., 1975. *The Mythical Man-Month*. Addison-Wesley, Reading, MA.

Chapter 17

Work Breakdown Structures

The previous chapter discussed status accounting and status reporting. This chapter follows logically from that by defining and discussing the kinds of tasks and groups of tasks that should be planned and tracked.

The key item in this kind of status accounting and reporting is the *work breakdown structure*, or *WBS*, the subject of the next section.

17.1 WHAT IS A WORK BREAKDOWN STRUCTURE?

A work breakdown structure (WBS) for a program or project is a set of tasks that must be completed. These tasks are grouped into a hierarchy or family tree. The WBS provides a conceptual framework that is used for planning and controlling the work on the project.

Effort is expended in performing the tasks or developing the products identified by the "leaves" of the WBS family tree and since effort is directly translatable to cost, these leaves can be used as focal points in the collection of data about these costs. The total cost of the program is the sum of the costs of the individual leaves. When looked at as a cost collection structure, the WBS is similar to the accountant's chart of accounts.

For each leaf of a WBS, an individual or individuals are identified as responsible for the completion of the task or product development that it defines. These individuals may then treat their assigned task as a separate program or project with its own WBS structure (provided, of course, that the basic rules imposed on this subordinate WBS are compatible with those for the project WBS).

17.2 GENERIC STRUCTURES

Because there are so many ways to arrange tasks and products for the purpose of cost collection and status accounting, confusion and incompatibility would quickly result if some limits were not placed on the general form of WBSs. The U.S. government has developed MIL–STD–881A [U.S. Department of Defense 1975] in order to control the development of WBSs for projects under its control. For software development, many companies, those doing custom development for the government and those doing commercial applications, take the next step by developing a "generic WBS." One particular generic form for the complete software development process is shown in Figure 17.1.

This generic WBS is not rigid in form and can be considerably tailored to project needs. The general structure and basic elements should, nonetheless, remain so that cost and time comparisons from project to project can be made without mixing "apples and oranges."

17.3 WBS ELEMENTS FOR SOFTWARE TESTING

A review of Figure 17.1 will show that test related elements are scattered about the structure and are quite high-level in nature; some considerable refinement of the WBS is necessary before usable cost-collection categories are defined. Experience has shown that software testing activities can generally be grouped into several specific categories, as described in the following sections. The allocation of these activities as leaves in the WBS tree will depend on the nature of the software development process in place for a particular developer. The elements described below are equally applicable to commercial software development and to custom projects for an organization like the U.S. government.

17.3.1 Software Testing Tasks

The task categories that are most generally encountered during software testing are described in the following sections.

Test management.   Test management is any activity that is directed toward allocation of resources, including equipment, manpower, and money,

Software Management	Software Product						
	Software Requirements Analysis	Preliminary Design	Detailed Design	Code and CSU Test	CSC Integration and Test	CSCI Integration and Test	Post Development
Program Planning and Control	System Architecture and Performance	Preliminary Design	Detailed Design	Code	Integration and Test	CSCI Testing	System Integration and Test
Subcontractor Planning and Control	Computer Resources	CSC1	CSU1	CSU1	Build 1	CSCI1	Customer (Beta) Testing
Software Librarians	Requirements Analysis	...	...	...	...	...	
	CSCI1	CSCm	CSUx	CSUx	Build y	CSCIn	
	...						
	CSCIn						
Software Development Plan	Interface Analysis	Test Planning	Design Walkthroughs			Test Report(s)	
	CSCI1						
	...						
	CSCIn						
Software Requirements Specification		Formal CSC Testing	Test Design	Test Descriptions			System Support
Manuals		Informal CSC Testing	Test Case Identification	CSCI Test Descriptions			
Administration		Informal CSU Testing	Test Software Development	CSC Test Descriptions and Procedures		Product (Release) Description	Training
Meetings				CSU Test Descriptions and Procedures			
Travel	Software Specification Review	Preliminary Design Review	Critical Design Review	Code	Test Readiness Review	Functional Configuration Audit	
Replanning						Physical Configuration Audit	
Other Direct Costs	Rework	Rework	Rework	Resork	Rework	Rework	Rework

Figure 17.1 A generic work breakdown structure.

for the accomplishment of the software testing effort as described in the Statement of Work (SOW).[1] Test management is commonly a level of effort activity[2] and care should be taken not to treat it as a "catch all" task for activities that are better allocated elsewhere.

Planning the test process.   All activity associated with planning the test process[3] is included in this task. The individual steps leading up to a complete plan may be identified as "subleaves." This task does *not* include the actual writing of the test plan document.

Requirements review.   Requirements review is the activity performed by the test organization in reviewing the customer's requirements documents (including system-level documents) for consistency, traceability, and testability. This task does not cover activity associated with allocating functions to system elements (which is a design activity) or the actual preparation of the requirements specification (see the Support Task associated with the Software Requirements Specification).

Requirements verification matrix.   Development of the requirements verification cross reference index[4] (VCRI) is a major activity within a program or project. The VCRI will drive the rest of the test effort. This task covers all functions associated with the preparation of the VCRI.

Write test plan.   The Software Test Plan document is generated after the program requirements have been developed and reviewed and after the verification matrix has been prepared. This task covers actually writing the plan. Depending on the nature of the project and the specific customer, the test plan and the test description may be tangled together in such a way as to make cost separation difficult. If the test engineer or WBS designer is unable to separate the tasks, it is probably better to collect plan and description data together under the banner of the test plan. As long as the nature of the project and the reasons for this combination are clearly identified, the cost data will be usable in the future.

Developing a build strategy.   The effort expended in identifying the number and content of the software builds[5] is collected in this category. On many programs, this task will not be used since build definition will be in-

[1] Refer to Chapter 2, "Software Development Process."
[2] See Chapter 16, "Status Accounting."
[3] As described in Chapter 4, "Planning the Test Process."
[4] See Chapter 4.
[5] See Chapter 10.

cluded in the Software Development Plan generated by the software development plan.

Design/code walkthrough.   The time used by the test team in attending design walkthroughs and code walkthroughs is accumulated in this category. Note that this leaf of the WBS frequently will be attached to the development branches.[6]

Generate test cases.   The time used to identify and design test cases and scenarios[7] is accumulated in this category.

Write test description.   The effort expended in actually describing the developed test cases (writing the Test Description Document) is accumulated in this category, unless, of course, it is being allocated to the Test Plan as described above.

Generate test input data.   The effort expended in generating (and debugging, if necessary) input data to be used during testing is accumulated in this category.

Generate test software.   All the effort associated in designing, coding, and implementing special test software is accumulated in this category. Note that on some programs test software may require formal verification or qualification in a manner very similar to the deliverable software. If this is the case, there may already be a cost collection category allocated for test software (sometimes called "software tools," etc.).

Write test procedures.   The expenditure of effort associated with writing and making editorial corrections to the detailed, step-by-step test procedures is accumulated in this category; the effort required to test the procedures is allocated to the next one.

Dry-run test procedures.   The effort expended in dry-running and debugging test procedures is accumulated here. The writing of minor corrections (called *red-lines*) in the procedure documents is included here, but major rewrites and any changes leading to republication of the procedures belongs under the previous leaf. Dry-running test procedures will be one of

---

[6] The test manager and the development manager should coordinate the planning of the walkthrough budgets. For most programs, walkthrough attendance will be a development activity, but it is possible for walkthroughs to be considered a test, or even a quality control, activity.

[7] See Chapter 8, "Test Case Design" and Chapter 9, "Scenario Generation."

the two or three largest test cost categories on a program since test procedure debugging frequently is where real testing takes place.

Conduct formal test.   Costs associated with the actual conduct of a formal test, including any contractually required dry-runs (as opposed to the debugging dry-runs described above) for Quality Assurance, will be collected in this category. Note that retesting in order to demonstrate that errors have been corrected does not fall under this category unless a complete rerun of the test is required. All other cases of retesting fall under the category of regression test.

Regression test.   Any activity necessary to demonstrate test-to-test system stability or to show that errors have been corrected is charged to this category. Testing here includes any form of test or demonstration that is not covered by delivered and approved test procedures but is required to complete a formal test.

Write test report.   Once a test is complete, its results must be documented in the form of a test report. Activity associated with the generation of this report is accumulated under this WBS leaf.

17.3.2 Informal Testing

On many programs, a great deal of testing is conducted informally, that is, without customer-approved test procedures. The costs associated with defining, preparing for, and conducting these tests are accumulated in separate categories from those for formal testing.

Define informal test.   This category is for costs of activities necessary to define the informal tests, including activities that might otherwise be considered planning and specification (or description) tasks.

Code informal test software.   Informal tests often require special test software for their conduct. Such software might include test *drivers* or special test *stubs*. The costs necessary to prepare and check out this software are included in this category.

Conduct informal test.   Costs incurred in the conduct of informal tests are accumulated in this category; this includes dry-run and retesting activities.

17.3.3 Support Software Tasks

In addition to activities that are directly related to testing, there are a number of software development and support tasks in which test engineers will assist. It is necessary to collect the costs associated with these activities also. The most frequently encountered ones are described below.[8]

Software development plan.   Depending on the specific requirements of the Contract Data Requirements List and the Statement of Work, the software test engineers may be required to contribute to the Software Development Plan. In any case, they will almost certainly be involved in the review of that document. Effort associated with this plan is collected in this category.

Software requirements specification.   A software requirements specification is prepared at the beginning of the development process. One section of that document addresses quality assurance and testing issues, and responsibility for its preparation is often assigned to the test team. Costs associated with the preparation and review of the requirements specification, including the review of sections other than those associated with testing, are accumulated in this category.

Design reviews.   Participation in design reviews is a normal function of the test team. Costs associated with preparing for and participating in the Preliminary Design Review, the Critical Design Review, the Test Readiness Review, and associated internal reviews are accumulated in this category or its "subleaves."

Witness formal module tests.   Module or unit testing is generally the responsibility of the software development team. However, members of the test team should witness at least some of these tests. The effort expended in witnessing these tests is accumulated here.

17.3.4 Other Categories

In addition to the activities defined above, others may occur to the test manager. He or she should feel free to add additional leaves to the WBS to support these. The only danger to be aware of is the creation of categories that overlap or duplicate parts of existing categories. This duplication creates

---

[8] Again, to avoid duplication of cost collection, the test manager should coordinate the use of these support categories with the development manager.

confusion and may make detailed cost tracking and future estimation difficult.

REFERENCES

U.S. DEPARTMENT OF DEFENSE, 1975. MIL-STD-881A "Work Breakdown Structures for Defense Material Items," Air Force Systems Command, 15 April.

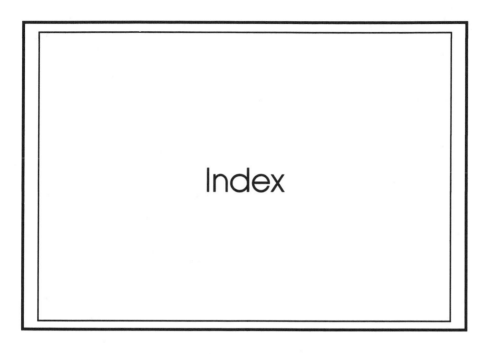

Index